Dancing BETWEEN Cultures

Praise for *Dancing between Cultures*

"*Dancing Between Cultures* is an engaging, practical, inspiring tool that takes the theory and research on cultural intelligence and makes it highly accessible to ministry coaches. Tina Stoltzfus Horst brings her extensive, first-hand experience coaching cross-culturally to offer a resource I look forward to recommending broadly."

—*Dr. David Livermore, thought leader on cultural intelligence and global leadership; President, Cultural Intelligence Center*

"When I began training as a coach, I quickly realized that coaching could become a game changer for me. But as an Asian, my first question was, "How will I translate this Western concept into my Asian, primarily Muslim, context?" Using illustrations from real life coaching experiences, Tina Stoltzfus Horst not only highlights the variables that define culture, but provides the practical tools needed to apply this understanding to coaching cross-culturally. I highly recommend *Dancing between Cultures* as an excellent resource, not only for the cross-cultural coach, but for the cross-cultural worker as well."

—*Celal, cross-cultural worker from South Asia, working in Central Asia*

"*Dancing Between Cultures* is that rare book that mates intellectual mastery of a subject with the nuance that only comes from extensive real-world experience. It's packed with meaty insights about the influence of cultural issues on coaching and well-illustrated with stories borne out of years of hands-on experience. I can feel the perspective shift inside me as I read it. And *Dancing Between Cultures* is organized around a values model that you can actually put on your desk and use to change the way you coach. If you are coaching across cultures—whether in different nations or just different subgroups of your own country—I'd highly recommend this book."

—*Tony Stoltzfus, Founder, Leadership MetaFormation Institute; Author of Coaching Questions*

"The challenge in writing about working cross-culturally is balancing explaining cultural dynamics and teaching how to successfully work within them. *Dancing Between Cultures* is a complete manual on cultural dynamics as they relate to coaching. The author explains each dynamic, but more importantly, how they matter to the coaching relationship. Loaded with practical tips and stories, *Dancing Between Cultures* fills a much-needed gap in the Christian coach's library. We'll all be better coaches by reflecting on and applying the wisdom in this book."
—*Dr. Keith E. Webb, PCC, Author, The COACH Model for Christian Leaders*

"This book is engaging at many levels: It's fast, fun and informative. The author's vast experience blends with an array of stories from herself and other professionals as they tell of their experiences living and communicating across borders. This well-researched guide is useful for all coaches who seek to understand the cultural nuisances of their neighbor – either across the street or across the world.
—*Dr. Michael J. Marx, Author, Ethics and Risk Management for Christian Coaches*

"*Dancing Between Cultures* is a journey extraordinaire. The author creates a thorough, thought provoking, and invaluable guidebook that is well structured and immediately applicable. It's a highly engaging, readable textbook, but has the heart and passion to not just focus on skills, but also the character and sustainability of a coach. I will be recommending this book for years to come! "
—*Sherri Dodd, Founder and Director of Advance Global Coaching*

CULTURALLY INTELLIGENT COACHING for MISSIONS and MINISTRY

TINA STOLTZFUS HORST, M.S.

Life Development Publishing

Acknowledgements

I could not have written this book without the support of my colleagues at Coaching Mission International, whose patience, courage, sacrifice, and commitment to engaging God for transformation has been a source of strength and encouragement. Thanks in particular to Paul Hillhouse, CMI's Professional Coach Training director, who has been an outstanding partner in ministry for a decade. I am grateful to the many cross-cultural coaches who consented to share stories, tips, and personal experience with me. Their insights have brought life and color to this book. Many of them work in areas in which their own and their family's security is at risk. In those cases, names and details have been changed to protect their identity.

Thanks also to my clients over the last fifteen years from whom I have learned much. Thanks especially to my missions clients who humbly and patiently taught me about their own cultures and contexts. I deeply admire your commitment. Walking with you in your transformation process has been my privilege, and I have been transformed in the process.

Thanks finally to my family, and especially to my husband Gary, coach and trainer extraordinaire, partner in ministry, best friend.

Introduction

On my first trip to India, I was asked by my hosts to meet with some of their friends and colleagues who did not have access to Christian life/leadership coaching or mental health counseling. I was trained in both at the time, so I quickly agreed. I live to help. Why wouldn't I use my skills if people had need of them?

With less than a week in-country, I began meeting with people. The first woman I met, Usha, was older than me by at least ten years and married with three sons, two of them adults. Her husband had a good job with a multinational corporation. It became clear early in our session that Usha, a talented, competent, and generous woman whom my hosts highly respected, felt stuck. She was not satisfied with her life at home, but saw few options for change. It was also clear that the men in her life had more power than she did and that everyone around her had expectations of her, about which she was ambivalent.

I used basic life coaching skills of intent listening, reflecting her words back to her, and summarizing. After we had explored her situation, I asked her about options for change. I asked vision questions. What do you see yourself doing when your last child leaves home? What do you see as your destiny or calling apart from your family? What is God saying to you about that?

I also asked questions to help her shift perspective. What would it be like if you felt more powerful in your marriage? What are some other ways to deal with your sons? I asked ownership questions. What do *you* want? What will *you* do to change this situation? What sacrifices will *you* make to get what you need? How will *you* change?

We got nowhere. At each point, Usha politely deferred or went around the question. Or she would offer something, then say it was not possible. She was very polite. I was very frustrated. At the end of an hour, no action steps had resulted. Going another half hour did not result in any either. At the end of ninety minutes, we said our polite goodbyes.

My sense at the time about that coaching conversation was that Usha was not ready to change. Years later, I have a very different perspective. Usha was taking a courageous step to talk to a stranger about her home life. There may have been much more going on than she shared in that session. In fact, I would guess there was a lot more. Coming from a culture that valued concealment of vulnerabilities and indirect communication, it's amazing she told me any details at all about her relationship with her husband. Because her culture was Status oriented, and I was younger with younger children, it was even more a step of faith for her to consult with me. She may have done it only to honor the recommendation of our mutual friend. In fact, the entire meeting with me was likely very much out of her comfort zone.

My expectations that Usha could imagine and articulate new ideas, develop action steps, and move forward decisively to change her destiny stemmed from my own direct and egalitarian cultural values that embrace individual autonomy, initiative, and straightforward communication.

Usha very likely entered the session with none of those expectations. In her culture, status is seen as fixed, and individuals have little ability to change or impact their destiny.

Furthermore, taking action without having the blessing of others, especially those of higher status, may not have been a part of Usha's thinking. Deciding to significantly change what she did with her time might be analogous to an employee in my own culture deciding, without the knowledge or approval of their boss, to simply change their job description from cashier to manager and begin managing the store, starting today!

Because of these fundamental differences in cultural values and expectations, many of my questions may not have made sense to Usha. For example, my asking her what she wanted to do *apart from* her family would have seemed a very alien concept. How does one answer a question like that when you have lived within a web of relationships that define your identity since birth? The concept that she could feel more "powerful" in her marriage may have seemed equally alien. Finally, an indirect orientation in her culture would have predisposed Usha to go around obstacles rather than to confront or change them directly, as I would be likely to do. Questions about how she could adapt might have been a better fit than those asking her what obstacles or challenges she could act on to change.

As I reflect on this encounter now, I realize I would coach Usha very differently if I had it to do again. I did not use poor coaching technique. Let me repeat that! I did not use poor coaching technique. In other words, I employed active listening, used great questions, moved the conversation towards options, decision, action, and so on. But my approach and my understandings did not fit Usha's culture. My own cultural expectations and values shaped my questions, the way I explained coaching, and my approach to the session. Therefore, I did not serve my client well. One of the things I most wish I had done is to have told Usha how honored I was that she confided in me. And I would have approached that session with ten times more humility the second time around.

As the founder and executive director of Coaching Mission International (CMI), an organization providing professional level life/leadership coaching and coach training to the missions world, I've spent the last decade learning how to adapt the coaching paradigm successfully in cross-cultural contexts. When I first began my training as a coach many years ago, I was an American with little cross-cultural experience or savvy. Within my first semester of coach training, God sent me clients who were living and working cross-culturally. These relationships grew and flourished, resulting in more opportunities to coach across cultures as well as invitations to teach, learn, and serve in Asia and Europe.

I learned to coach across cultures through trial and error as I worked with clients from six continents, logging thousands of hours of coaching and training. The people I learned most from were my own clients, both expats (expatriates or those who live in a country that is not their own) and indigenous leaders, passionately serving God around the world. Walking alongside these often-lonely leaders gave me a deep passion to see them resourced and supported. CMI was born as a result. Since its inception in 2006, CMI has provided tens of thousands of hours of coaching and coach training to leaders from over sixty countries in more than a dozen languages.[1]

If we want to serve all our coaching clients with excellence, we must learn to adapt our coaching skills and paradigms cross-culturally.

This book is about faith-based coaching. Specifically, Christian coaching. Christian coaches operate out of the awareness that God is the one who initiates and invites growth in people's lives. As Christian coaches, we get front row seats for the Spirit-inspired change process. Our goal is to be aware of and stay in step with what God is doing—God's pace, God's timing, and God's purposes—and to help the coachee become aware of and congruent with God's action in their lives. Jesus just did what the Father was doing, and that's what we get to do too.

---

1 For more information on Coaching Mission International, go to <u>www.coachingmission.com</u>.

As coaches, we want to imitate Christ in attitude as well as in our actions. As my brother, Tony Stoltzfus, director of the Leadership MetaFormation Institute, and author of the bestseller *Leadership Coaching: The Disciplines, Skills, and Heart of a Coach*, often reminds us, we want to see our clients with God's eyes and to believe intentionally and concretely in the potential God has placed within them.

Before we go on, let me first introduce just what life and/or leadership coaching is to any reader not familiar with the terminology. For many, the term "coaching" raises a visual image of sports coaching. A sports coach yells directions from the sidelines or drills their team on a particular skill or play. But the terms "coach" and "coaching" have widened tremendously in this century beyond just sports coaching. Many roles that used to have consultant, pastor, or mentor in their title or job description now use the term "coach". Coaching can be a great method of helping people grow in a variety of contexts. Yet coaching is not simply mentoring, consulting, pastoring, or discipling under a different name.

The type of coaching addressed in this book is coaching that comes alongside another person, team, or organization to help them reach their potential. In this kind of coaching, coaches are not necessarily experts on a particular subject who might advise clients on action (as a therapist or mentor might), drill them on skills (as a sports coach or trainer might do), or even teach them better understanding (as a disciple-maker or pastor might). Life and leadership coaches are experts in the process of growth. They help coachees grow more effectively, quickly, and deeply, maximizing client potential. The coach's job is to provide encouragement, support, and accountability as the coachee determines goals and subsequent action steps. This kind of "coming alongside" is present and future oriented. It results in action, development, and change. Coaches can help coachees grow externally in their performance and effectiveness, transformationally in their character and inner resources, or both.

Part of the coach's expertise is managing the coaching conversation to aid in the growth process. The client leads in terms of direction: setting goals, developing options, deciding on action. The coach provides a conversational structure that leads towards growth. The conversational model referenced in this book is the "coaching funnel". The coaching funnel is a visual representation of the stages in a coaching conversation, including goal setting, exploring, options, decision, and action steps. After the first session, reporting/reflecting on progress also happens at the beginning of the funnel. For a great explanation of this model for the coaching conversation, consult *Coaching Questions*.[2]

---

2 Tony Stoltzfus, *Coaching Questions: A Coach's Guide to Powerful Asking Skills* (Redding, CA: Coach22, 2008), 30-31.

Coaching is at heart walking alongside the coachee, helping them reach for their potential in a new area, achieve a goal they have dreamed of for years, or struggle through a difficult transition and come out more virtuous, grateful, or resilient. We partner with God when we walk alongside others and help them grow.

I believe that coaching's time has come. Our world is increasingly multi-cultural, and coaching is uniquely suited to cross-cultural relationships. Our clientele is becoming—and will continue to become—more diverse. Greater mobility means we can serve those who've come from other cultures to our communities, churches, and organizations as new neighbors, partners, students, and visitors, and we can also travel to other places to coach among new people groups and nationalities. Continuing innovation in information and communication technologies means we can connect with new clients from other countries and language groups over Skype, cell phones, video conferencing, or webinars. Our teams and businesses will continue to become more multicultural. As Christians, being conversant with other cultures not only broadens our effectiveness with clients, but deepens our understanding and experience of God. And so, the necessity to understand culture and its global variants is a foundational skill for the twenty-first century coach.

To tackle this new frontier, great coaching technique and great heart are not enough. We cannot get by just by being great coaches. I am continually surprised when I hear otherwise savvy and experienced coaches tell me that they don't adapt their coaching style or approach when coaching someone from another culture. From my perspective, that's like refusing to switch from driving my car on the right side of the road in North America to driving on the left British-style on the streets of Ireland, India, or South Africa. Roads and motor vehicles may be similar in both scenarios, but refusing to adapt from my own culture's driving regulations is likely to end in a painful traffic collision. We shouldn't assume, as I did with Usha, that because we know how to coach in our own culture, the process, assumptions, or procedure for doing so will be the same in another culture.

Developing the cultural intelligence needed to coach excellently in cross-cultural settings requires inner transformation as well as new understandings and skills. I want to join God in his fierce love for all people. To do that, I must be willing to be changed in the process. As coaches, we know that growth takes time, commitment, and the humble willingness to learn from our mistakes. If we want to serve our coaching clients well and if we hope to help others reach their potential, grow in character and Christlikeness, increase impact, and develop their gifts, we must learn to adapt our coaching skills and paradigms cross-culturally. That will require perseverance and sacrifice.

Are you a Christian coach working in your church or community, in business, with executives, in missions, in education, in health services, or some other niche? Is it your desire to become equipped to serve others with culturally intelligent coaching? Then this book is for you. Multiculturalism is here. Don't miss out!

This book is intended both as an introduction to faith-based culturally intelligent coaching and a continuing reference for new situations and cultures that the Christian cross-cultural coach might encounter. If you are a coach who has never coached cross-culturally, my hope is that in reading this book you will begin to understand and deepen your cultural intelligence. May you catch as well the incredible excitement and potential of cross fertilization that coaching across cultures brings.

If you've coached across cultures and been frustrated or wondered if you've failed, I hope you'll gain confidence, anticipation, and curiosity for what faith-filled, culturally intelligent coaching can look like. You will also learn practical ways to be effective in your cross-cultural coaching relationships. And if you already love coaching cross-culturally, I hope you'll pick up new insights and techniques, deepening your vision and anticipation of the positive impact culturally sensitive coaching can have.

It's important to note that the concepts in this book go well beyond coaching and can be useful for cross-cultural conversations and cross-cultural leadership in general. If you are not a coach, but are working or living cross-culturally, understanding and applying the principles and values in the following chapters will result in increasingly fruitful conversations across cultures.

The book is organized into sections for easier reference. Section One will answer the following basic questions as they relate to cross-cultural coaching: What is culture? How does it relate to faith? What is cultural intelligence, and how can it be developed? What are cultural values? Why are they important? These chapters are foundational to understanding the rest of the book.

Section Two is a set of chapters on various cross-cultural values. This section can be read in its entirety, or you can simply use it as a reference when you are coaching others with differing cultural values. These chapters identify the principles and basic understandings about each value continuum, then go into detail about how to apply these in coaching. You'll discover how cultural values actually look and sound in the coaching relationship along with tips and stories from a multitude of coaches who are working cross-culturally. Depending on who and where you are coaching, some chapters may be more applicable to your needs. Any time you begin coaching a new client whose culture or values are unfamiliar to you, you can use these values chapters to gain understanding of what issues might arise.

Finally, Section Three covers virtues and skills that are critical for the cross-cultural coach. This includes character qualities like flexibility and skills such as assessment. We will also discuss the vital need for self-care in order to finish well in the challenging arena of culturally intelligent coaching.

How you read the book is as important as its content. As you peruse the material, I encourage you to experience it rather than approach it studiously or academically. God welcomes us to enjoy him through a growing relationship with him. Approach this process in similar fashion. Rather than thinking of culturally intelligent coaching as a discipline to be mastered, a course to be studied, or a skill to be obtained, allow yourself to approach it the way you might look forward to gaining a new friend. Growth comes as you learn to know and appreciate a new person over time.

Similarly, when it comes to cross-cultural coaching, expect fits and starts rather than smooth, upward progress. Gaining cultural intelligence means growing and allowing oneself to be transformed in the process. You won't accomplish that just by reading a book. As a coach, you know that learning happens when motivation combines with relationship, reflection, vision for the future, concrete goals, and practical application.

To help you internalize the material, you'll find questions for reflection and exercises to practice at the end of most chapters and sometimes in the middle. I also highly encourage you to find someone to coach cross-culturally while reading the material so that you have a context for application and insight. And of course, find a peer coach or mentor coach to walk with you. Doing the reflection exercises with a peer will help you apply new discoveries and understandings.

Take it slow. Read, reflect, apply, and practice. Gain vision and set goals. Read some more. Talk to other coaches who are on this journey. Consider starting a mastermind group. Coach cross-cultural clients. Read. Apply. Practice. Learn. And enjoy!

The Basics of Cross-Cultural Coaching

Chapter One

Diving into Culture

At 9:00 a.m. EST, I put on my headset, open my computer, and tap on my GoToMeeting invitation. It's time for the CMI (Coaching Mission International) quarterly staff meeting. We always meet at 9:00 a.m. because it's the only time that works. It's 6:00 a.m. for our west coast staff, 6:30 p.m. for those in Southeast Asia and 9:00 p.m. for those in the Far East. Jeremiah has the worst connection, and sometimes it's hard to catch all his ideas because of the static on the line and the cadence of his African-flavored English. We spend the first minutes sharing stories, laughing, and commenting on current events and headlines. After the meeting, our action steps are posted on our common project page, which we can all access online.

Ten years ago, our far-flung virtual organization would not have been possible. Today, with staff and partners on three continents and trainees on six, we communicate, meet, and work together almost entirely over the internet for little or no cost.

Our twenty-first century world has the technology to interconnect across national boundaries easily, quickly, and for the most part cheaply. Ideas travel the globe over the web. We Skype or phone partners, friends, and colleagues on the other side of the world instantly. Fashions, fads, news, and products move across the planet at lightning speed. We are connected at an unprecedented level.

All this multicultural mixing, high-speed communication, and crisscrossing currents of globalization might lead us to believe that cultures are becoming more and more alike and that the concept of unique "cultures" is on the wane. To the contrary, many experts believe that culture becomes even more important in the face of globalization. People and societies find national, religious, and ethnic identity in their traditional local culture. In fact, culture in many ways is more owned and celebrated now than a few decades back. Locally grown food, locally made products, and local businesses are increasingly perceived as important.

Customs and languages are recorded and celebrated. Businesses talk equally of globalization and "localization" (tailoring a product or service for a local market and culture so that the product/service looks and feels as if developed locally). In an increasingly confusing and fast-paced world, culture and cultural values provide a sense of identity and security. Professor of missions Dr. James Plueddemann states in his book *Leading across Cultures*:

> While the externals of clothing, food, music, transportation and the internet are changing and making the world more homogeneous, deep cultural values seem to be ever more stable and enduring. Globalization might make us look more alike on the outside, but localization reinforces the deepest inner being of our identities . . . The more we interact with each other, the more we need to understand each other's underlying cultural values.[3]

What is Culture?

So, what exactly do we mean by the word "culture"? Culture is the distinctive characteristics—including values, attitudes, beliefs, and behaviors—shared by a group (region, nation, people group, social group, or organization). I like Across Cultures, Inc. founder and president Brooks Peterson's definition in his book *Cultural Intelligence*:

> Culture is the relatively stable set of inner values and beliefs generally held by groups of people in countries or regions and the noticeable impact those values and beliefs have on the peoples' outward behaviors and environment.[4]

Let's look a little more closely at these definitions:

- Culture is what makes different groups distinctive.
- Culture starts at the internal level of attitudes, values, and beliefs, which then shape externally noticeable behaviors and customs.
- Many types of groups can be said to have a "culture". We can talk about national culture, regional culture, a church's culture, or organizational culture.

That last point is particularly important. The concept of culture does not just apply to nations or people groups, but also to organizations, denominations, corporations, and churches. Learning about culture can be helpful to us as we cross

---

3   James E. Plueddeman, *Leading Across Cultures: Effective Ministry and Mission in the Global Church* (Downers Grove, IL: IVP Academic, 2009), 73.

4   Brooks Peterson, *Cultural Intelligence: A Guide to Working with People from Other Cultures,* (Boston, MA: Intercultural Press, 2004), 17.

religious and generational boundaries. Understanding the concept of culture and gaining familiarity with cultural values will serve us well if we move from one region of our own country to another region. Or if a ministry takes us to a variety of different churches or back and forth between denominations. Perhaps you are an executive coach who coaches leaders from several corporations or an organizational coach who works with a range of NGOs. Or perhaps like me you are a missions coach who serves leaders from many different sending and aid organizations. In any of these situations, the understandings of culture we gain now will apply and help us to better serve our coaching clients.

Take a Minute

- *Think back to the first time you entered a particular culture. What do you remember about that initial encounter?*
- *Take a minute to re-immerse yourself in that situation. What did you notice? What caught your attention in the first minutes or hours?*

I remember the first time I exited the airport in India. After a flight of more than eighteen hours, I emerged bleary-eyed from a surprisingly easy walk through security. Clutching our luggage tightly to our sides, my companions and I followed the flow of passengers towards the outside doors and the night sky. Our friends would be meeting us in the parking area for the three-hour drive to their flat in a neighboring city.

Nothing prepared me for the mass of people jostling and pressing against the barricades as we exited those doors. The outside lights hurt my tired, jet-lagged eyes, and I squinted to try to see our friends amidst the crush. People were shouting in what sounded like a variety of languages. I could not tease out any meaning; it was just a wall of sound. The heat and humidity hit me. Smells of sewage, sweat, curry, and exhaust fumes swept over me.

I could not see our friends, and the momentum of those behind us was carrying us right into the crowd. I tried to draw back as hands reached out to us, but we were surrounded. Then our friends, who had waited from behind the crowd, extracted us with confident ease, greeting us with "Namaste!" (a common Hindi greeting), warm smiles, and water bottles as they led us to their car and driver. Ah! Welcome to India!

Often what stands out when we arrive in a new region or encounter a new culture through a new client are the external behaviors and customs. We notice that people maintain a foot or so of personal space in public places—or not. They eat plain, non-spicy food—or not. They employ drivers and maids—or not. Different ways of dressing. Different rules about personal space. Different food. Different art and music. Different pace. Different smells and sights. Different greeting rituals. These evidences of a different culture that we encounter with our five senses are what we will generally notice first.

The most crucial characteristic of culture to understand here is that the internal level of cultural values, beliefs, and norms powers the external customs, manners, and behaviors that we see and experience.

However, the most crucial characteristic of culture to understand here is that the *internal* level of cultural values, beliefs, and norms powers the *external* customs, manners, and behaviors that we see and experience. Some of you might be thinking at this point: "Okay, enough. This is sounding way too complicated, and I've got lots of tools in my coaching toolbox already. Frankly, reminding me of how it feels to enter or experience a new culture is uncomfortable and provokes anxiety. I think I'll just stick with 'my own kind'."

It is a common human drive/behavior to want to hang out with like-minded friends and colleagues. But in this era of globalization, new and unfamiliar cultures are hard to get away from. As coaches, we know that growth and change are uncomfortable. This is equally true with growing in cultural intelligence, so expect to experience some discomfort.

Others of you might be thinking instead: "Blah, blah, blah. I know this stuff already. I've traveled a lot, and I know how cultures are different."

But do you? As I've talked with those who've traveled extensively and even lived in other countries for years, it's surprising how often they do not understand the deeper internal issues of culture. Or they have learned through trial and error about the hidden values of the country they have lived in for a decade, but they still don't know the principles behind those values. Understanding those principles would enable them to quickly identify deep cultural differences, thereby allowing them to enter (or coach!) a brand-new culture with relative ease.

For instance, an expat may understand that in Uzbekistan leaders are not openly challenged and subordinates are expected to follow instructions. The expat may have adapted well to this. When leading, he/she does not delegate easily and expects subordinates to follow through on given instructions. When following, this expat does not take initiative or challenge the group leader in public.

But what this expat does not understand is that these ways of leading and following are powered by a value for hierarchical relationships rather than flat or equal relationships. They reflect a deep belief in the principle that hierarchy brings stability and security at all levels of society. The expat may not realize that national cultures as diverse as France and China hold this value. Or that a whole set of identifiable beliefs that power behaviors is associated consistently across cultures with this particular value.

Beneath the Waterline

So, how can we get to those crucial internal realities that power the external differences we see, hear, touch, taste, and smell every time we enter a new culture? One helpful way to visualize this is to think of an iceberg.

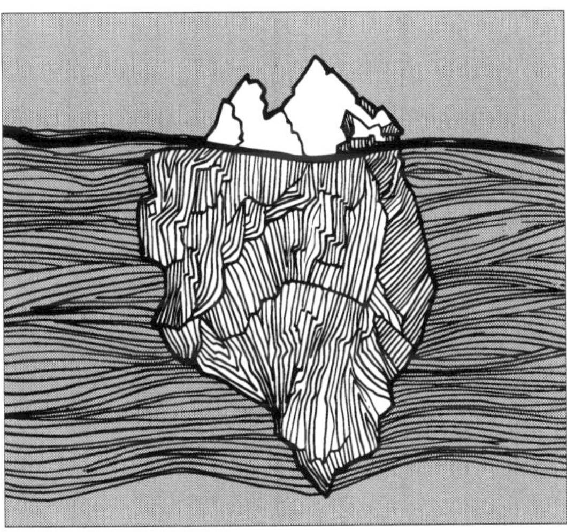

Generally, only one-tenth of an iceberg is visible above the waterline. This makes it difficult to judge accurately the shape of the remaining ninety percent that is underwater simply by looking at the part of the iceberg that is visible. Ships are often sunk, not because of that part of the iceberg sailors can see, but the part they can't see.

When it comes to culture, the underlying, internal factors like beliefs, values, and unspoken expectations determine the external behaviors and customs. In the coaching relationship, we are more likely to run aground or sink the relationship when we ignore the part of the iceberg that is below the waterline. We must intentionally bring what is normally unconscious and below the waterline into our awareness.

So, what's down there under the water? Many psychologists visualize personality as being a "below the waterline" construct. Personality preferences measured with standardized tests or structured interviews such as the Myers Briggs Temperament Indicator (MBTI), the Big Five, the DISC, or even the motivational gifts list from Romans 12 help us understand ourselves and others as individuals.

Cultural values are the other main "below the waterline" component. Culture is learned from the external world. It is picked up from an individual's environment, family, experiences, even the structure of one's first language. The aggregate sum of this learning becomes a largely unconscious set of values that operate internally. We'll delve deeply into cultural values in Section Two of this book. As with personality, it is critical that we understand our *own* cultural preferences as well as those of our clients.

The influence of these hidden components of the iceberg cannot be underestimated. Culture shapes how we relate to each other, how we express emotion, how we deal with conflict, how our teams function, how our homes and cities are laid out, how people are governed and participate in that government. Culture touches every aspect of our lives and relationships.

The Culture Box

One of the clients I coach regularly is a highly-motivated planner who always shows up to his appointments on time and nearly always has his action steps completed. He is prepared for the appointment and generally has already taken time to reflect on what he has learned in the last month leading up to our session. This client is from an Event oriented, Non-Crisis culture which values flexibility over punctuality and spontaneity over planning. However, my client is by personality a highly organized, attention-to-detail STJ on the Myers Briggs Type Indicator. In other words, he is a thinker who is concrete and lives in the present; who thrives in a controlled and organized work environment.

In this case, understanding the client's personality style was more helpful than understanding the cultural values in his environment. It is important to pay attention to cultural patterns, but also to pay attention to the gifts, personality, and experiences that motivate and shape our individual cross-cultural clients.

As we discover more about the power of culture in following chapters, the temptation may be to fit everything into the "culture box"—i.e., to consider all issues the client faces as being derived from cultural issues. Don't do it! God in his infinite creative ability made all of us human and yet all of us unique. We are each someone who brings particular value to his family. We are layers of personality, gifting, and culture with a dose of common humanity, salted with the image of God and overlaid with the development of skills and gaining of experience throughout our lifetimes. As you work with your clients, don't lay down your other coaching tools. Coaching expert Dr. Keith Webb, founder of Creative Results Management, states:

> It's critical for coaches working with culturally diverse clients to understand basic differences in culture. However, it is not necessary to be a cultural expert. The more important thing is to embrace two contrasting mindsets: a) each person is unique, with his own values, personality, and motivations; and b) there are broad cultural similarities that make people similar.[5]

Remember too that cultural values are what make groups distinctive. Simply because an individual belongs to a particular people group or organization does not mean that individual will share the values of that group. I recently took the CQ Self-Assessment survey, which is a self-inventory of cultural intelligence capabilities and cultural value orientations available from the Cultural Intelligence Center.[6] Though I am an American from one of the most highly individualistic cultures in the world, I had an extremely high score in "collectivism" (or Community orientation), the opposite of individualism. Because I believe passionately in gift-based ministry, I place a high value on working in teams and making decisions that draw on the gifts and perspective of each member. My values about community are more typically in agreement with my Asian clients than my neighbors in Indiana.

So, while we can state, for example, that the American culture is highly individualistic, we cannot assume that every individual in the United States shares this value or shares it to the same degree. Dr. David B. Peterson, Director of

---

5   Dr. Keith E. Webb, "Cross Cultural Coaching," In *Coaching in Asia: The First Decade*, edited by Denise Wright, Anna Leong, Keith E. Webb, and Sam Chia. (Singapore: Candid Creation Publishing, 2010), 21.

6   Self-Assessments provide feedback on how individuals view their own CQ capabilities. Participants complete online surveys and receive a feedback report on their CQ capabilities.

Executive Coaching and Leadership at Google, writes in his article "Executive Coaching in a Cross-cultural Context":

> An understanding of a culture may tell you a lot about a given group, (but) it does not necessarily tell you much about any given individual.[7]

Learning about culture gives you new tools for your coach's toolkit. But the tools are there to help you find out more about your individual client, not to rigidly stereotype according to culture.

For example, n-Culture, a network of practitioners offering training in faith-based inter-cultural intelligence, in its *Faith & Culture* curriculum, describes the importance of recognizing that for certain populations such as expatriates, Third Culture Kids (TCKs), and internationals (those who have spent much of their life moving between cultures) "you cannot describe people in terms of national culture when this is your audience. When you work with a client like this, you must identify individual worldviews and value dimensions." n-Culture calls this concept "inter-cultural intelligence".[8]

One interesting point to understand as we delve deeper into this book is that our cultural background itself will influence how valid we find concepts about cultural values and cultural intelligence. Those from individualistic (Autonomy) cultures will be more likely to link the roots of behavior to individual factors like personality or character. If we come from an individualistic culture, which many Western cultures are, we may resist the idea that some of our behaviors are culture based and not solely determined by our uniqueness or our own conscious choices. On the other hand, if we come from group cultures, we need to keep in mind that individual attributes such as personal experience, values, and personality can significantly influence cultural norms and behaviors.

As we read, learn, and apply new knowledge, we need to remember that culture is only one way to understand ourselves and our clients. All of us are multi-layered, and all of us are more than our culture.

Becoming Self-Aware

When I trained as a coach, I spent a whole semester focusing on life purpose coaching. The process went beyond knowledge to personal application. That semester I wrote my own mission statement and identified my own core values.

---

7   David B. Peterson, "Executive Coaching in a Cross Cultural Context," *Consulting Psychology Journal: Practice and Research* (December 2007), 262.
8   www.n-culture.com

Many of us have gone through a similar process in coach training. My mission statement, retooled a couple times, still hangs over my desk, and I refer to my ten core values frequently. For instance, I have a strong value for gift-based teams, and that has shaped the organization I founded in significant ways. I continue to choose ministry opportunities based on the possibility of working with a team. I feel naked without teammates around me.

Take a Minute

- *Identify a core value of your own and take a few minutes to think about how that core value powers your behavior.*

Clinical psychologist and coach Gary Collins writes in his book *Christian Coaching*:

> Effective coaches know themselves . . . Good coaches are aware of their own core values and beliefs long before they get involved with clients who may have different values.[9]

All of us who have gone through a thorough process of coach training know how crucial it is for coaches to be growing in self-awareness, to continue to learn, and to be aware of their own values. Coaching is built on relationships, and the person of the coach is key in the coaching process. Understanding and owning our own sense of mission as well as identifying our core values are both important because these shape who we are and how we respond to the world. But what I did not learn in coach training was that my values, for instance my value for gift-based teams, were not only shaped by my personality, gift set, experience, and understanding of Scripture, but by deep-level cultural values.

In fact, I've come to recognize that even how I understand Scripture itself is shaped by my cultural heritage and milieu. My understanding of what it means to function as a team is rooted at a deep level in my culture. For instance, I like to work in teams of equals, therefore I prefer collaborative decision-making. To me such collaboration seems inherent in the very concept of gift-based teams. Colleagues from other cultures also share a value for gift-based teams. But their

---

9   Gary Collins, *Christian Coaching: Helping Others Turn Potential into Reality*. 2nd ed. (Colorado Springs, Nav Press, 2002), 34.

cultural background influences their expectations about what this will look like. For them, hierarchy within the team is assumed. Since I am the director, they look to me as the person who will make decisions and wield influence. For them, hierarchy is inherent in the concept of gift-based teams.

My own original coach training included no mention of culture and the deep and profound impact this has on my own expectations and behaviors. However, as we delve into coaching relationships with those from other cultures, it is absolutely crucial that we develop self-awareness about our own cultural background and values as well as a basic understanding about how that background and those values shaped us. What assumptions, motivations, values, and beliefs power our own behaviors? If we are not aware of these, we cannot adapt to the needs of our clients or learn to leverage our own and our clients' values for growth and transformation. As professor of anthropology Sherwood Lingenfelter writes in his book *Ministering Cross-Culturally*:

> For the Christian who seeks to serve . . . another culture, knowing one's cultural bias is essential to effective ministry. Once we have understood the power of our cultural habits over us, we are more ready to call on the spiritual power and freedom we enjoy in Christ to break the habits of our culture, to let go of them, and to enter into another culture to help those people encounter Christ.[10]

Remember Usha, the first South Asian client I coached? I failed to effectively help her because not only did I not understand *her* cultural context, I did not understand *my own*! I had not examined my own cultural assumptions and beliefs, so I did not see how they influenced my coaching style and even the questions I posed to her. As you continue this journey towards cultural understanding, please do not focus only on your clients. Take the time to think through your own cultural values. Become aware of the ways those values shape your behavior, attitudes, and beliefs, even the way you approach Scripture. Learn to know *yourself* in a deeper and more profound way, so that you will be a more effective instrument of God as you serve others through coaching.

---

10   Sherwood G. Lingenfelter and Marvin K. Mayers, *Ministering Cross-Culturally: An Incarnational Model for Personal Relationships*. 2nd ed. (Grand Rapids, MI: Baker Academic, 2007), 12.

Chapter Two

Faith and Culture

Romans 1:20: For since the creation of the world God's invisible qualities—his eternal power and divine nature—have been clearly seen, being understood from what has been made.

Ephesians 5:2, *The Message:* Mostly what God does is love you. Keep company with him and learn a life of love. Observe how Christ loved us. His love was not cautious but extravagant. He didn't love in order to get something from us but to give everything of himself to us. Love like that.

My dad was a biologist. One of the things he loved to do as a family was share his curiosity about the natural world. In the spring, he'd gather up all five of his children, bundle us into his old tan-and-brown station wagon, and head for the mountains to find and identify wildflowers. Once we arrived, we would trail through the forested hillsides, Dad out in front scouting for the good finds. Picture five children under the age of nine, all kitted out in jackets and boots, grubby and rambunctious, paper bags in hand for collecting our treasures. Dad would turn over musty, decayed logs to show us insects. He'd spot the least obvious of tiny flowers. I believe his satisfaction was simply in loving and enjoying creation and sharing it with us.

This is the kind of joyful curiosity and delight I believe God, our heavenly parent, has in the diversity of creation and the diversity of his people. Becoming a culturally intelligent coach is one of the most fun and rewarding journeys around. There is always something new to learn—and coaches love that, right? But what motivates me most is joining God in his great love for his people around the world. Becoming a culturally intelligent Christian coach means learning to not just accept, but love and delight in the diversity of culture expressed in God's people.

One of my South African friends, Carl, works in the Middle East. He is passionate about his work, but even more passionate about the people—now his people—whom he coaches and works with. Carl loves his people and finds great joy and care in coaching them. Here is his account of being adopted by the Middle East:

My previous experience was in Africa, and I had very little appreciation and understanding of Arab culture. Twenty years ago, I went to Jerusalem and met a ministry leader I knew there. We traveled into the old city of Jerusalem. The noises, the people, the smells all hit me. I was really impacted by watching how this guy interacted with the people. I decided to stay for a while and moved in with a local family. I remember I had a lot of trouble adjusting, especially to the food. It was so weird! And I hate olives. There were no sweets except this sweet cheese mixture, fried with roasted stuff in it. Oh, it was disgusting. It made me feel sick. The first year was really difficult. I thought, "I won't be here long. This is just a transitional place." I thought I would end up in China, but everything closed up and I went home. While there, I received a word from a friend that the Arab people would become my people, my family. That even the food would become part of me. When I came back, there was something different in my heart. The olives became my passion. Even the sweet cheese was good. I came alive. There was a difference in my heart. I knew this was my inheritance, the people God had called me to. I looked at the individuals in the context differently. There was a tremendous change inside me.[11]

Carl had a heart change that enabled him to embrace the Arab culture with the kind of passionate love God has. Love is the foundation stone for culturally intelligent relationships.[12] Loving as God does makes the learning and discovery process inherent in working cross-culturally not just possible, but joyful. The Bible is chock-full of examples of God's great love for all of creation. Let's take a closer look at what Scripture has to say about culture and faith.

The Old Testament

In the creation story, which we find in the first chapter of Genesis, God started it all off by taking a dark and unformed earth and separating day and night. From

---

11   Carl, Personal Communication, Permission granted on August 2, 2015.
12   David A. Livermore, *Cultural Intelligence: Improving Your CQ to Engage Our Multicultural World* (Grand Rapids, MI: Baker, 2009), 19.

the start, he began creating diversity and called it good. Just think about how many species there are of plants and animals. The vast number of stars in the sky and grains of sand on a beach. The diverse molecules, muscles, and neurons that make up our complex and extraordinary bodies.

The sheer inventiveness of our Creator is amazing to consider. He seems to have delighted in imagining crazy things like anteaters and giraffes, black holes and galaxies, colors and birdsong. Just how much God loves the earth and those who live on it is expressed through the natural world. God expects us to steward nature and care for it.

The Bible's record of diversity and culture doesn't end with the creation story. Certainly, the Old Testament is filled with cross-cultural conflict, exhortations to Israel to remain separate from other cultures, and some blatant intolerance. There are plenty of cross-cultural horror stories, but the Old Testament also includes the thread of redemption for all: God choosing to reveal himself in/through one people group (the Israelites) in order to welcome and bless the nations. Rev. Dr. Isaac Canales in his book *Multi-Ethnicity* calls this "a theology of welcome".[13] Beginning in Genesis, we find a hint of this trajectory: "all peoples on earth will be blessed through you" (Genesis 12:3). This thread appears again in the book of Isaiah, chapter 56, where the Lord explicitly welcomes the foreigner who chooses to serve Him and declares: "My house will be called a house of prayer for all nations" (Isaiah 56:7b).

The Israelites were God's chosen people, and his primary focus throughout the Old Testament was on them. But God also reminded Israel that he loved the aliens among them. Yahweh expected his people to also love strangers and aliens, bearing in mind their own experience as foreigners in Egypt (Deuteronomy 10:18-19). As God welcomed his chosen people repeatedly despite their repeated sin and disconnection with God, so Israel was to welcome those who were "other".[14]

God's long-term objective was a cross-cultural mission that would bring all people together to worship him. Jonah was sent out to proclaim God's message to another people group, the Assyrian city of Nineveh. Abraham was told that all nations will be blessed through him. In Isaiah 66:19, God told the prophet his plans for the nations:

---

13   Isaac Canales, *Multi-Ethnicity, Global Issues Bible Studies.* Edited by Stephen Hayner and Gordon Aeschliman (Downers Grove, IL: Intervarsity Press, 1990), 11.

14   Ibid., 12.

> I will set a sign among them, and I will send some of those who survive to the
> nations—to Tarshish, to the Libyans and the Lydians, to Tubal and Greece, and
> to the distant islands that have not heard of my fame or seen my glory. They will
> proclaim my glory among the nations.

When you think of creating a culture of welcome, what comes to mind? What comes to my mind is my daughter Rosie. Throughout her entire life, she has welcomed into her heart others who are different. When she was a child, we marveled at her ability to move among friend groups. Rosie was friends with extroverts and introverts, band geeks and science nerds. She had close friends among both boys and girls. The collections of people she brought together were so disparate that at times it created friction. When she was a college student at a Christian school, one of her best friends was an Iranian Muslim, despite ongoing tensions between Rosie's own birth culture (USA) and Iran.

Being a person who embraces an attitude of welcome means embracing discomfort at times, being challenged in one's assumptions, and going way outside of one's comfort zone. Jonah wasn't pleased at being sent to Nineveh, and sometimes we are not so happy about leaving the comfort and security of hanging out with those just like us. Remember my friend Carl's discomfort during his first sojourn in the Middle East? Despite our discomfort, God invites us to create with him a culture of welcoming others who are on the outside, a mindset that sees diversity—and leans in.

As we look back at the Old Testament, we can see throughout the thread of a God who created and enjoys diversity. We learn of a God whose welcoming love for Israel models the love he has for all. Yahweh exhorted his chosen people to welcome the alien and the stranger, a foreshadowing of his ultimate intent to gather all nations and people to worship and enjoy him together.

The Example of Jesus

And then there is Jesus. God's purposes, character, and love for us are made clear to us through who Jesus is. The meaning of "incarnation" is a person who embodies (expresses or gives visual form to) another person, quality, or concept. Jesus embodies/incarnates who God is and what his purposes are. We understand God and his purposes by looking at Jesus. I've been captured by Dr. David Livermore's phrase expressing this concept: "God speaks in Son".[15]

What do we see when we look at Jesus? What can we learn from him? Sherwood Lingenfelter in *Ministering Cross-Culturally* writes:

---

15   David A. Livermore and Julie Slagter, *CQ Ministry Kit,* (Cultural Intelligence Center, 2013),22.

Jesus was a learner. He was not born with knowledge of language or culture. In this respect, he was an ordinary child. He learned the language from his parents. He learned how to play from his peers. He learned the trade of a carpenter from Joseph . . . The implications of Jesus' status as a learner are seldom discussed, let alone understood or applied. God's son studied the language, the culture, and the lifestyles of his people for 30 years before he began his ministry.[16]

Jesus' divine stature as God's son is clear, yet Jesus chose to come to Earth as an ordinary, peasant-class human baby. This truly was a sacrifice made from love. One of the most important things we can learn from Jesus' example is humility: taking the posture of a learner as we enter cross-cultural relationships. We'll explore this more deeply in the chapter on Virtues of the Culturally Intelligent Christian Coach.

Jesus was fully human and fully divine. He came from heaven, but made his home on earth in first century Palestine. He was thoroughly immersed in Jewish culture and acutely aware of that culture's intersection with the Roman occupation (turning the other cheek, going the extra mile, giving to Caesar what is Caesar's). He moved between village culture and the cosmopolitan culture of urban centers like Jerusalem, whose elite had been strongly impacted by Greek values and customs.

But while Jesus constantly made reference to local culture, using examples, metaphors, and values from first century Palestine as he taught, ate, and walked with his followers, he also spoke constantly of the heavenly kingdom to which he belonged. In his well-known Sermon on the Mount (Matthew 5-7), Jesus refers to the kingdom of heaven or to heaven sixteen times in one long teaching session. But even those stories centered around his heavenly kingdom are filled with familiar cultural articles and activities—bread making, lighting a lamp, being forced to march with a soldier, tax collectors, familiar birds and wildflowers. Jesus was a master at dancing between cultures.

Jesus was tuned in both to kingdom values and to the values of the culture around him. He could function fully on earth while keeping his citizenship in heaven. He affirmed his listener's culture through his own full immersion into that culture. He honored his listeners by drawing examples from their own everyday lives. He shared life with them.

He also gave up some significant perks to become part of his listener's world. He gave up heaven! Yet Jesus also kept one foot in the heavenly realms. His ears

---

16   Sherwood G. Lingenfelter and Marvin K. Mayers, *Ministering Cross-Culturally: An Incarnational Model for Personal Relationships.* 2nd ed. (Grand Rapids, MI: Baker Academic, 2007), 16.

and heart were tuned to his Father's voice, and he only did what he saw his Father doing. His ministry was to call his listeners to recognize the heavenly kingdom from which he came and to join fully in God's family.

Jesus' sacrifice did not end with giving up heaven. He also gave up his life to establish full and sweet communication between us and our heavenly Father. Jesus with his own body became a bridge from our earthly culture to our heavenly inheritance, the ultimate act of love for us.

What can we learn from this? We can never fully live up to Jesus' example because we don't have the capacity to be perfect as he is. But to the best of our ability, we can honor the cultures we work with and minister to. Becoming a culturally intelligent coach has a lot to do with finding ways to appreciate and even love other cultures. But being a cultural bridge—a "world Christian", as some authors term it—sometimes means laying down our own comfort, our own desires and values, our own preferences. It involves sacrificial love.[17]

Furthermore, although Jesus was immersed in the culture of first century Palestine, his first allegiance was to the kingdom of heaven. Jesus was willing to challenge culture and cultural values when they clashed with kingdom values. There are times when he certainly did not hold back. Think about the culture in the temple at the time with money changers and animal sacrifices. Jesus' declaration to those doing commerce in his Father's house (Matthew 21:12-13) as he drove them out of the temple, overturning their tables and benches, was definitely not politically correct. In fact, I'd say it was politically disastrous!

Often the values that came through in Jesus' teaching felt foreign to those who listened. They continue to feel foreign to us today. This is because Jesus was living the values of another kingdom, and he was calling his listeners to be part of that kingdom while continuing to be a part of daily local culture on earth.[18]

As we encounter culture in our coaching work and ministry, we will discover God reflected in new and beautiful ways in other cultures. We will also encounter distortion of that beauty. As missions professor Dr. James Plueddemann says in his book *Leading Across Cultures*: "God is at work in every culture, but Satan is too."[19] Jesus' example shows us that our first allegiance is not to our own culture or our client's culture, but to God's values and purposes.

---

17   Ibid., 25.
18   Livermore, *Cultural Intelligence*, 36-7.
19   James E. Plueddeman, *Leading Across Cultures: Effective Ministry and Mission in the Global Church* (Downers Grove, IL: IVP Academic, 2009), 65.

Culture in the New Testament

Culture is a pretty big theme in the new Christian church, formed after Jesus' death. Reading through the book of Acts is like going on a cultural odyssey. In chapter two of Acts, the joyous event of Pentecost kicks off that journey (Acts 2:6b-11):

> A crowd came together in bewilderment, because each one heard them speaking in his own language. Utterly amazed, they asked: "Are not all these men who are speaking Galileans? Then how is it that each of us hears them in his own native language? Parthians, Medes and Elamites; residents of Mesopotamia, Judea and Cappadocia, Pontus and Asia, Phrygia and Pamphylia, Egypt and the part of Libya near Cyrene; visitors from Rome (both Jews and converts to Judaism); Cretans and Arab—we hear them declaring the wonders of God in our own tongues!"

Peter addresses the bewildered cross-cultural crowd with a quote from the Old Testament prophet Joel (Joel 2:28-32), announcing that God's spirit will be poured out on all people. The redemptive thread of welcome to all that runs through the Old Testament now comes to fruition, mediated by Jesus' blood and sealed with the Holy Spirit.

But cultural tensions very quickly engender conflict within the new church and persecution from the prevailing culture. Peter and John are hauled before the Sanhedrin. Stephen is martyred. Peter receives a vision about what is clean and unclean. He begins eating with uncircumcised believers who have received the Holy Spirit and is in turn both welcomed and criticized. At one point, the Jews in Philippi bring the apostle Paul and his preaching companion Silas to the magistrates, claiming:

> These men are Jews and are throwing our city into an uproar by advocating customs unlawful for us Romans to accept or practice (Acts 16:20b-21).

In Acts 15, "sharp dispute and debate" also ensues in the young church over who can be saved and what customs and cultural practices are necessary. As the believers begin to embrace the reality of welcoming the stranger and living out of the new covenant, the church opens its arms to new believers from non-Jewish (Gentile) backgrounds. The hard work of sorting out what is essential to Christianity and what is simply cultural preference begins to take place.

The apostle Paul, missionary to non-Jewish people groups throughout the New Testament, is a figure of great cultural intelligence. In his New Testament writings and sermons, Paul brings light to cultural discussions and navigates constantly between cultures. His own example of sacrificial love for those from other cultures is inspiring. After his conversion, Paul travels to Arabia, Greece, Macedonia (Eastern Europe), Syria, Turkey, Judea, Samaria, Cyprus, Italy, and Crete. Paul wields his Roman citizenship masterfully when necessary (Acts 22:25-29). Similarly, he uses his Jewish heritage to gain audience with the people in Jerusalem after he is arrested (Acts 21:39). Paul's attitude towards those from other backgrounds and cultures is loving, powerful, and sacrificial (1 Corinthians 9:19-23):

> Though I am free and belong to no man, I make myself a slave to everyone, to win as many as possible. To the Jews, I became like a Jew, to win the Jews. To those under the law, I became like one under the law (though I myself am not under the law), so as to win those under the law. To those not having the law, I became like one not having the law (though I am not free from God's law but am under Christ's law), so as to win those not having the law. To the weak I became weak, to win the weak. I have become all things to all men so that by all possible means I might save some. I do all this for the sake of the gospel that I may share in its blessings.

The example of Paul inspires me. It's a high bar. In and of myself, I don't think I could live out this kind of sacrificial love. But as Christians, it is Jesus' resurrection power in us that enables us to incarnate this kind of radical cultural intelligence.

Take a Minute

- *How have you welcomed or not welcomed others who are culturally different from you or your family? If God's purpose was that our homes, families, churches, businesses, and organizations reflect a culture of welcome, what would need to change in your sphere of influence? What is one thing you can do about that?*
- *What is the most humbling thing for you about being a learner in a new cultural setting or relationship? What will you have to give up to learn deeply and well?*
- *Think about a cross-cultural client you are coaching right now. Flesh out how you could apply Paul's formula (becoming "like" your client) to your coaching of that client.*

Chapter Three

Lining up with Love

I John 3:18: Dear children, let us not love with words or tongue but with actions and in truth.

Love is a powerful word. It is also a biblical concept. While the Bible speaks a lot about love and a good bit about patience, bearing with one another, and unity, I find little in Scripture about tolerance as we define it in the twenty-first century. In fact, tolerance as we currently understand it is a lukewarm concept. I don't think God is asking us to be more tolerant of other cultures and other people. I believe he is asking us to love them.

Love is a different standard. For one, it's a lot more work. Love is not the same as political correctness. It's not avoidant. It's not defaulting to the lowest common denominator. Love is strong and sure, but graceful and meek. Love balances between justice and mercy. Love embraces the tension between knowing and understanding our own culture, knowing and understanding another's culture, and giving first allegiance to God's kingdom. Love allows us to begin to master dancing between cultures.

Love allows us to begin to master dancing between cultures.

As we start to explore, understand, and extend love towards other cultures and peoples, I am not advocating that we each abandon our own culture. We coach best when we know and understand ourselves. Becoming a culturally intelligent Christian is not about rejecting who we are, but embracing our own culture and the cultures of others.

But we cannot stop there. Culture is varied and beautiful at its finest, but not everything in every culture is good. Giving first allegiance to God means that we measure cultural values, customs, and worldviews—both ours and others—by God's standards. Leading missiological anthropologist Paul G. Hiebert says in his book *Anthropological Insights for Missionaries*:

> The gospel serves a prophetic function, showing us the way God intended us to live as human beings and judging our lives and our cultures by those norms.[20]

Remember the Iceberg

That is a lot harder to do than it seems. Much of our own cultural values, norms, and beliefs are below the waterline. Nor are they in our conscious awareness much of the time. We interpret Scripture through the screen of our culture, and it is hard to escape this influence. Mark Powell, author of *What Do They Hear? Bridging the Gap between Pulpit and Pew*, studied how Christians from Tanzania, the U.S., and Russia read the parable of the Prodigal Son in Luke 15. Each group was asked, "Why was the prodigal son in the pigpen?" North Americans responded that it was because the prodigal son squandered his inheritance. Russians that it was because of the famine. Tanzanians because no one gave him anything to eat.[21]

The first time I heard this study, I am embarrassed to admit that I laughed inwardly at how the Russians and Tanzanians answered. "What famine?" I thought. "And of course, the Africans would be thinking group responsibility instead of individual responsibility!" I was humbled when I read the full text (Luke 15:13-16):

> Not long after that, the younger son got together all he had, set off for a distant country and there **squandered his wealth** in wild living. After he had spent everything, there was a **severe famine** in that whole country and he began to be in need. So, he went and hired himself out to a citizen of that country, who sent him to his fields to feed pigs. He longed to fill his stomach with the pods that the pigs were eating, but **no one gave him anything.**

Powell goes on to describe how translation and meaning differences influence interpretation of this parable in vastly different ways among these three cultural groups. That chapter alone is well worth the price of his book. There are many other examples of how we "read" our own culture into Scripture. Adjusting our

---

20   Paul G. Hiebert, Anthropological Insights for Missionaries (Grand Rapids, MI: Baker Academic, 1985), 56.

21   Mark Allan Powell, *What do they hear? Bridging the Gap Between Pulpit and Pew*, (Nashville, Abingdon Press, 2007), 11-27.

perspective culturally as we read biblical texts can bring new light to old stories. What if we looked at the story of Zacchaeus through the lens of Status/Equality values or a Mediterranean honor/shame dynamic?[22] What if the excuses of those invited to the great banquet in Luke 14 were an indirect rebuke to a host who was not honoring the expected stratified social structure (Status, Community, and Indirect communication values)?[23]

Our cultural "lens" is real! And though we may see and interpret things differently, at times each perspective is correct. As the Quakers would say, there is "that of God" in every culture, and every culture brings something unique and special to the banquet table of the Lord. Hiebert writes:

> Not only are all cultures capable of expressing the heart of the gospel, but each also brings to light certain salient features of the gospel that have remained less visible or even hidden in other cultures. Churches in different cultures can help us to understand the many-sided wisdom of God, thereby serving as channels for understanding different facets of divine revelation, truths that a theology tied to one particular culture can easily overlook.[24]

So, we are back to the example of Jesus beginning as a learner with humility. But at times, we will see the side of a culture that does not reflect God. For example, in some cultures, male children are valued over female. In some places, infanticide or abuse is common. Where life is not valued or abuse is tolerated, it is clear that God is not being reflected in the culture. These are complex issues to be approached with a great deal of prayer and humility. We'll deal more deeply with evaluating and transforming culture in the chapters on skills of the culturally intelligent coach.

What Does an Ideal Cross-cultural Coaching Relationship Look Like?

We've identified the love that God has for all of creation and the welcome he creates for all. We've examined the humble learner posture of Jesus and his graceful ability to dance between cultures, tuning into the values of both earth and heaven while maintaining allegiance to the kingdom. We've discovered the New Testament church's struggle with culture and unity and read Paul's inspiring

---

22   Richard L. Rohrbaugh, The New Testament in Cross-Cultural Perspective (Eugene, OR: Cascade Books, 2007), 77-88.

23   Ibid., 147-168.

24   Paul G. Hiebert, *Anthropological Insights for Missionaries* (Grand Rapids, MI: Baker Academic, 1985), 55.

words on adaptation and sacrifice. We've recognized that God asks us to imitate his love for others, and we've begun to sense the humility needed on our part in the work of transforming culture. What does all this look like in a coaching relationship? Let's return to my friend, Carl. Here's what he shared with me recently about his coaching:

> I love being a learner when I come into these [cross-cultural coaching] contexts. I coach Arabs mostly, but also some Scandinavians, Koreans, Africans, and Americans, most of them living in this region. There is so much richness to appreciate and learn from. But in my region, especially, there is so much turmoil and so many negative news reports, it just hurts my heart. I see a whole different picture. One way I see this is in the Palestinian and Arab value for family; it reflects the heart of God.
>
> Sometimes I feel like the decision-making process gets dragged on and on with consultation and talking to people and so on. I've had to wrestle with that in coaching, it's stretched me. I am more prone to an individual Autonomy focus. But I have to put my bias aside. I see this one person in front of me, but my coachee sees everybody around him, so I need to see through his eyes. There is so much more potential in coaching because your coaching will not just impact one, but the whole community. It goes bigger and broader, not just with coaching, but for the kingdom of God. There is exponential potential to multiply, and that's what motivates me, the potential that is locked up within. I must respect their Community value and how long the process takes, even when it drags on. Now when it happens, I just see impact. No need to rush.[25]

Carl inspires me. To me, he is a visual picture of what a coach looks like who has God's heart amidst cultural diversity. He crosses back and forth between cultures gracefully and humbly. He has learned to look through his coachee's eyes. He has recognized one of the particular ways that the culture he lives in reflects God's best, even when that value is in opposition to what he grew up with and operates out of himself. In several conversations I've had with Carl, he's expressed a sense of loss when he has seen Arab friends move to Autonomy cultures and lose their sense of family, or when he has observed others insisting on Arabs adopting an Autonomy approach in business or ministry. He writes:

> Those who have been submerged in the expat circles start to lose their Community orientation and become more individual, and this is something I don't want

---

25   Carl, Personal Communication, Permission granted on August 2, 2015.

to see multiplied in the community through my coaching. This connectivity in the community is very powerful and can bring far greater impact when you are coaching the client, but also through them, multiplied impact on the host culture also.[26]

Isaac Canales in Multi-Ethnicity says:

The church's distinguishing feature can become our determination to live life together as our Lord intended in a world whose solutions include segregation, violence, and polite toleration. We can freely affirm our variety (a key characteristic of our Creator's work), enjoy one another's cultures, and learn from the interplay of our strengths and weaknesses . . . meeting, working, and living together as partners keeps us in a position of submission before God and one another. In this way, we truly become light in the darkness, a living proclamation of Yahweh as Creator and Lover of all peoples and cultures.[27]

Carl's choice to live in a violence-prone area with constant security concerns is a response of obedient sacrifice to God's call to him as an individual. It has resulted in a life of joy, discovery, meaning, and value as he functions within his own culture and that of those he serves. Whether we coach in the Middle East or the Midwest United States, we can all embrace God's call to love the stranger and to discover what is godly and beautiful in their culture, while maintaining our allegiance to God and his kingdom.

Whether we coach in the Middle East or the Midwest United States, we can all embrace God's call to love the stranger.

Summary

God is the loving Creator of the culture of welcome. His purposes for us are for all to be gathered together and worship before his throne. He sent Jesus to us to incarnate his purpose. To show us what it means to learn deeply about how to love and embrace others who are different. To invite us to become kingdom citizens. The account of the early church in Acts and the remainder of the New Testament includes stories of adaptation, cultural tension, and the power of God to live sacrificially among others. As we delve into cross-cultural coaching, we take with us a powerful inheritance as God's daughters and sons. We enter into this inheritance as we let love be our standard and humility our guide.

---

26   Ibid.

27   Isaac Canales, *Multi-Ethnicity, Global Issues Bible Studies.* Edited by Stephen Hayner and Gordon Aeschliman (Downers Grove, IL: Intervarsity Press, 1990), 17.

Take a Minute

- *What have you discovered in your cross-cultural client's culture that was unexpected or new to you, but is godly and beautiful? How does that broaden your understanding of God?*
- *When have you encountered an ungodly aspect of culture in your coaching practice? How did you respond?*

Chapter Four

Cultural Intelligence 101

In 1978, I embarked on a thirteen-week service/learning semester in Haiti as part of my undergraduate experience. Before leaving, our group underwent several orientation sessions. The group leaders did their best to prepare this group of twenty-five eager and inexperienced young adults for life in the "majority world". Referenced more commonly in the last century as the "third world" or "developing world", the term "majority world" highlights the fact that it comprises more of the world's population than the so-called "first" or "developed" world. In our orientation, we learned about Haitian culture, languages spoken (French and Creole), and what to expect of our host family and the program itself.

The faculty couple leading our group encouraged us to open our hearts and minds to a new people, a new country, and new rhythms of daily life. We were introduced to the concept of culture shock and warned that we'd feel both alone and different when we arrived. Other students who had already finished their service-learning semester advised us that we would see our own country through different eyes when we returned. Excited, eager, and anxious, we boarded a bus to Miami to catch our flight to Haiti and begin the adventure.

When we arrived in Port-au-Prince, we were each met by our host family. I was scared silly to think I would be living with strangers who spoke another language for six weeks. During those first days in Haiti, everything felt new and raw. Walking to classes each day was an education in itself as I encountered beggars, crazy traffic, the smells of street food and jasmine, sweat and sewage. Then there were the outrageously dangerous sidewalks. I learned to watch my feet so I would not fall into inexplicable meter-deep holes at irregular intervals. In the evening, I walked home to my host family for plates and plates of rice and beans and conversations with my host sister, Helene.

In week seven, our group left the city for service assignments. I was excited about working with Mennonite Central Committee (MCC) in north-central

Haiti in the field of nutrition education. This involved walking many miles with the MCC nutrition coordinator, knapsacks of supplies on our backs. We forded wide, shallow rivers on foot. We steadfastly ate lots of memorably bitter "green leaves" (full of vitamins missing in the diet of that region). We weighed and cradled many malnourished babies of mothers with few resources. After a day in the villages, I often returned to our clean and roomy villa shell-shocked and grief-stricken.

As a twenty-year-old college student, this experience impacted me profoundly. It changed my perspective about ministry. About wealth, poverty, and service. About God. And about myself as well. In many ways, the orientation program prepared us well for a life-changing experience. I continue to be deeply grateful for the opportunity I had as a young adult to live and learn briefly in the majority world.

But as I look back now on that significant semester from the vantage point of a decade of cross-cultural coaching, I am also aware of what I did *not* learn during that first immersion in cross-cultural life and relationship. I was not prepared for and did not understand that Haitians thought and experienced the world in fundamentally different ways than I did. I could see the "above the waterline" differences. These became clearer and clearer as the weeks went by. Different diet. Different clothing. Different language. Oh, how I struggled with language! Different pace of life.

I could see the conditions and lack of expectations created by poverty and by scarce resources. I no longer expected hot water. I saw with grief that not everyone could go to school. I saw that it was difficult to maintain vehicles, buildings, and roads without resources. I experienced my host mother's desire to see me become plump and "healthy". My host sister's carefully defined and bounded world. My host brother-in-law's expectations of Americans (rich and immoral!). When I served in the villages of northern Haiti, I experienced the loss of hope for small babies who were malnourished and felt devastated for their moms.

Much of what I experienced as different, I attributed to poverty and lack of resources. I did not understand that another dynamic was also at work. I did not recognize that what I experienced as loose time management was a value for spending time rather than saving it. I did not understand that the lack of planning I experienced was a cultural preference for living in the moment rather than planning for possible negative outcomes that might not actually happen. I did not understand the depth to which my behavior reflected on my host family because I did not understand the web of relationship in which my host family lived. I continued to wear my own cultural lens, and because I lacked knowledge and sufficient motivation, I failed to fully enter my host family's world.

When two decades later in my forties, I began to coach missionaries, both Americans and those from Europe and Asia, I was profoundly impacted by their loneliness along with their desire to serve God and their neighbors with grace and excellence. These solitary leaders, often living many hours from anyone of their own culture or language, were living out the calling of God on their lives to minister, serve, and sacrifice for others in ways I deeply admired. God ignited in me a passion to serve these leaders.

As I did, I began to see, feel, and hear the depth of my ignorance about the cultures and worldviews of others. I began to open myself up to learn deeply about how my clients experienced the world. I confessed my ignorance and asked lots of questions. I welcomed their perspective about my culture and discovered with surprise how they experienced me (none of my American friends or family would *ever* have described me as relentlessly cheerful and optimistic!). I heard and pondered their comments about the American "Lone Rangers" they had worked with in the past. I began to read about cross-cultural issues.

My relationships with my clients taught me about the narrowness of my assumptions about life, about Scripture, about lifestyle, and about leadership.

My relationships with my clients taught me about the narrowness of my assumptions about life, about Scripture, about lifestyle, and about leadership. Delving deeply into their worlds began to bring clarity to my own values, beliefs, and motivations. I began to interpret both their behavior and my own differently. I became more flexible. Some gray areas became grayer, and others became much clearer. I became more open to other viewpoints. I began to adapt my coaching style, my schedule, the pace of the session, and even the questions I asked to fit more effectively into my clients' cultures.

Becoming a culturally intelligent coach is a process of transformation. As coaches, we already know about the change process. After all, we are change experts. The elements in the process of becoming a culturally intelligent coach will be familiar. Coaches know that the change process is powered by motivation, deepens with perspective and application, and results in new strategies and behaviors.

As Christian coaches and leaders, we also know that true transformation begins with God's initiative. God draws us into awareness of our need for change. He provides new motivation and perseverance and at times brings divine understanding and strategies. Deep change takes time. In adults, such change draws from and builds on experience and application. As Christians, we believe that as we grow and become more like Christ, fruitfulness and multiplication result. You'll see all these elements at work as we talk about cultural intelligence.

I want to invite you to take this change journey seriously and joyfully. It's a whole new adventure in learning and growth. And I fully expect that as you become more culturally intelligent, you will also become more fruitful and effective as a coach and as a leader.

Why Do I Need Cultural Intelligence (CQ)?

As Christians and as Christian coaches, our mandate is to reach out to those we serve with the transforming love of God. Dr. David Livermore in *Cultural Intelligence* writes:

> Love is the primary reason cultural intelligence is an essential competency in the life of twenty-first-century ministry leaders . . . The goal isn't cultural intelligence in and of itself. Instead, cultural intelligence is the pathway for moving us along in the journey from the desire to love the Other (those who are not like us) to the ability to express that love in ways that are meaningful and respectful.[28]

Without CQ, our ability to effectively love and serve others across cultures is limited. Our coaching and, in consequence, the transformation that could result from that coaching will be weakened by misunderstanding and lack of humility and flexibility. For instance, as coaches, we learn to rely on our EQ (emotional intelligence) to hone in on red flags, pick up inconsistencies, and read non-verbal signals. However, in cross-cultural situations, CQ is a greater predictor of success in relationships than EQ, which relies on picking up cues which are usually related to (differing) cultural values.[29]

And, there's more, according to David Livermore in *The Cultural Intelligence Difference*:

---

28   David A. Livermore, *Cultural Intelligence: Improving Your CQ to Engage Our Multicultural World* (Grand Rapids, MI: Baker, 2009), 14-15.
29   David A. Livermore, *The Cultural Intelligence Difference: Master the One Skill You Can't Do Without in Today's Global Economy* (New York, American Management Association, 2011), 13.

Those with higher CQ will adjust more successfully cross-culturally. CQ is related to greater flexibility, ability to work with multicultural teams, and even to foster collaborative environments across cultures.

CQ increases job performance. Networking across cultures, anticipating and managing risk, and making complex decisions that involve cultural dynamics are all impacted by CQ.

Higher CQ decreases stress in cross-cultural situations. Those with higher CQ enjoy the process of traveling and working internationally more than those with lower CQ. Higher CQ results in less stress and burnout for cross-cultural workers.

CQ increases profitability. Individuals with CQ earn more on average.[30]

So, how does all of this apply to coaching? You can expect that developing your CQ will allow you to adjust more easily and quickly to coaching others of different cultures. It will increase your effectiveness as a coach for both individuals and teams. It will increase your enjoyment and decrease your stress in the process. Those are big wins. For those who coach for profit, earning more is an added benefit.

Coaching cross-culturally also involves assisting our clients with *their* cross-cultural adjustment. How many of our expat clients would benefit from decreased stress, increased flexibility, and greater enjoyment of their cross-cultural work or missions assignment? Understanding the concept of CQ and how to develop it adds value to the coaching process as we walk alongside clients grappling with cross-cultural issues and cross-cultural adjustment themselves.

Finally, without CQ, we run the risk of not only being ineffective coaches, but of undermining the value of the coaching process and inoculating cross-cultural clients to the benefits of coaching. In *Values Sensitive Coaching: The DELTA Approach to Coaching Culturally Diverse Executives*, the authors write: "culturally uninformed coaching techniques are ineffective at best and damaging and costly at worst."[31] When we do not take the time and energy to understand our client's cultural setting and values, when we do not employ appropriate questions and strategies, and when we do not adapt our behavior in order to walk effectively *with* our cross-cultural clients, the change process is undermined. What a loss for the kingdom of God!

---

30   Ibid., 12-18.
31   Chris W. Coultas, Wendy L. Bedwell, C. Shawn Burke, and Eduardo Salas, "Values Sensitive Coaching: The Delta Approach to Coaching Culturally Diverse Executives," *Consulting Psychology Journal* 63, no.3 (September 2011): 155.

What is CQ?

Researchers, including Dr. Livermore and colleagues at the Cultural Intelligence Center, have pioneered understanding of CQ as a specific type of intelligence. CQ measures a distinct form of intelligence that relates to our ability to adapt and function effectively in a variety of cultural settings.[32] Throughout this book, we'll use the language of Cultural Intelligence or CQ. CQ applied to coaching is simply your capacity to coach effectively with understanding and respect across cultures. Just a few points to keep in mind about CQ:

- CQ can be developed. Although some may develop it more easily than others, it is not a given. Unlike your personality profile or motivational gifting, CQ can be changed, gained, and increased across your lifetime.[33]
- CQ is more predictive of cross-cultural adjustment than is age, gender, or IQ.[34]
- CQ is more than head knowledge. It includes motivation, strategy, and action.
- CQ is real and relevant. Research suggests that CQ can predict "adjustment, well-being, cultural judgment and decision making, and task performance in culturally diverse settings".[35]

CQ identifies four important elements or learning modes, which will be familiar to coaches:

- Drive or Motivation
- Knowledge
- Strategy
- Action or Behavior

Notice that knowledge is only one component of CQ. We often think of knowledge or insight as the magic pill that will transform. Again, as coaches, we know that deep change results when a combination of factors and learning modes are present. In this book, for instance, you will often find sections that will ask you to *stop* and deploy other methods of learning like reflection, experimentation, and

---

32   Livermore, *The Cultural Intelligence Difference*, 3.
33   Livermore, Cultural Intelligence, 47.
34   Livermore, *The Cultural Intelligence Difference*, 13.
35   Cultural Intelligence Center, 2008.

application to increase your retention and integration of the material.

What we must keep in mind here is that these four elements are all interdependent. You can have tremendous drive to be culturally intelligent, but if you have no knowledge about cultural values, you'll have a rough road. You can have a lot of knowledge about culture and speak several languages, but if you don't apply that knowledge and change your behaviors, you will not coach with cultural intelligence.

Take a Minute

Think through these questions before moving on.

- *What experiences has God provided you with recently that have resulted in your interest in cross-cultural coaching?*
- *How is God partnering with you right now to develop your cultural intelligence? Ask Him if you aren't sure.*
- *What's your biggest motivator to learn about cross-cultural coaching?*

Chapter Five

Becoming a Culturally Intelligent Coach

We've already discovered that CQ has four components: Drive, Knowledge, Strategy, and Action. We've explored why you need CQ and that gaining it will be a process of transformation. As we start on that transformational journey, let's take a closer look at CQ Drive, Knowledge, Strategy, and Action and how to intentionally increase each of those components as we coach others.

A great way to find out where you are starting in this journey is to take the CQ Self-Assessment available when you purchase *The Cultural Intelligence Difference*, or directly from the Cultural Intelligence Center. This assessment will give you some baseline data about your level of CQ in each of the four component areas. A quick four question scale is available online at the site, or contact the CIC to take the full assessment.

CQ Drive

When I lived and served in Haiti as a twenty-year-old, I was not motivated to really understand the experience of my host family. Admittedly, I was distracted at the time by my relationship with a fellow student (who later became my husband). While I enjoyed my host sister, I saw no benefit in entering my host family's world since I would be with them for only six weeks. I was turned off by my host brother-in-law and wanted to avoid him at every possible turn. And since my host mother spoke only Creole (my French was bad enough; my Creole nonexistent), I had little confidence in relating to her.

Drive is the component of CQ that coaches would call motivation. Drive is a combination of interest, confidence, and perseverance. As coaches, we know that when our clients are not motivated, change doesn't happen and goals and action steps are not finished. And when our clients lose their confidence, growth is stalled. It's the same way with CQ Drive. Without it, not much will happen.

My experience in trying to relate to my host family in Haiti illustrates some of the components of CQ Drive: interest, enjoyment (or avoidance), seeing the benefits of cross-cultural interaction, and the level of confidence you have in those interactions. Those with high CQ Drive will be drawn to cross-cultural coaching and other cross-cultural experiences and will be energized by them. They will expect success in cross-cultural settings and feel a sense of competence rather than worry or anxiety.

Thankfully, my CQ Drive increased when I began coaching cross-cultural workers. However, as with most significant growth goals, there is a cost to becoming more culturally intelligent. We'll delve into that in the chapter on finishing well.

Increasing Your CQ Drive

Coaches know how to increase motivation, and many of the techniques we use are applicable here. Choose one or more of the following strategies that will work for you.

Picture a desired future: Imagine the benefits of increased CQ in your coaching. Review the list of CQ benefits found in the section titled "Why do I need Cultural Intelligence?" in the previous chapter and how they relate to coaching. Pick the item on the list that motivates you most. Either in your journal or with your coach, spouse or friend, flesh out in detail the result of having attained the item you chose. Use your five senses to really imagine yourself in the future.[36]

Develop an action item: Often in coaching we encourage our clients to celebrate successes and build in rewards. What reward would motivate you to work on developing your CQ? Develop a specific action step (i.e., a clear, concrete course of action, including a deadline) that implements your decision.

Establish accountability: Set action steps with your coach or a trusted friend and ask them to hold you accountable. Coaches know how much accountability can increase successful goal attainment!

---

36   Ibid., 54.

Set achievable goals: Gain confidence by setting small goals and experiencing success. As coaches, we're aware that sometimes all it takes for our clients to gain confidence is to score a small win. Set an achievable goal. For instance, tackle a cross-cultural situation that is only a tiny bit uncomfortable like learning to greet your client in their language or checking out a cultural event in your area. Build on small wins to increase your confidence.

CQ Knowledge

Let's look next at the second element of cultural intelligence: knowledge. When I first began coaching South Asian and British clients, my coaching felt flat. It seemed like my clients and I were doing the mechanics of coaching, but not getting to the heart level. I was getting bored. I questioned whether my clients were interested in deep change or whether I was doing a good job in serving them.

Learning about the cultural value for Vulnerability vs. Concealment (we discussed this concept in my first illustration back in the introduction) helped me understand what was going on. I am an American from a "Vulnerability" culture (i.e., a culture that values candidness and sharing internal thought and feeling). Coaching, which was developed primarily in the United States, assumes a certain level of vulnerable sharing. Britain and India are Concealment cultures (i.e., cultures that value reticence and conceal weakness). The British are famously reserved. My Indian clients learned early in life to "save face". Neither was inclined to open up to me easily or quickly in the way I had come to expect from my American clients.

CQ Knowledge is awareness of how culture influences behaviors, relationships, and worldview, both our own and that of others. Knowledge can come from experience or from formal learning such as classes, seminars, reading. One of the most important components for me in my own journey towards CQ was gaining knowledge about differing cultural values. This enabled me to understand a client's responses and behaviors at a deeper level.

It is critical for a coach to understand cultural values.

I cannot overemphasize how important it is for a coach to understand cultural values. In fact, we'll be spending a great deal of time in Section Two on various cultural values that impact the coaching process and coaching relationship. Cultural values reveal so much about the way people think and behave. Often simply identifying the differing cultural value will bring light to a misunderstanding in the coaching relationship, reveal which coaching technique is appropriate in a given situation, or cast an entirely new perspective on an obstacle and possible solutions.

But awareness of the client's values is not enough. As an example, I had a northern European client who was working in Asia. As our relationship became deeper, my client mentioned that at the beginning of our coaching relationship, he'd felt uncomfortable with how cheery I was. My constant encouragement and the celebration of progress I offered at the beginning of each coaching session had felt to him inauthentic and uncomfortable. I was shocked. I had never before been described as overly optimistic. In fact, my personality inclines me towards seeing problems rather than possibilities. I had worked hard at becoming more optimistic and encouraging in my coaching relationships.

So just what was going on here? The way I had expressed encouragement to this client revealed my belief that the client's individual actions were powerful and significant and that singling these out for praise would be motivating. In contrast, my client's background and current cultural context shaped his own belief that success was often dependent on circumstances and that humility was therefore a virtue. My enthusiastic celebration of his progress felt artificial and even wrong to him. As I came to understand how I appeared from my client's perspective, I learned something about my own cultural values.

Another crucial aspect of CQ Knowledge for the coaching leader is self-awareness—i.e., understanding one's own cultural values and the impact of "below the waterline" beliefs on one's own behaviors. Brooks Peterson, founder and president of Across Cultures Inc., states in his book *Cultural Intelligence*: "Self-awareness and awareness of others are built in an ever-increasing cycle, each enhancing the other."[37] In chapter one we discussed the importance of self-awareness for coaches. Without self-knowledge, we can easily get in the way of our coachee's process. Knowledge about our own cultural values can come in "aha!" moments when reading, observing others, returning home from another culture, in a cross-cultural team setting, or when others give us honest feedback.

But CQ Knowledge is not just about seeing ourselves. It is about seeing our *culture* with different eyes. When I was in Haiti, my host brother-in-law, who had lived briefly in the U.S. and constantly watched American TV, made clear to me his belief that American women were obsessed with sex, makeup, and materi-

---

37   Brooks Peterson, *Cultural Intelligence: A Guide to Working with People from Other Cultures* (Boston: Intercultural Press, 2004), 162.

alism. No amount of conversation with me convinced him otherwise, and his actions towards me were based on his internal beliefs. Needless to say, that made any interaction with him very uncomfortable.

Whatever area of the world we come from, others around us will make assumptions about us based on our culture. Sometimes those assumptions will be accurate. Sometimes they will not. But they *will* impact our relationships with those we coach. Being aware of how others view our culture is an important, though sometimes uncomfortable, part of developing CQ.

Another aspect of CQ Knowledge concerns manners and customs. While not as foundationally important as understanding cultural values and being self-aware, basic understanding of manners and customs helps pave the way to trust within the coaching relationship. On my first trip to India, I quickly learned not to show the soles of my feet to others and to greet others with an honorific (Dr., Reverend) vs. adopting a first-name familiarity (Hi, Tom! Hey, Nancy!). Such customs are connected to a cultural value for Status and for showing respect to others. But there is no way I could have discerned these particular customs simply by knowing that India's culture values Status over Equality.

Learning particular customs and manners relevant to those we are coaching is especially important at the beginning of the coaching relationship as we build trust and rapport. Learning these formalities is like learning formulas in math class. They may not make sense, but we had best memorize them because they will come in handy later. Coaches cannot be expected to know all these rituals for every culture. But we can ask our clients how they would like to be greeted and invite them to help us learn the essential dos and don'ts in their culture that might impact the coaching relationship.

Lastly, understanding the language of a culture can be a very important element of CQ Knowledge. Dr. Cory Lemke, Ph.D., an American coach who has lived and worked for over a decade in Ukraine and does most of his coaching in Russian, shared this story illustrating the importance of language in adapting to culture:

> People effective in Eastern Europe are those who begin to understand and assimilate into the culture. You become a little schizophrenic as you assimilate. I had to learn the Russian language. As I learned it, I consciously adapted my speech, phrasing, ideas, and thought processes to reflect Russian and Ukrainian cultural values. Every time I spoke Russian, I intentionally tried to integrate the values. If I had just adapted the Russian to my English thought processes, they

still wouldn't have understood the ideas I was trying to communicate. It had to be intentional. I thought it through. I worked at it. That allowed me to be schizophrenic in a healthy way. I didn't try to adopt and adapt to the Ukrainian cultural values when speaking in English.[38]

Beyond the simple ability to communicate, the structure of a language itself often reveals and reflects cultural values. Word choice or the absence or proliferation of certain words is also instructive. One example is that in English there is no formal "you" conjugation, as can be found in many other languages. English speakers use the same form of "you" when referring to everyone from a young child or their housekeeper to their boss, leader or the president/queen. In contrast, some languages have many, many forms of "you" based on differing relationships with the person being addressed. The singular form of "you" in English reveals the deep value for Equality that the English-speaking Western world typically shares.

Increasing Your CQ Knowledge

We'll be spending a lot of time on self-awareness and learning about cultural values, both of which are essential parts of CQ Knowledge, in later chapters. But here are some other ways you can increase your CQ Knowledge:

- When you have a new client from a culture you have not worked with before, spend some time researching your client's culture, country history, and customs.[39]
- Follow your curiosity. This common coaching concept is a powerful tool for the cross-cultural coach. Ask your client about their culture and heritage. Ask about family. Ask about their cross-cultural experiences. Ask how their culture typically views persons from your culture. Use curiosity.
- Learn a language. Delve into another way of communicating.[40]
- Experience the art, literature, or entertainment valued in your client's culture. My husband learns a lot about his clients' cultures and values by going to their host country's sports events with them. A leader doing short-term ministry trips to Brazil brushed up on her Portuguese by watching soccer matches on Brazilian cable TV.

---

38   Dr. Cory Lemke, Personal Communication, Permission granted on July 3, 2015.
39   Livermore, *The Cultural Intelligence Difference*, 82.
40   Ibid., 98.

CQ Strategy

So, what do you do with your CQ Knowledge once you have used your Drive to obtain it? This leads us to the third component of cultural intelligence: CQ Strategy. Let's go back to my experience with South Asian and British clients. I became aware (CQ Knowledge) of the differing cultural value for Concealment (being reserved or saving face) that my clients had. CQ Strategy kicked in when I reflected on these differences outside of sessions and began to plan for them. I changed my expectations about how quickly my clients would be comfortable with vulnerability. I decided to let them set the pace for revealing personal weaknesses and settled in for a longer focus on performance goals that were less interesting to me.

I also became aware of the specific ways my clients avoided vulnerability or admitting to weakness during our sessions. With the Brits, this might be through changing the subject or using humor. On the part of the South Asians, this could be by moving the discussion to extenuating circumstances or consistently focusing on performance rather than transformational goals. I became aware of my frustration with this while it was happening. This in turn allowed me to assess my success during the session based on my new CQ Knowledge, my strategy plan, my client's responses in the moment, and at times the prompting of the Holy Spirit.

CQ Strategy is all about metacognition, another word with which coaches are generally familiar. Metacognition is becoming aware of what you are thinking and doing while you are thinking and doing it. It's self-awareness with a kick. CQ Strategy is this metacognitive awareness paired with the ability to plan ahead for effective cross-cultural functioning.

As coaches, we know that metacognition takes some effort. Some of us may be more naturally gifted at this ability than others, but we can all grow in it. When we are going through coach training, we become more adept at being aware of what was going on in the coaching session at a process level, rather than a content level. For instance, a common experience in coach training is becoming aware of when we are talking too much and the impact this has on our client identifying their own solutions.

When we work with a coaching supervisor or mentor coach, we are also working at a metacognition level. We are becoming more aware of how we responded to our clients and why we responded that way. Reflection is an important part of the process. Processing our reactions or responses and why we responded the way we did, either verbally or through journaling, increases the depth of this "thinking through" process.

Planning is the second component of CQ Strategy. Again, this component may come more easily to some personalities (and cultures) than others, but it is an essential part of CQ Strategy. Planning our responses so that they are culturally appropriate may mean anything from thinking deeply about what multistep techniques in our toolbox are appropriate with a particular cross-cultural coaching client and how we will deploy these over time to simply putting a post-it note in a client's folder or a flag on their file as a reminder to ask about their family before diving into the progress report.

At the beginning of a typical coaching session, we ask our clients how their action steps went and what they learned. Sometimes we may find that our clients decided to do something different than we'd talked about, based on new information and new circumstances. In similar fashion, CQ Strategy must also include real time assessment and evaluation of what is working and what is not. Our cross-cultural coaching clients are unique and complex individuals, and a variety of factors influence their behavior and responses at any moment during the coaching session. Culture is only one of these. Strategies and plans that seemed effective when we wrote them in our journal or discussed them with our mentor coach might not be right in the moment.

Cross-cultural strategies must be held loosely, and we must be ready to adapt spontaneously. As Christian coaches, we must also be aware of the Holy Spirit's direction while coaching. Perhaps there will be a time that you sense God prompting you to ask a direct question to a client from a culture that values indirectness. God knows much better than we do what our clients need.

Increasing Your CQ Strategy

Strategy and planning is something we help clients with, but often don't talk much about as coaches. However, some of the ways to improve CQ Strategy will be familiar to us. Here are some ways to increase your CQ Strategy:

Be willing to be stretched. As coaches, we often use the phrase "follow the process" to remind us that even when we can't see how the session or issue our client brings will be resolved, our experience with coaching and our belief that God is working in our client remind us not to take control or lead. This helps us manage our uncertainty and allow the client to remain in the lead. In similar fashion, coaching conversations with clients who have very different cultural values may prove to be uncomfortable at times. We need to practice withholding judgment or jumping to conclusions at a whole new level. Working with cross-cultural clients challenges our "categories" and our willingness to have our deep assumptions and expectations tested and changed. After a taxing session, journal or process with your peer coach or supervisor the things your client said or did that most challenged your worldview.[41]

Stay with the client. As coaches, we discipline ourselves to listen deeply and stay in the present moment with the client. In cross-cultural situations, staying focused in the moment will help us notice things we might not otherwise notice. Awareness sets the stage for planning, and it is also a necessary ingredient in real-time assessment. Choose three upcoming cross-cultural coaching sessions in which you will focus intentionally on deep and intense listening.[42]

Hire a coach supervisor or mentor coach. This should be someone who is familiar with culturally intelligent coaching and with whom you can enter into an intentional reflection process. The process of supervision coaching in particular focuses on metacognition and helps you increase your awareness of process. Evaluate your plans and your real-time adaptation of those plans with your supervisor.

Make a strategy plan. When there is a lot of "cultural distance" between myself and a client on a cultural value continuum, I've found it helpful to write out some strategies that would work with that client's cultural value preference. We'll discuss this in much more detail in the Values chapters in Section Two of this book.

CQ Action

Action is our fourth and final component of CQ. Coaches love action. A coaching appointment is not a coaching appointment without action steps. We can have all the drive, knowledge, and strategy in the world, but no action means no fruit. CQ Action is closely related to Strategy, but it's different. CQ Action references specific behaviors we must cultivate to coach more effectively cross-culturally.

---

41   Ibid., 117.
42   Ibid., 120.

Coaches with high CQ Action have a set of flexible cross-cultural coaching behaviors available to them that they can use at the appropriate moment. These actions are both verbal and nonverbal. They include general across-the-board adaptations like rate of speech, adapting to a client's cadence and word use, greeting skills, eye contact, and conversational topic. But they also include the implementation of specific strategies we may have planned and developed.

One of the best pieces of feedback I personally have received while doing cross-cultural coach training offers a good example of a general nonverbal CQ Action. During my teaching session, a wonderful Dutch coach, Miranda, implored me very gently to slow down.[43] My desire to share every last bit of material during the short time I had with these particular trainees had impacted my rate of speech. I was imparting information at a speed more in keeping with a hotdog eating contest at a U.S. county fair than an appropriately respectful and understandable cross-cultural training class. Especially considering many of the trainees had learned their English as a second, third, or even fourth language.

Miranda's gentle reminder sounds so simple. But a year later, I admit I am still struggling to slow down. Slowing down your pace of communication is helpful for your trainees and clients. But it also helps you as the coach or trainer to have room to notice more of what is happening while you are communicating.

Increasing Your CQ Action

So how do we increase our CQ Action? To begin with, we need to implement our specific strategy plans, continually refining and testing them. We'll talk more about this in coming chapters. When we discuss skills of the culturally intelligent Christian coach, for instance, we will focus on specific competencies such as assessment, utilizing diverse cultural viewpoints, and juggling cultures in the coaching appointment. But there are some general CQ Actions we can all put into practice:

- Adapt to your client's pace, cadence and word use. If your client says apartment instead of flat, use apartment. If your client's language cadence is rhythmic and beautiful, don't stop yourself from a subtle adjustment of your own cadence to match.
- When coaching in a language that is not your client's first language, speak slowly and watch your word choice, avoiding slang and colloquialisms.
- Adapt your handouts, visuals, and exercises ahead of time for different cultures you may routinely coach.

---

43   Miranda, Personal Communication, Permission granted on July 7, 2015.

CQ is a concept we'll continue to reference throughout this book. Much of the information in this chapter was built on concepts and ideas from Dr. David Livermore in his excellent books *Cultural Intelligence* and *The Cultural Intelligence Difference*. Check them out for a more in-depth look at cultural intelligence from both Christian and business perspectives.

Take a Minute

- *Reflect about your own CQ. Of the four components of CQ (Drive, Knowledge, Strategy, and Action), which is your strongest? Which is your weakest?*
- *Go back and read the suggestions for increasing the component of CQ in which you are the weakest. What strategy appeals to you most?*
- *What is one action step you are willing to commit to?*

Chapter Six

Cultural Values

Andrew, a South African coach, recounts the following story of coaching a South Asian woman:

> I don't fully get the culture she is from. It's very different than mine, and the bulk of my clients are from another area of the world. This client has a very successful teaching ministry, but has been dealing with intimidation and fear. She went into teaching with so much trembling, even though she was teaching on faith! Whenever a negative evaluation would come in, she would lose all steam. But as we talked, I realized that she is a younger leader teaching older persons, and I came to understand that that was strange in her culture and intimidating for her."[44]

Coaching cross-culturally is difficult. But that makes it even more rewarding when we cross the cultural divide and really connect with our client's hearts. So how do we get there? Andrew offers a good example. Though he did not fully "get" his client's culture, he listened to her concerns without dismissing them or rushing to a wrong interpretation through his own very different cultural lens. He could easily have used his EQ (emotional intelligence) to conclude that his client's feelings were not logical, that she was overreacting, that she was not assertive or confident enough, or that some trauma in her past needed healing.

Andrew could also have pointed out the dissonance in teaching on having faith and trusting the Holy Spirit while walking in so much fear, a coaching technique that might have been valid with a client of his own culture. He could have explored character issues about developing faith. Instead, Andrew "caught" the cultural value difference and so could understand and empathize with his client about what in her context was a very real concern and pressure for a young leader.

---

44   Andrew, Personal Communication, Permission granted on August 2, 2015.

How did Andrew notice what was really going on? He acknowledged that he was no expert on South Asian culture. But he understood *cross-cultural value differences*, so he was listening closely with an educated ear. Through his client's emotive words and fearful voice tone, he picked up the deeper language of culture and could immediately identify "Status culture" language and understandings (differing cultural values for Status vs. Equality are among the cross-cultural variances we'll be exploring in coming chapters). This enabled Andrew to empathize with his client and to interpret correctly what was happening.

Understanding of the basic cultural value continuums—i.e., the ways cultures often differ, such as in dealing with Status—helps us as coaches to:

- ask great questions that fit the client's context.
- interpret the answers correctly according to the *client's* cultural values grid and not our own.
- help the client design actions appropriate to their context.
- assist the client in looking through different cultural values lenses (leveraging cultural values) to create new options, insights, and possibilities.

We don't have to be experts in every culture to be able to do these things. But we *do* need a basic framework of cultural understanding in order to more quickly and accurately spot and respond to cultural differences in the coaching relationship.

For our purpose as coaches, the single most important way to gain CQ Knowledge—a basic framework of cultural understanding—is to understand the concept of cultural values. Values operate "below the waterline" of the culture iceberg and give us information that allows us to understand, make sense of, predict, and generalize from culture to culture.

Many books and resources on specific cultures give tips and advice on what to wear, how to greet people, whether to make eye contact, etc. These resources are helpful when we are immersed in one particular culture or have a new client from a culture with which we are unfamiliar. But memorizing all these details if we are coaching clients from many cultures on a daily basis can be overwhelming, even impossible. Learning instead the underlying values that power "below the waterline" cultural dynamics gives us the ability to spot those differences that power "above the waterline" behaviors. We may still make mistakes with greeting skills or eating with the wrong hand, but our ability to "get" at a deep level just where our client is coming from will prove much more valuable for both ourselves as coaches and our clients.

The Power of Working at the Values Level in Coaching

As coaches, we understand the power of working with personal or core values. Being able to bring light to those inner attitudes and beliefs that shape our client's behaviors and responses can help resolve dissonance and internal obstacles. It also helps discover unseen options and possibilities. Similarly, understanding and being able to unearth hidden cultural values does not just allow us to adapt to our client's cultural context, empathize more fully, and offer questions and co-design actions appropriate to their culture. This process also enables us to leverage those cultural values to help our clients gain new perspectives, options, insights, and opportunities.

Understanding cultural values and being able to bring them into conscious awareness can open new worlds in the coaching conversation.

This works no matter the cultural distance between us and our clients. Whether that distance is large or small, understanding cultural values and being able to bring them into conscious awareness can open new worlds in the coaching conversation. We'll talk more about leveraging and perspective shifting when we reach Section 3, and explore the skills of the culturally intelligent Christian coach.

Cultural Value Continuums

Cultural values are those underlying understandings that a group of people share about what is good, right, just, acceptable, and valuable. They are perhaps the most important component of "culture". These values are most often unconscious and unexamined. We may *say* that we know others think and believe differently than we do. But because these values are at such a deep and hidden level, we often unconsciously assume that others think and value the same things we do.

Values are expressed as a continuum from one pole, or extreme, to another. For instance, the Direct/Indirect value continuum refers to the way people communicate. Those whose value inclines them to speak directly and bluntly will fall towards that end of the continuum. Others whose communication is more indirect will be towards the other end.

Continuums are quite different than dichotomies. Dichotomies and continuums both contain two different concepts or values. But when we use a dichotomy to describe two characteristics, you are either one or the other. Those of us who regularly use the Myers Briggs Type Indicator (MBTI) are familiar with the concept of a dichotomy. One can be, for example, either an extrovert or an introvert. Dichotomies have two subsets and there is a firm line separating them. Furthermore, in the MBTI, your preference for one or the other does not change. It is stable over time.

A continuum, on the other hand, is like moving from black to light gray on the spectrum of color.

There are many gradations moving from simple black to charcoal, to medium gray, and finally to the lightest gray. It may be helpful to think of a cultural value continuum as a scale or line between two points with gradations in between. You could plot yourself at any point on that scale or line, based on how strongly you prefer one end of the continuum or the other. And the point where you fall could change over time. In fact, many of the cross-cultural workers I coach find that their cultural values shift somewhat after living or working in another culture.

Many cultural values assessments use lines, graphs, and scales to plot results. The Cultural Intelligence Center's CQ Self-Assessment, Marvin Mayers' Basic Values Questionnaire, and Philippe Rosinski's Cultural Orientations Framework Assessment (COF) all rely on scales or graphs to plot cultural preferences. These visual pictures of a continuum help us understand that there are many points of "gray" between the two value poles on any given continuum. Some individuals we coach will have a very clear preference for one pole or the other. Some will fall towards the middle.

Cultural Distance in Coaching

The concept of cultural distance, or deep level diversity (differences in values, beliefs, and attitudes), is important for us in coaching. Cultural distance applied to the coaching relationship is the degree of difference between your cultural values and your coachee's. For instance, I have had many clients over the years who live in India. One of those clients, Pat, is ethnically Indian, but grew up in Tanzania, Africa, as well as Mumbai, India, living mostly in urban areas. She went to graduate school as I did. Pat has traveled extensively, married an American, and works in an international environment. If we plotted where Pat and I fall on a number of value continuums, our values would be similar.

Another client, Liza, is Italian and has lived in a remote region of India for a decade. She is a businesswoman, and the employees in her small business are all Indian from the region in which she works. Her children were born in India. Liza goes home to Italy about once per year and maintains some business ties there. If we plotted Liza and me on the values continuums, there would be some significant differences, but also some close similarities.

The concept of cultural distance helps us understand how much of a gap in cultural beliefs, values, and attitudes to expect with our clients.

A third client from India is Rajesh, who is also ethnically Indian. He grew up in a village and is married to a woman from a nearby province who did not have the opportunity to go to school. He has lived in the same region of India for much of his life. Rajesh's underlying cultural values would plot very differently than mine. But they would also be very different than Pat's, even though Rajesh and Pat are from the same country.

In terms of cultural distance, I am closest to Pat and farthest from Rajesh with Liza somewhere in the middle. However, my cultural distance from Pat is large compared to the distance from another client who is a fellow American. Kimberly grew up in rural/small town Midwestern U.S., just as I did, went to the same Christian college, and belongs to the same Christian denomination. The cultural distance I experience with Kimberly is almost solely generational, since she is almost thirty years younger than I am.

The concept of cultural distance helps us understand how much of a gap in cultural beliefs, values, and attitudes to expect with our clients. When I coach Kimberly, I can expect that culture will not be much of an issue at all. It will be a bit more so when I coach Pat. In contrast, when I coach Rajesh, the cultural distance between us will be significant, so I will need heightened awareness and sensitivity to potential value differences.

The Basic Value Continuums

Cultural values have been studied by anthropologists and social scientists for decades. Experts have created many different systems for understanding cultural values, which can be confusing to the layperson. Often the language and labels used are difficult or complex. Some experts in cross-cultural values theorize between five and eight main categories of values or value themes. Others name as many as twelve or add subsets to the main value themes. Global coaching expert Philippe Rosinski in his book *Coaching across Cultures* identifies seven categories of values and seventeen dimensions for those values.[45] In its *Faith & Culture* curriculum, n-Culture names twelve dimensions of culture and three overarching worldviews that color cultural preferences.[46]

Whatever the number of value themes, it is well accepted that cultures have different value sets and that these influence behavior profoundly. These value continuums have been adapted in one form or another to leadership and team development. They have also been used extensively in such areas as business, expatriate adjustment, and international consulting.

For readers who are pragmatic and just want something useful you can use as you coach, the chapters in Section Two will provide scope for developing your CQ Knowledge regarding value sets. They will give you some strategies and exercises to increase your CQ actions and behaviors as well. For others who want to go deeper, I've personally been influenced by and can recommend:

- Geert Hofstede's groundbreaking research as found in *Cultures and Organizations: Software of the Mind, Intercultural Cooperation and its Importance for Survival*, McGraw Hill, 2010.
- Marvin Mayers' Basic Values Questionnaire as explained in Sherwood Lingenfelter's book, *Ministering Cross-Culturally*.
- Cross-cultural coaching pioneer Philippe Rosinski's *Coaching across Cultures*.

There are many other excellent books on cross-cultural issues. Digging into research on the topic and its application is a fascinating exercise, and I highly recommend it if you have time and inclination. Check out the footnotes in this book for a starting point.

The value sets in this book are not exhaustive. Depending on what culture you and your coachee are from or are working in, other values continuums or subcategories may bring further insight. However, I've attempted to identify and explain those value continuums that I feel will be most helpful for *coaches*. While they are not exhaustive, they will give you a solid grounding for coaching issues. In the following chapters, we'll explore:

---

45   Philippe Rosinski, *Coaching Across Cultures: New Tools for Leveraging National, Corporate & Professional Differences* (London: Nicholas Brealey Publishing, 2003), 49-73.
46   www.n-culture.com

- Values related to identity, power, and responsibility (Autonomy/Community).
- Values related to change and planning (Risk/Caution; Crisis/Non-Crisis).
- Values regarding organizational arrangements (Status/Equality)[47].
- Values regarding thinking patterns (Dichotomistic/Holistic; Conceptual/Practical).
- Values related to purpose (Task/Relationship).
- Values related to communication (Direct/Indirect; Concealment/Vulnerability).
- Values related to time (Time/Event; Long Term/Short Term).

Basic information on each continuum can be found in the Appendix, the Cultural Values Chart. The Chart draws from and expands on many sources but I am particularly indebted to Sherwood Lingenfelter and Marvin K. Mayers' work, as found in the excellent book, *Ministering Cross-Culturally*. The Cultural Values Chart is informed by their work.[48]

Each of the following chapters will delve deeply into the application of these values concepts to coaching. Practical details about how to introduce coaching, begin the relationship, apply cultural values to the coaching conversation, and much more will be explored. We'll see how cultural values impact the different stages of a coaching conversation using the common coaching session management tool, the coaching "funnel": from setting a goal, to exploring, developing options, making a decision, and finally, taking action. Stories, tips, and insights from seasoned culturally intelligent coaches will be included in each chapter. For more information on the coaching funnel style of managing a coaching conversation, check out *Coaching Questions*, pp. 30-31, by author and master coach Tony Stoltzfus.[49]

Let me reassure you that you don't need to commit all this material to memory. Instead, simply use the second section of the book as a reference. Explore Section 2 for help in envisioning practical ways to apply values to coaching conversations in a particular cultural context. Due to overlap between different value continuums, you'll often need to use your own creativity and lean on the Holy Spirit's

---

47   The term "organizational arrangements" comes from Philippe Rosinski, *Coaching Across Cultures: New Tools for Leveraging National, Corporate & Professional Differences* (London: Nicholas Brealey Publishing, 2003), 54.
48   Sherwood G. Lingenfelter and Marvin K. Mayers, *Ministering Cross-Culturally: An Incarnational Model for Personal Relationships* (Grand Rapids: Baker Academic, 2007).
49   Tony Stoltzfus, *Coaching Questions: A Coach's Guide to Powerful Asking Skills* (Redding, CA: Coach22, 2008), 30-31.

inspiration to decide what is best in your own context and with your own clients. Use the values chapters as a reference and beginning point in your own adventure of developing and applying CQ in coaching.

As you read through the values chapters, expanding your CQ Knowledge to develop Strategy and Action, here are some things to remember:

- Values chapters on Autonomy/Community and Status/Equality are longer and contain more descriptive information as these are critical values to understand and may also be the ones in which the coach and client potentially have the most cultural distance.

- Gaining self-awareness about your own underlying cultural values is just as important as gaining awareness of your client's values. Don't neglect to apply the material to yourself.

- The generally accepted values of your coachee's home culture will not necessarily determine their behavior. Individual personality, differences in experiences and beliefs (such as a decision to join a minority religious group, regular trips to another culture, or friends from diverse backgrounds), personal values, generation, and cross-cultural awareness will all interact to determine your coachee's values, behaviors, and preferences. You'll need to use your curiosity to find out where your individual clients fall on the values continuums.

- Don't neglect the "Take a Minute" exercises. Gaining CQ Knowledge is not enough. You must apply what you've learned in putting together new strategies and gaining new behaviors to be an effective and culturally intelligent coach.

Cultural Values in Coaching

- Autonomy and Community Values
- Applying Autonomy and Community Values to Coaching
- Risk and Caution Values
- Crisis and Non-Crisis Values
- Status and Equality Values
- Applying Status and Equality Values to Coaching
- Dichotomistic and Holistic Values
- Conceptual and Practical Values
- Task and Relationship Values
- Direct and Indirect Values
- Concealment and Vulnerability Values
- Time and Event Values
- Long Term and Short Term Values

Autonomy and Community Values

 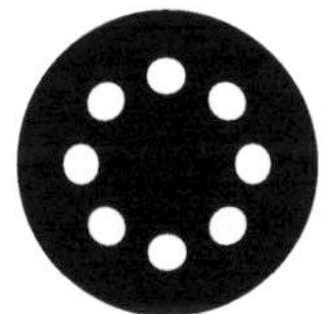

One of the first missionaries I coached was an American who had spent his entire adult life in South Korea and had returned to the United States when his mission organization closed their ministry project there. All of George's adult relationships had been with Koreans. His community was there. In many ways, he had adopted his host culture at a deep identity level. George contracted with me as a coach to help him with life purpose—i.e., what he should do now that he was at home.

George spent much of the first 8-10 sessions grieving his relationships in Korea and expressing feelings of betrayal by his organization. His childhood friends had either physically moved or moved on emotionally. His mother's health was failing. He barely knew those in his home church. He would spend half the night awake, talking to Korean friends and colleagues on Skype. He felt the mission organization had abandoned them and him. He was literally unable to engage with life purpose issues. As a coach, I felt hamstrung and became frustrated with his inability to move forward. To me, George seemed dependent and immature.

As I think back now on that coaching relationship, I can see there was much going on besides George's struggle with re-entry and grief. What I did not understand then was his loss of the sense of belonging in a web of relationship when he left Korea. I can now feel that loss with him more acutely. I also did not understand the depth of his feeling of abandonment by his mission organization. Given the loyalty factor in Community cultures, I now understand that George expected the mission organization, his "we" group (which included the national staff), to fulfill their family obligations to him. He had served the organization for all his adult life, and he expected more than a few days of debriefing from them. He expected they would take care of him in the same way that he took care of his ailing mother.

Cultural preference for Autonomy or Community is one of the most important for a coach to understand. The Autonomy/Community continuum influences both where power for decision-making and change reside and where identity comes from. The impact of these values on the coaching process and the coaching relationship is hard to overestimate. Deep change is powered by internal transformation. Our desire as coaches is to connect at an identity level with our clients to create conditions for that deep change. Decision-making that leads to life-changing action is the heart of what coaching is about.

Value for Autonomy or Community influences many other factors in the coaching relationship. Due to its significance, we'll take extra time with this particular continuum. A visual representation of the two ends of this continuum is found in the icons at the beginning of the chapter: a single individual dot standing alone for Autonomy; and dots which together create a circle, for Community. See the portion of the Cultural Values Chart pertaining to Autonomy/Community, below, for a quick written summary.

● Autonomy (identity/power/responsibility) Community ⦿	
My identity comes from my individual characteristics.	My identity comes from membership in a group (family, tribe, or community).
I believe that, for the most part, my choices determine my destiny.	My destiny is most often the result of my circumstances and background.
I'm responsible for my own failures.	Circumstances and destiny are often responsible for failure.
I value my independence.	I value the interdependence and dependence in my group/community/tribe.
I am responsible for my own decisions and how they impact me.	Making decisions is best done in my family/community/tribe, benefitting all.
I believe that I have distinctive and unique qualities.	Harmony and fitting in with others are most important.
My relationships evolve based on my location, job, and circumstances.	My relationships are stable; most come from family/tribe/community.

Once we're immersed in these values, we'll apply what we've learned (CQ Knowledge) to the coaching relationship and coaching process and develop new CQ strategies.

Remember the iceberg? These values are of absolute importance in coaching, but are often unspoken and unconscious. Your client may very well not be able to verbalize these values. This means that to effectively facilitate a client's progress towards their goal, you must be aware of your own preferences and able to recognize when the client's values are different than yours.

Take a Minute

As you read through this chapter and all the following chapters on values, be deliberate about trying to identify your own values and the relative strength of your preference. Self-awareness is one of the keys to great cross-cultural coaching. Take a few minutes right now and do the following quick exercises:

- *Underline or note which phrases in the Cultural Values Chart for Autonomy/Community most appeal to you or match your own beliefs.*

- *Think about the relative strength of your preference for either Autonomy or Community. Plot a point on the line below that represents where you are on the Autonomy/Community continuum. Continue to keep this in mind as you read the chapter.*

Autonomy   Community

Brief Explanation of the Value Set

I was recently out in my vegetable garden with an axe and a shovel, trying once again to uproot new aspen shoots. Seventeen years ago, I had blithely planted a single aspen tree fifteen feet from our vegetable garden, thinking as an Autonomy-minded tree planter that the aspen would eventually shade one corner of the garden as it grew. What I did not know was that aspens form groves through an underground network of roots. My single aspen thrived, developing over time into an aspen grove with new trees shooting up from thick, established roots thirty to forty feet in all directions. The young trees coming under the axe that day measured only three to five feet high, but the roots attaching them to the mother tree were up to four-plus inches thick.

In my estimation, there are few things lovelier to the eyes and ears than a grove of gold-leaved aspens fluttering in the autumn breeze. But they are also unstoppable! In fact, one aspen grove nicknamed "Pando" is the largest single organism known on earth. This grove is connected by a single root system and covers over

a hundred acres. Though the roots of the aspen grove are not visible, their power and connectivity are substantial and far-reaching.[50]

Identity is the basis of personality. It influences everything we do, how we relate to others, and how we think about ourselves. Those from Autonomy cultures find it difficult to "get" the web of relationship in which the identity of clients from a Community culture is rooted. An aspen grove is a great way to visualize the Community value dynamic.

In Community cultures, an individual's identity is linked to the community like a grove of aspens is linked together. The child grows in the context—i.e., attached to the root—of the community around her. Children in Community oriented cultures in Africa, Asia, and Central/ South America grow up rooted in a sense of "we", a tangible and ever-present web of relationships that forms the structure of identity and security. Typically, your group is one you are born into. Children and adults considered to have good character are those who adopt the opinions of the group, care for other group members, and contribute to group or family success and harmony. Who you are is defined in relationship to others. Your story begins with your grandparents' story or the story of your tribe. In school, children are expected to respect the wisdom of the teacher and the traditions of the culture, thereby promoting harmony. Work is more likely to be done as a group or in small groups. There is a beautiful connectedness that is woven into the heart of who you are as a Community value person.

This sense of "linked-in-ness" continues into adulthood. Community culture adults may identify strongly with their team or organization. This applies especially to new Christians who have found it necessary to leave their cultural

---

50   "Pando (tree)" Wikipedia.com, last modified January 30, 2016, https://en.wikipedia.org/wiki/Pando (tree).

"we" group to become part of the Christian community. Success and failures are owned by the group or attributed to nature or birth. Interdependence and dependence are expected and are a sign of mentally healthy adults. The icon of individual dots which together form a shape, finding their identity as a part of the circle, is another way to visualize Community value.

🙂 The Wedding in the Village

I heard the following story from an expat coach working in Asia. One day he entered a village to find a hubbub of activity as everyone prepared for a festive event to be held the following day, which was the wedding of two village young people. Special food was being prepared, clothing laid out, and excitement filled the air.

"Who's the bride?" asked the visitor.

"Oh, we don't know yet," said the village elder. "There are many eligible young women who could be the bride tomorrow."

For this village, it was not the significance of an individual that was important, but the value for the group and the group event.

In contrast, Autonomy value children grow up with a sense of independence and aloneness. Here's an example from nature:

Eaglets are born in late spring from individual eggs the size of a fist. Families are small, an average clutch no more than 1-3 eggs. The baby eagles grow for thirty-five days inside the egg. Once the eaglets are born, the mother and father eagles bring food to the nest, which is located high in the treetops or on rocky cliffs. When the parents judge that the young eagles are nearly ready to leave the nest, they begin to bring less food so that the eaglets' motivation to fly increases. Sometimes the parent eagles will fly close to the nest with a choice rabbit or other food in their talons, but glide on without sharing it with the young.

When it's time to fly, eaglets must learn to use their own wings to avoid a catastrophic crash. Flying lessons are not included in this package, and about forty percent of young eagles do not survive their first flight. Those that do survive return to the nest, but continue their practice flights, using the rest of the warm months to learn to hunt on their own. Surviving the first winter independently is crucial for an eagle's survival. Soaring high above the trees with a wingspan of 5-9 feet, a mature eagle in flight is a magnificent sight.[51]

Children from Autonomy value cultures such as the U.S., Australia, and much of western Europe grow up instilled with the belief that they are in charge of their own destiny and have an identity as a unique individual apart from others. Though children are dependent on the nuclear family while young, independence is expected and rewarded. Children in Autonomy cultures are praised for taking initiative and standing up for themselves. Identity is defined based on individual personality and experiences. An individual's story begins at their birth. In school, children choose friends based on their own preferences and desires. They are expected to interact verbally with the teacher and to "think critically", question, and even debate. Autonomy value persons grow up with a beautiful sense of freedom and uniqueness that is woven into the heart of who they are.

Autonomy culture teens and young adults are expected to make their own way and create their own destiny. Adults are expected to live independently. Either success or failure is the responsibility of the individual. The height of mental health is seen as independence and self-actualization (the fulfillment of one's own talents and potential). The individual dot in the middle of the Autonomy icon stands alone and independent, as do Autonomy culture individuals.

It is difficult for those born into Autonomy cultures to imagine the ever-present connectedness of the Community culture person. It is equally difficult for those born into Community cultures to imagine the profound aloneness and independence of the Autonomy culture person. Our daughter recently arrived in Africa for a service assignment. She wrote in her first email home that "being with people all the time is stressful." I laughed. In many parts of Africa, one is not left alone because if you are alone, you might get lonely.

In the U.S., by contrast, children and adults are given their own rooms and their own space. International students who arrive in the U.S. from Community cultures often feel *very* alone, insecure, and disoriented. They are expected to go

---

51   "Bald Eagle Nesting & Young," BaldEageleInfo.com, last modified 2016, http://www.baldeagleinfo.com/eagle/eagle4.html.

to class alone, find others to eat with in the cafeteria on their own, and go home to their own rooms. It's a lonely existence for someone who is used to connectedness with a group at all times.

These differences in "we" and "I" are deeply imbedded in culture, in education, and often in language itself. In Chinese, for instance, there is no word equivalent for "personality" in an Autonomy culture sense. Rather than personality being defined by individual characteristics, personality is defined only in relation to context[52]. Social psychologist Richard Nisbett writes in his excellent book *The Geography of Thought*, about the differences in early reading materials used in American and Chinese schools. Dick, Jane, and their dog Spot were the stars of the American version. Of them, Nisbett writes:

> The first sentences are "See Dick run. See Dick play. See Dick run and play." This would seem the most natural sort of basic information to convey about kids to the Western mentality. But the first page of the Chinese primer of the same era shows a little boy sitting on the shoulders of a bigger boy. "Big brother takes care of little brother. Big brother loves little brother. Little brother loves big brother." It is not individual action, but relationships between people that seem important to convey in a child's first encounter with the printed word.[53]

Take a Minute

- *Based on what you just learned about Autonomy and Community cultures, what qualities do you expect each to look for in a promising young leader?*
- *Having specific situations in mind is helpful when growing CQ. Take a moment before reading the next chapter and identify a situation in which you coached (or related to) someone of the opposite value than yourself, either Community or Autonomy. Think back to the dynamics of that relationship. Is there anything you would interpret differently now based on your new CQ Knowledge? For an example, refer to the story of George at the beginning of the chapter. At the end of that story, I share what I would interpret differently now based on CQ Knowledge.*

---

52   F.L.K. Hsu, "Psychological Homeostasis and Jen: Conceptual Tools for Advancing Psychological Anthropology," *American Anthropologist* 73 (1971): 23-44 as quoted in Hofstede, Hofstede, and Minkov, 114.

53   Richard E. Nisbett, *The Geography of Thought: How Asians and Westerners Think Differently....and Why* (New York: Free Press, 200), 50.

Chapter Eight

Applying Autonomy and Community Values to Coaching

We just learned a lot about how Autonomy and Community cultures function. That was the CQ Knowledge section. Now we need to deploy CQ Strategy, applying what we've learned to the coaching relationship and coaching process. Remember that CQ Strategy is about employing metacognition (thinking about what we are thinking) to analyze and interpret what is going on culturally. Our next step will be to begin the process of planning and then responding appropriately (deploying Behavioral CQ) to adapt our behavior as we coach cross-culturally.

Beginning the Relationship: How to Gain Clients

Lis wanted to implement leadership coaching in the nonprofit organization she led. Though Lis herself was from an Autonomy culture, her organization and the Asian host culture she worked in had a definite Community orientation. Lis was strongly convinced of the need for coaching to be provided to her leaders, but the leaders she worked with in her Asian host culture were not familiar with the coaching model. Lis contacted a coaching organization from a Western Autonomy value culture to help implement her vision. She painstakingly explained that what she was after was "a wave of influence". This would involve soliciting input from influential leaders in her host culture organization. A trial period of coaching would take place for them. Key leaders from the Western-based coaching organization would visit her host country, where they would be introduced and vouched for personally by Lis.

After the trial period, feedback would be sought from participants. Testimonies of the impact of coaching and the personal transformation leaders had experienced would be gathered and shared, obstacles discussed and dealt with. If all went as planned, widespread coaching could be offered within a few years. While the coaching organization envisioned a quick start-up with feedback happening mid-stream, Lis planned for a slow and steady beginning with buy-in opportunities at each step, creating the wave of influence that she needed in order to implement a completely new program successfully in her context.[54]

In Community cultures, relationships are strong and longstanding. So, what happens when a new person wants to join a "we" group? It's a long process! Brad Bridges, VP of the Malphurs Group, writes of his experience in Uruguay, "It could take a decade or more to 'cross the line' in our host country, and really be accepted as part of the group."[55] Trust-building over a period of time is necessary. Often an intermediary or a trusted person in the group is needed to vouch for a new person or organization (as Lis did). Once the new person is in, the relationship is expected to last with loyalty, protection, and care shared mutually. Trust in business dealings cannot be assumed when the business partner is not part of the "we" group.

In contrast, in an Autonomy culture, it does not take long to get in, but it also does not take long to get out. Establishing a trust relationship in an Autonomy culture is not difficult when there is mutual benefit or a mutual task to work on. But even when an authentic, deep relationship is formed, there is no assumption of protection or longevity. The relationship may end when geographic, task, or other variables change. This could happen quite abruptly. Because loyalty cannot be assumed, business is done with detailed contracts which spell out the duties of each party.

So how will these differing values impact beginning coaching relationships? For Autonomy value coaches who want to offer coaching to Community value clients, beginning coaching relationships may be difficult. Coaches who live in the community and have already become part of the "we" group have a distinct advantage over those offering coaching from a distance or those who are new to the community.

If you want to offer coaching within a Community culture, here are a few tips:

---

54   Lis Cochrane, Personal Communication, Permission granted on June 30, 2015.
55   Brad Bridges, VP of the Malphurs Group, Personal Communication, Permission granted on October 10, 2015.

- Gain a personal recommendation from other members of the "we" group you are targeting or an intermediary. If possible, share testimonies from those who are already part of the "we" group who have had a positive experience of coaching.
- Offer team or group coaching. Help the group or organization in question to understand how coaching will benefit the *group*, rather than just individuals in the group.
- Begin the coaching relationship without a long, formal contract you may be used to. Use a simpler "agreement" or introduce the contract later in the relationship, rather than at the first session.

Conversely, for Community-culture coaches offering coaching to Autonomy-culture clients, keep in mind that you do *not* have to enter the in-group in order to offer coaching. You will most likely be convincing individuals rather than groups that coaching is a great option for them. Even if you have a contract with a group, you should not assume that all the individuals in the group will agree with the idea of getting coaching. Selling the concept of coaching will be based on the value it brings to the individual.

Here are some tips for dealing with Autonomy-culture clients:

- Ask your potential client what *they* want out of coaching and help them see how you can help them attain their own personal goals.
- Gather and share testimonials about your coaching from any of your previous clients.
- Be prepared with a detailed contract and explanation of confidentiality. Autonomy-culture clients are likely to be very concerned about privacy and will want assurance that you will not share information with others.

Goals, Decisions, and Action Steps

There is a well-known African proverb: "If you want to go fast, go alone; if you want to go far, go together." Decision-making of any kind in the coaching appointment, whether it is setting goals, choosing among options, or deciding on action steps, is greatly impacted by Community vs. Autonomy values. Remember Carl, who coaches Arabs in the Middle East, and his initial frustration with how drawn-out consultations could lengthen the process? He writes:

> Consulting elders gives security; wait patiently on the processing that will need to be done with others outside the coaching relationship.[56]

---

56   Carl, Personal Communication, Permission granted on August 2, 2015.

The coach who ignores a Community coachee's need to consult others within their web of relationship risks stalling out the coaching process.

Consultation with the coachee's community may not just change the timeline of the goal, but may actually change the goal itself. In teams and workplaces, collaborative decision-making or fitting in with the group decision is expected. When Lis described creating a "wave of influence", she was describing how to enact change effectively in a group culture. Decision-making in Community value clients is centered around the "we" group's welfare and ownership. When the group they belong to is long-term or lifelong and provides their identity, protection, and relational (sometimes financial as well) security, loyalty to that group is expected to take priority. The coach who ignores a Community coachee's need to consult others within their web of relationship risks stalling out the coaching process.

In Autonomy cultures, relationships are much looser. Individuals operate largely as free agents, moving between groups and relationships according to preference, need, or circumstance. It's expected that group, team, or organizational goals will coincide with individual goals, and when they do, support will be given. When they don't, individuals may protest or they may leave. Decision-making is based on the individual's preferences, and other people's needs are often not a factor.

For Community value coaches, it can be hard to believe that your Autonomy value client has not shared the goal of radically changing his job description with his boss or his goal to move cross-country with his own wife. Here is where we can assist our clients by leveraging (using the value on the opposing end of the continuum for the client's benefit). Philippe Rosinski, in *Coaching across Cultures*, makes extensive use of the concept of leveraging cultural values.[57] According to Rosinski, leveraging means making the most of differences by "coaching from multiple perspectives, in order to shift views, in a kaleidoscopic manner, to look at issues from various angles, each with potential merits, to facilitate progress."[58] For more on leveraging, see Chapter 22, Walk around the Castle section.

We can leverage the opposite end of the value continuum by asking our Autonomy client perspective questions such as:

---

57   Philippe Rosinski, Coaching Across Cultures: *New Tools for Leveraging National, Corporate & Professional Differences* (London: Nicholas Brealey Publishing, 2003), 23.
58   Ibid.

- What would your boss say about this change? What impact will this have on him/her? On your colleagues? On the workflow in your office/workplace? How can you best ensure a great reception for these proposed changes?
- If you could create an outcome that was a win/win for everyone involved, what would that look like?

Similarly, leveraging with Community value clients might sound like this:
- What would change in your perspective about this situation if you felt your action could make a real impact?
- What has God given you passion for?

Steve K., who coaches mission clients in South Korea, says that introducing the possibility of "a more autonomous perspective can also help Community value clients get in touch with what they personally are most passionate about and then can lead to them appealing to their elders or community in a humble but clear way."[59]

Take a Minute

Given what you have learned so far about Autonomy and Community clients, what differences in conversational pace might you expect from an Autonomy client vs. a Community client?

Options and Outcomes

Alana, an Autonomy value client working for an Autonomy value business in a Community culture, came to her coaching appointment tired and discouraged. She vented: "I feel so much guilt about being unproductive. I have so much to do, but I am so tired. Yesterday I just took the day off and sat on the couch. Now I have wasted another day. I don't see my colleagues struggling with this much guilt."

Alana described a punishing round of meetings required by her employer, an international firm doing business in Europe. Currently juggling multiple roles due to budget cuts, she had also been asked to do a significant amount of in-

---

59   Steve K., Personal Communication, Permission granted on June 30, 2015.

ternational travel. The coach asked Alana what in her schedule she had control over and what she didn't. Alana came to realize she was feeling unconsciously responsible for many things that actually weren't her responsibility and couldn't be changed.

The coach then asked Alana directly if her expectations for herself were realistic. With a sigh of relief, Alana admitted they were not. This helped her to focus in on what she *could* change. Her action steps included taking needed time off and beginning to listen to her own body's need for rest and sleep.

In Autonomy cultures, the individual is perceived to have power to effect change on their own. They feel responsible for both success and failure to achieve their objectives, often despite obviously adverse or biased circumstances as in Alana's situation. In contrast, in Community cultures, change is consensus-based and stems from group norms and opinions. When Lis was introducing coaching into her organization, she did not legislate it. Instead, she created a wave of influence with carefully crafted steps of input and agreement built in.

At a deeper level, Autonomy clients generally believe they have power to impact their destiny and life choices, while Community clients may not. There is a Chinese saying: "There is nothing you can do about it!" A Community oriented client in a similar situation to Alana might attribute their failure to meet objectives to circumstances or fate. The downside of this is that for someone who strongly believes in the influence of fate, developing options for change may seem foolish.

Here are some tips for working on options with Community oriented clients:

- Help the client find options within their own cultural experience rather than trying to envision "out of the box" scenarios. Ask what they have seen others do or what is *possible* within their team or organization.

- Limit time spent on brainstorming and decrease the number of options you ask the clients to come up with (for instance, instead of five, ask for three). Dave Houser, coaching in India, where one's future marriage, work, and economic status can be determined by the tribe you are born into, says, "Too many options can be overwhelming for someone from a tribal culture."[60]

- Help the client discover options that benefit the community, tribe, or team, thus increasing motivation. Kevin Sutter, an American who has a very influential international role in his organization and coaches leaders

---

60   Dave Houser, Personal Communication, Permission granted on July 13, 2015.

from many countries and regions writes: "The willingness to take initiative and work toward change may not be strong. Help the client envision the benefits of positive change and how it can benefit the community."[61]

Here are some tips for working on outcomes with Autonomy oriented clients:

- Help your client to weigh the impact of circumstances they can't control when planning outcomes. Autonomy clients will tend to downplay or even completely overlook the importance of external circumstances in projected outcomes.

- Use perspective questions to assist the client who is weighed down by guilt over a failure to see the external or immutable circumstances which impacted that negative outcome.

- In weighing options and outcomes, ask, "What is under your control? What is not?"

Motivation and Accountability in Coaching

Motivation for change and accountability in the change process will be different based on where your client falls on the continuum from Autonomy to Community. We just discussed the negative motivator of guilt (a personal internal negative emotion) impacting Autonomy clients. The negative motivator of shame (which is experienced in relation to others) is particularly significant for Community clients.[62]

In coaching, we aim to use positive motivation. However, as in the example above of Alana, it is also important to understand the role that negative motivation can play in our client's lives. Being able to identify it and talk about it is employing CQ Knowledge and metacognition (CQ Strategy) to help clients turn awareness into new actions (CQ Action). Leveraging, perspective questions, and direct questions can be helpful.

In terms of positive motivation, we have already noted that Autonomy clients will tend to respond to questions designed to increase individual success: "How will attaining this goal prepare you for your future? How will *your* success impact others?" In contrast, Community clients will respond to questions that increase

---

61   Kevin Sutter, Branch of YWAM focused on long-term work among unreached people groups, Personal Communication, Permission granted on July 16, 2015.

62   n-Culture, in its Faith & Culture curriculum identifies "three Colors of Worldview" where Innocence/Guilt, Honor/Shame and Power/Fear are the paradigms or drivers that compose someone's worldview. They are seen as "lenses" that give us insight into cultural motivators and demotivators. www.n-culture.com.

group benefit: "How will your continued effort contribute to your team goal? to your family's success? How will the *group* attaining this goal benefit everyone?"

To maximize client goal attainment, coaches will also help design processes and accountability questions for client action steps in terms of group or individual motivation. David B. Peterson in his article "Executive Coaching in a Cross-cultural Context" says it well:

> In collectivist (Community) cultures, accountability is provided by a sense of social obligation whereas in individualistic cultures accountability will more often come from an individual's personal commitment to a goal. [63]

Your Community client who has processed his/her goal with their team, family, and leader has more built-in accountability, therefore may be motivated by social obligation or bringing honor (rather than shame) to the group. For Autonomy clients, ask what the client needs in terms of accountability, both inside and outside the coaching relationship.

At times, Autonomy coaches may be frustrated by what they perceive as the Community client *not* taking responsibility for failures (or for instance, action steps not being followed through). Lindsey Bridges, director of communications at the Malphurs Group, explains how this has impacted her coaching with Spanish-speakers and while church planting in South America. The structure of the Spanish language itself exemplifies a culture that deeply values relationships and not "losing face". Instead of saying "I broke it", the correct grammatical construction is "it broke itself". In this case, the language signals that the fault lies with fate or circumstances, rather than the individual.[64]

Lindsey suggests using questions such as "How have you seen other teams approach this differently?"[65]Another approach integrates the importance of relationship generally embedded in the Hispanic culture by asking, "How was the team/family/group affected by this situation?" Or "If someone else were to approach this situation, what advice would you give them?" Conclude by asking what the client can do to help bring healing or benefit to the group.[66]

---

63   David B. Peterson, "Executive Coaching in a Cross Cultural Context," *Consulting Psychology Journal: Practice and Research* 59, no. 4 (December 2007): 261-271.

64   Lindsey Bridges, Director of Communications at the Malphurs Group, Personal Communication, Permission granted on October 27, 2015.

65   Ibid.

66   Ibid.

Coaching for Life Purpose

Coaching for Life Purpose is significantly impacted by Community and Autonomy values. Here's an example of an Autonomy coach working with a firmly Community client. Patty is an experienced coach who lives and works in China. She often does educational seminars for Chinese and Westerners. She also coaches expats and occasionally Chinese as well. She related the following story:

> My friend Li Na was interested in life purpose coaching. When we met to begin coaching together, I shared how God has made each of us uniquely with gifts, strengths, and unique experiences. I spoke about how wonderful I thought it was to explore what is unique about each of us and that finding out how we are made as individuals can help us focus on the unique calling God has for us. After several minutes of this, with my using the word "unique" several times, there was silence. My Chinese coachee finally said, "I don't want to be unique. I want to be like other people."[67]

While Patty, her American coach, reveled in the concept of God making each of us uniquely, Li Na did not want to be unique. In her culture, a common saying is that "the nail that sticks up gets hammered down." In Community cultures, fitting in is more important than being unique or standing out.

Here is what Patty shared about the end of her first life purpose session with Li Na:

> From my perspective, it's a great pursuit to look at how you are different than others: that makes you special! From Li Na's perspective, that makes her odd! So, we had a discussion about that, and it was really helpful to me. To go about life purpose coaching, you must have a completely different approach, in order for an Asian to engage in it meaningfully. Chinese often say, "We Chinese think . . ." instead of "I believe . . ." or "I think . . . " This is so deeply ingrained! I learned how to frame life purpose differently with my Asian coachees.[68]

You may have noticed that Patty, being an outstanding coach, used great coaching technique when this cultural faux pas surfaced. She followed her curiosity, listened intently to her client, and learned more about how her coachee experienced the world. With this CQ Knowledge in hand, she came up with a more effective plan (CQ Strategy) for life purpose coaching with other Asians.

---

67   Patty, Personal Communication, Permission granted on July 17, 2015.
68   Ibid.

Here's what Patty did going forward:

> I definitely changed the way I talked about life purpose and the words/language I used. I also changed some of the material to reflect more emphasis on the origins of life purpose within the group context and web of relationships. Now I ask my Asian clients, "Given the community God placed you in and the family God put you in, how did that shape you? What values became a part of who you are? What are you good at because of your milieu? What did your community do to shape you? What are you good at within your community? What does your community recognize that you do that brings value to the community?" While I wouldn't just take American life purpose materials and work through those as is, I do use the concepts because the concepts and principles are right; they just need cultural translation."[69]

Ending the Coaching Relationship

Ditmar, a German coach working in Brazil, shares:

> There is an expectation in Brazil—a Community culture—that even after the coaching goal is achieved, the coach and coachee will maintain a strong relationship and talk frequently. This is not to say that the client has become dependent, but simply that he expects that the coaching relationship—marked by vulnerability—would naturally evolve into a friendship. Ending the official relationship can be pretty challenging in such a culture, since it may come across as uncaring and cold. I remember a phase when I needed to end a number of coaching relationships. It was challenging. But since I have a busy travel schedule, I would naturally delay returning phone calls, and the travelling was a culturally understandable excuse. After a while, it became clear to the client that we simply couldn't maintain the same regular, intense relationship.[70]

In contrast to Ditmar and his clients, when Lisa came to the end of a year of phone coaching sessions working on deep transformation, she thanked her coach Cindy for walking alongside her in such a significant way. They celebrated the goals that Lisa had successfully achieved. They exchanged affirmations and shared what they had learned from each other. Cindy and Lisa prayed for each other at the end of the session. Cindy never heard from Lisa again.

---

69   Ibid.
70   Ditmar Pauck, Personal Communication, Permission granted on September 16, 2015.

For Autonomy value clients, ending the coaching relationship is pretty straightforward. When the client feels they have achieved their individual goals or completed the number of sessions for which they have contracted, they will readily finish their coaching, and their coach may never again have contact with them. The client will likely be quite satisfied with this.

This may sound cold to the Community oriented coach, but an Autonomy client will not experience it this way. So, when you sense a client is nearing goal completion, do not hesitate to ask how they can maintain their progress outside the coaching relationship. It can often be especially affirming for your client if you offer to stay in touch after the coaching relationship ends (if they want to and at their initiative). Your Autonomy client may experience this as particularly caring and supportive since it will be unexpected.

If you are dealing with Community value coachees, remember that once you are "in" their "we" group, you are in. Finishing coaching goals does not mean finishing the relationship. The relationship is expected to continue. Sometimes this will make it difficult to determine when the coachee is done with coaching, as they may not have an expectation that the coaching will end. We'll address this dynamic more when we discuss Status/Equality and Relationship/Task values.

Learning to transition the relationship from coaching to a less formal connection is a key skill for a coach working with Community value clients. Ditmar found a culturally appropriate excuse to change the *level* of the relationship from one of intentional coaching to a much more informal type of relating. Another way to transition to a more informal relationship with distance clients is to suggest staying in touch on Facebook, which enables mutual sharing of family updates and photos as well as occasional comments or messaging. Living in the community in which your coachee lives will allow for other informal options such as meeting for coffee or inviting the former coachee to church or community events.

Dealing with Coach Discomfort

As coaches, it can be tempting to want to move our clients subtly towards our own value orientation on this continuum. Autonomy coaches may want their Community coachees to become independent. After all, this is a sign of maturity and responsibility, right? Community coaches may feel their clients should become more interdependent with others. I mean, selfishness is bad, isn't it? But our ultimate goal is to help our clients follow God. While we may leverage other cultural values to help increase our client's range of options, we must resist the temptation to feel that *our* value orientation has all the "right" answers.

There are many other stress points in working with clients different than you on this continuum. Pace, for instance. Or the way conflict is handled within and outside the coaching relationship. Dealing with responsibility, guilt, and shame. In coping with these, self-awareness, a great supervisor or mentor coach, and good self-care are helpful.

What is important to keep in mind is that of all the value continuums you must understand as a cross-cultural coach, this one is in the top two or three. Dr. Keith Webb, Master Coach, and Trainer of Creative Results Management, says of the Autonomy/Community value continuum:

> If you don't value this grid, what's the downside? For me, the downside of getting this grid wrong is really big, whereas getting the Time/Event continuum wrong doesn't have as many liabilities. But if you take an individualistic, autonomy oriented approach when coaching a Japanese client, that can wreak havoc in the client's setting."[71]

Gaining CQ Knowledge, interpreting client behavior and words with CQ Strategy, then deploying CQ Action as you coach is essential in serving your clients with excellence on this continuum.

For more information on how Autonomy and Community values impact coaching for conflict, go to www.dancingbetweencultures.com.

Take a Minute

- *Review the statements you underlined in the Values Chart and where you placed yourself on the continuum of Autonomy/Community. Is there anything you need to change?*
- *What new strategies have you thought of that would help you coach your cross-cultural client more effectively? What is one action step you are ready to commit to now because of identifying those new strategies?*

---

71   Dr. Keith Webb, Founder of Creative Results Management, Personal Communication, Permission granted on July 6, 2015.

Chapter Nine

85

Risk and Caution Values

One of the bewildering things about values continuums for the layperson is that they sometimes overlap, or seem like they *should* overlap. This can make it hard to identify what value continuum is in operation during any particular time of the coaching appointment. This is particularly true for the Risk/Caution and Crisis/Non-Crisis continuums, which we will be discussing in the following two chapters. With both these continuums, tolerance for ambiguity is a factor. In Risk/Caution, *change*, which in itself brings uncertainty and ambiguity, is avoided or embraced. In Crisis/Non-Crisis, ambiguity regarding *planning* is the issue.

Risk/Caution and Crisis/Non-Crisis are also similar in that they are focused on how our clients relate to the present and future. In this sense, Risk/Caution and Crisis/Non-Crisis could be said to relate to time orientation, which includes a separate set of continuums we'll be discussing later. However, as you read on, you'll also see distinct differences between Risk/Caution and Crisis/Non-Crisis. Additionally, you'll note variations between these two continuums associated with change and planning vs. those continuums dealing directly with time orientation.

To see the basics of Risk/Caution and Crisis/Non-Crisis values, refer to the Appendix, Cultural Values Chart or to the chart below. The visual representation of Risk/Caution is the parachute, denoting Risk; and the umbrella, used to shield against rain or sun, which signifies Caution. The Crisis icon is an outline with A,B, and C noted in order; the Non-Crisis icon is a question mark, representing an openness to making a decision when the moment happens rather than having a detailed plan ahead of time.

Risk	(change)	Caution
I value flexibility and adaptability.		I value rules and reliability.
I embrace change and make decisions quickly.		I prefer to have a long time to make a decision and don't change quickly.
I like to try new things and methods rather than stick to the routine.		I like to stick to what is proven and stable; I value a routine.
I value innovation: I prefer less rules and guidelines.		I value tradition: I want more rules and guidelines.
Changes and differences are interesting.		Changes and differences can make me a bit anxious.
I can handle nonlinear change.		I prefer slower, incremental change.

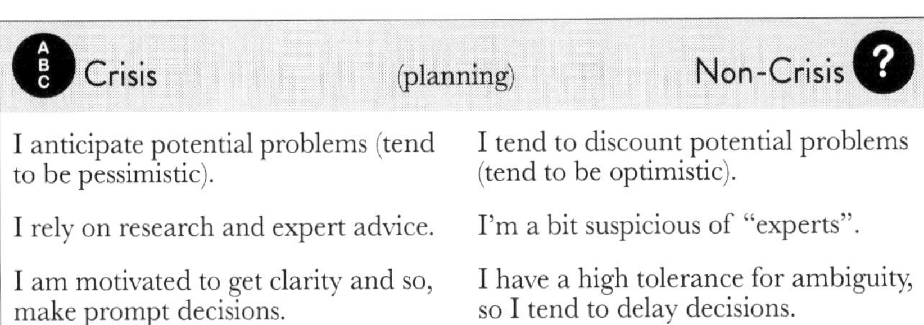

I anticipate potential problems (tend to be pessimistic).	I tend to discount potential problems (tend to be optimistic).
I rely on research and expert advice.	I'm a bit suspicious of "experts".
I am motivated to get clarity and so, make prompt decisions.	I have a high tolerance for ambiguity, so I tend to delay decisions.
I stick to the plan when the crisis hits.	I improvise when a crisis hits.

Take a Minute

Self-awareness is key to great cross-cultural relationships. Take a few minutes right now and do the following quick exercises:

- *Underline or note which phrases in the Cultural Values Chart, the Appendix, for Risk/Caution and Crisis/Non-Crisis most appeal to you or match your own beliefs.*

- *Think about the relative strength of your preference for either Risk or Caution. Plot a point on the line below that represents where you are on the Risk/Caution continuum. Do the same for Crisis/Non-Crisis. Continue to keep this in mind as you read this chapter, and the following chapter on Crisis/Non-Crisis.*

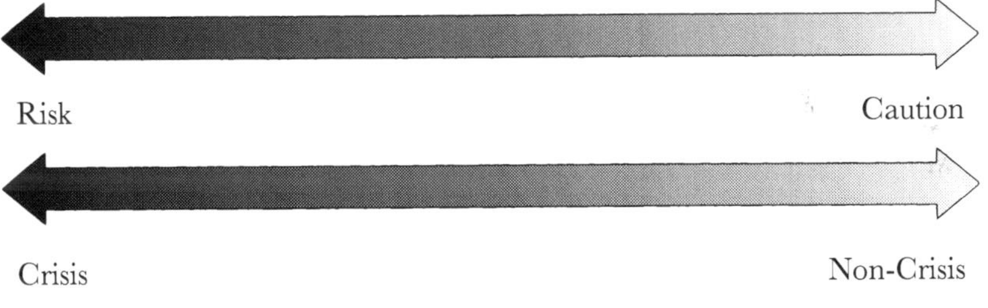

Risk and Caution Values

An American coach who lived for many years in Eastern Europe and continues to coach there shared the following story that illustrates the Caution side of the Risk/Caution continuum:

> I have a coachee, Alexander, who has a chronic terminal disease. We've been meeting for coaching twice a month for a year. Before coaching, we had been

good friends for a decade. He has been the pastor of a church in his home country for many years, and while I lived in the region, I found him to be one of the most progressive pastors I knew. Yet with all of this and the fact that his disease is worsening, he is resistant to any kind of change.

Over time, it became slowly obvious that Alexander was not able physically to do everything needed for his role as pastor. So I cautiously asked him how he would pastor as his physical condition worsened. We had talked openly about this happening sometime in the future, but now I wanted to be available to listen and active in helping him take proactive steps to cultivate a leader to be the next pastor.

Well, we still have not solved that issue! We have talked around it for a year, and only last week did he want to address it head on. I'm still not sure how he will deal with it, but it has taken him that long to address it. I know there are other issues involved, like family, kids, status, and other things. But it just takes a long time in his culture to respond, to think ahead, and be willing to change the status quo."[72]

Conversely, one of my own clients illustrates the Risk end of this value continuum. I've been coaching Vanessa, a wonderful young American woman, off and on for several years. She is single and in her late twenties, very creative and talented. At the time of our last session, Vanessa had been involved in an innovative Christian community and was managing a music store, a job that had given her security, stability, a good income, and lots of contacts in the music field.

When we met again after several months, Vanessa caught me up on her life. After two years at the music store, she was increasingly restless. She felt a tremendous draw towards writing and performing music. She had decided to quit her job and had already turned in her resignation. She was planning on taking the next two months off to visit family and friends, pursue some leads in the music industry, and just see what would happen.

Though I kept my feelings to myself, I was a bit anxious when I learned that Vanessa had no other job in the works, was not currently in a music band, and had no fallback plan or alternate source of income. It turned out Vanessa was a bit anxious about this, too.

"I value stability," she told me, "but don't want to just do the same job every day!"

---

72   Dr. Cory Lemke, Personal Communication, Permission granted on July 3, 2015.

I asked Vanessa to tell me more about that. She could delineate clearly to me and to herself that what she really wanted was to play music, write, and perform. Our session ended with Vanessa making a list of what she might risk losing if she carried through with her decision (security, success, roots) and what she might gain (a sense of wonder, being engaged in things that mattered to her, unexpected surprises, enjoying the process, and potential adventure).

In the end, Vanessa's takeaway was: "I want to pursue music, and this is what I have always wanted. Yes, there is a risk, but I want to take it. I'd rather take the risk of leaving this job than go another decade without trying."[73]

Risk/Caution is a continuum that appears in some form in most published studies on cultural values. Risk and Caution are related to the concepts of "low uncertainty avoidance" and "high uncertainty avoidance", which were the original terms used by Geert Hofstede in his pioneering research on cultural values.[74] The Risk and Caution continuum is important for the coach to understand because it influences openness to change and the desire for/discomfort with trying new things.

Brief Explanation of the Value Set

The two previous coaching stories demonstrate some of the differences between Risk and Caution orientations. Alexander was slow to think about and address change, and his coach was having to deal with the slower decision-making process of Caution orientation. Alexander will likely want to make small, incremental changes in his responsibilities and in raising up a new leader. Alexander's coach is wise to understand that this process will take time despite the trust and relational rapport he has with his client.

Vanessa, on the other hand, has initiated a radical, discontinuous change in her life. Although she loved some aspects of her job, she was not drawn to its routine and found energy in anticipating "unexpected surprises" and "adventure". Her plan to pursue some leads for two months and see what would happen displays flexibility and adaptability. She is willing to trade financial stability, roots in a community, and "success" to take a risk on her dreams. The icon representing the parachute is apt for Vanessa: she'd be willing to skydive – it might be interesting!

---

73   Vanessa, Personal Communication, Permission granted on November 30, 2015.
74   Geert Hofstede, Gert Jan Hofstede, and Michael Minkov, *Cultures and Organizations: Software of the Mind, Intercultural Cooperation and its Importance for Survival.* 3rd ed. (New York: McGraw Hill, 2010), 188-190.

Risk and Caution each have their advantages and disadvantages. The stories above highlight the strengths of Risk and the disadvantages of Caution. But of course, there is another side. Those with Caution orientations don't change for change's sake, and they draw on the tried and true experience of tradition. Leaders with such orientations can provide stability and continuity for those they work with. On the other hand, those with Risk orientations may throw caution to the wind, consequently reaping relational or ministry disasters. Leaders with such orientations may wear their followers out with constant innovations and over-the-top risks.

> *One's generation, rural or urban location, educational level, or profession might be as relevant as nationality in influencing a person's Risk/ Caution values.*

Connections, Disconnects, and Politics with Risk/Caution

Countries and even well-defined regions that cluster together on other characteristics are often split on this particular value continuum. Within Western Europe, for instance, Belgium is quite high on the Caution side, while Austria, Switzerland, and Germany are moderately Caution, and Great Britain, Ireland, Sweden, and Denmark are highly Risk. Japan is a Caution culture. China, on the other hand, is further on the Risk side than the U.S. or Australia. African and Arab countries cluster towards the middle, but Eastern Europe, Central America, and South America are split. It's a puzzling pattern.[75]

The Risk/Caution continuum may have interesting national political and social ramifications. Some writers see societies with high Caution value as being less tolerant of other religions, immigrants, and minorities. Nations with high Caution value tend to have more laws and unwritten codes of conduct in place. Countries with high Risk value will have fewer laws and unwritten rules, but citizens' ability to protest laws and their relative trust in government may be higher. There are some rather flagrant exceptions to this, such as China.[76]

One's generation, rural or urban location, educational level, or profession might be as relevant as nationality in influencing a person's Risk/Caution values. Think about the differences in this continuum between generations in the United

---

75   Ibid., 195.
76   Ibid., 216-221.

States; for instance, Millennials tend towards Risk while the parents of today's Baby Boomers (the so-called "Silent Generation" that grew up during the Great Depression) tend towards Caution.

Applying this value continuum to churches, organizations, and denominations is also instructive. YWAM, for example, is a pioneering, risk-taking organization and would definitely fall on the Risk side. Many denominations and sending organizations I've worked with are firmly on the Caution side. Risk and Caution are values that will impact your client and the teams and organizations you coach in a variety of areas. But catching just where your client falls on this continuum takes some intentionality. Consider the following reflection questions to help you become more aware of this continuum as you read on.

Take a Minute

- *Based on what you just learned about Risk and Caution cultures, what kind of retirement planning would you expect in each? What about response to emerging leaders?*
- *Having a real life situation in mind will help you apply CQ Knowledge to your own coaching conversations. Before reading further, think of a cross-cultural situation (preferably a coaching situation) you are presently in where both Risk and Caution values are operating. Jot down some factors related to these values that might be relevant to this situation. As you read through the next sections, identify new behaviors or strategies you could deploy to be a more effective coach in the scenario you've identified.*

Applying Risk and Caution Values to Coaching

Let's turn now to increasing our CQ Strategy and Behavior by examining how Risk and Caution values impact the coaching relationship, coaching funnel, and coaching goals. We'll start by looking at how to establish relationships that can result in transformational coaching conversations and how to introduce the concept of coaching itself into a new culture or organization.

Introducing coaching into a Risk culture vs. a Caution culture is vastly different. In Caution cultures, which include many older Christian organizations and denominations, and with Caution culture clients, coaching is best introduced slowly and incrementally, using concepts or stories that are already familiar to listeners. Finding a tradition already present in the culture and linking it to coaching is ideal. Kevin Sutter, an American working in an influential role for a Risk value organization, often interacts about coaching with grassroots leaders in Caution cultures. He introduces coaching by using the familiar story of Barnabas in Acts 11: 22-4, relating Barnabas' activities in Antioch to those of a coach—observing/listening, caring, encouraging, empowering, and inspiring.[77]

Conversely, in Risk cultures, a quicker route can be taken. Referring to coaching's cutting-edge role in business and management and appealing to the Risk culture's desire to try new things are ways to make coaching instantly interesting. When you pitch coaching to a Risk culture organization, they will make a quick decision, so be ready.

Motivation and Options

These differing strategies for Risk vs. Caution clients are also useful for fanning the flames of motivation in your clients as well as helping them to develop options. Risk value clients will be motivated by innovating and trying new things. When motivation is flagging, ask the client how the plan can be changed. Probe for new ideas. Ask "what if" questions that push the envelope of what they know or have experienced. When they are stuck in developing options, ask them to brainstorm about what would be possible if they had no constraints and could try anything. How could they make their ministry or organization more cutting-edge? More innovative? Ask them what their options would be if they could start fresh.

The opposite will be true of Caution value clients. Caution clients will be motivated by reliable systems, building on traditions, and minimizing uncertainty. When your Caution client is losing motivation or seems overwhelmed, probe for a small step they would feel secure taking. Ask how the goal they are working on connects to some of the traditions that are most dear to them. When stuck in the options phase, inquire about traditional or "tried and true" methods that might be employed or methods they may have seen other respected leaders use consistently. Ask how might they make the system/team/organization more reliable.

Pace and Embracing Change

An obvious difference in coaching Risk vs. Caution clients is in the pace at which they embrace change and can tolerate uncertainty, risk, and new developments. Heather Hicks, who was working with an international relief and develop-

---

ment organization, relates the following story, which not only highlights this value, but also the reality that the coaching situations we encounter will likely have more than one factor (e.g. cultural value, personality, and experience) in play:

> I was coaching an Indonesian woman, and she was explaining her concern about being impatient and her desire to work on this quality. I found that her Community orientation often conflicted with her temperament tendencies. She really is a strong J on the Myers Briggs (she likes order, structure, and sees things in black and white), but her desire to honor and do what is right with the group created a great deal of internal frustration. We did a lot of exploring about the issues that were important to her, the reasons why, how it related to her faith, and where the resistance from the group was coming from. We looked at who in the group was important to honor and began talking about her boss. It seemed as we talked that her boss was from a Risk orientation and that he was making decisions quickly, changing his mind, seeking to do new things and try new things. He enjoyed change—a lot of change! But that made my client very uncomfortable. His approach felt reckless to her and dishonoring to the traditions of the past. So, mixed with her Community orientation and personality, she was struggling internally and in the end it was the "Caution and Risk" values that seemed to be the most important issue to her. So, we explored the perspective of a "Risk" orientation (not using that language) and the pros and cons of that approach. We explored her fears as well. Then we found examples in her own life and culture where the kind of action her boss had taken had helped people grow and break out of patterns they were stuck in, even creating new and good ways of doing things. She began to see that her boss's orientation wasn't wrong…and as she began to see the other perspective, she softened and found that she was less threatened and more able to ask questions, and to share her concerns or hesitations.[78]

This story is a lovely example of a coach helping a client see both sides of the value continuum and learn how to relate to the opposite value. In doing so, this client indirectly assisted the larger organization to function more effectively with better team relationships and balanced perspectives, drawing on both value orientations.

The Risk/Caution continuum can often create tension when organizations and teams, whether business or ministry oriented, cross cultures. One missionary

---

78   Heather Hicks, Personal Communication, Permission granted on October 14, 2015.

The Risk/Caution continuum can often create tension when organizations and teams, whether business or ministry oriented, cross cultures.

described the constant pressure he felt from the home office because of the slow pace of change on the field. This long-term missionary had to explain over and over to his leaders in the U.S. that the lack of change was not due to lack of effort on his part, but due to the Caution oriented society that he was working in.

Caution value coaches working with Risk value clients may feel that the action is getting out of control as their clients push for faster change. Caution value coaches can help risk-taking clients slow down and evaluate the impact of change. Risk value coaches may become frustrated at the slow pace of Caution value clients, but with patience can help the Caution value client see the risks of waiting too long to take action.

Structure, Stability, and Certainty

Heather Hicks shares this example:

> I was coaching a North American leader working in Bangladesh. He wanted to mentor his senior leaders in healthy management skills, but there were huge barriers to overcome. There was already a management system in place, and among the local leaders there was very little ability to be adaptive and flexible. The leaders' supervisees wanted clear steps to be laid out for them and followed each time. They did not want to consider potential alternatives to the ways they had learned to manage in the past. Ideas the North American shared created anxiety and great concern from his core leadership.[79]

When working with Caution clients, it's helpful to let them know clearly what is expected of them in coaching and how you will be working with them. Providing written guidelines that the client may refer to later may be useful in some settings. The client's comfort and ease in the process will increase as you follow the same format and structure in each session. One Asian leader I know explains to new coachees that he is switching from a mentoring role with them to a coaching role because he has seen so much growth in them as leaders and feels they are ready to move into a bigger sphere of leadership. He carefully explains that he will be asking them a lot of questions as he coaches them, which is not normally a part

---

79   Ibid.

of their culture, because he knows they are ready to make more decisions themselves. He steadfastly affirms them and his ongoing commitment to relationship with them. He provides stability through affirmation and continuing relationship as he transitions to a different format in his helping role.

In contrast, Risk clients will stay interested if your appointments do not fall into a routine. While communicating initial expectations is important with any client, Risk clients will appreciate being able to meet at different times of the day, alternating in-person with Skype or phone, and the ability when needed to break with the stated goal to process another agenda. They will likely be open to the suggestion of doing a longer session when needed or to having a longer or shorter time between sessions. They will not be confused by a departure from the coaching funnel when it's called for. If you are a coach who follows a set routine when coaching (for instance, greeting, asking after the client's health and family, asking for prayer requests, praying for the client, asking for a progress report, and then moving into the coaching funnel), try changing up that routine for your Risk clients.

When working with Risk and Caution clients on goals that involve structure or lack of structure, help your clients gain what they each need to lessen stress. For Caution clients, a clear action plan with incremental steps laid out will help them decrease anxiety. For Risk clients working on long-term change, give them opportunities to innovate at each step in the process.

Dealing with Coach Discomfort

Caution value coaches will need to be braced for a wild, uncertain, and fast-paced ride with their Risk clients. Risk coaches will need to be willing to settle in for slow, stability-enhancing changes with their Caution clients. Goals for the Risk client may be grand and innovative, while for the Caution client, they may be smaller and more incremental.

In either case, managing the difference in style may be stressful for the differently-valued coach. Caution coaches may find they are quite uncomfortable with the pace of change in their Risk clients and will need to hold lightly their sense of foreboding or threat. Risk coaches will find themselves extremely frustrated at times and will need to exercise patience with a slower tempo.

Take a Minute

- *Recall a situation when you coached (or related to) someone of the opposite value than yourself, either Risk or Caution. Think back to the dynamics of that relationship. Is there anything you would interpret differently now based on your new CQ Knowledge?*
- *What new strategies have you thought of that would help you coach your cross-cultural client more effectively? What is one action step you are ready to commit to now as a result of identifying those new strategies?*

Chapter Ten

97

Crisis and Non-Crisis Values

Many years ago, I coached a majority world leader who was the country director for a mission organization. This leader was an affable man, warmhearted and good-humored. Passionate about his people and about helping them to succeed, Peter used his influence in a variety of societal spheres to help promote his own fellow citizens. He persevered in coaching despite many technological obstacles. I respected him deeply.

I was relatively new to cross-cultural coaching when I began working with Peter and was determined that we would have clear goals for our coaching. After all, coaching is about action and making progress on goals. And Peter did indeed make progress. He just tended to make progress on whatever particular thing we were working on that day. I would press him to set future oriented goals, and he would do just that. But invariably during the first five minutes of our Skype session, he would express the need to debrief concerning a team disagreement, a problem with a leader he had to deal with, or a financial crisis needing attention.

We would end up focusing on this current issue without ever getting around to Peter's continuing or series goals. His action steps from one coaching session to another rarely had any relation to each other. He seldom followed through on a longer-term plan for more than a session or two. Peter valued the coaching and told me many times that he did not know who else he could process these current issues with. But as a coach, I felt I was not serving him well, since he was not accomplishing the overarching goals I considered to be most important.

Coaching Jack, an American organizational-change consultant, through his dissertation process was a different story. Jack had been working on his doctoral degree for several years and was not getting it finished as quickly as he wished. Jack explored with his coach what was holding up his progress, identifying a host of obstacles, including time, courage, energy, and a variety of distractions. He then spent time with his coach planning for each one.

The following year passed with slower movement than Jack had hoped. After meeting with his dissertation advisor and investigating thoroughly what was needed to graduate by January, Jack arrived at his next coaching appointment ready to stick to a rigid schedule and eliminate other distractions. He recognized he would have to seriously limit business travel in the next few months and had taken steps to clear his schedule. Jack produced a detailed spreadsheet of activities needed to take him to a January graduation date. His plan succeeded, and Jack celebrated his graduation as planned with his wife and family.[80]

---

80   Jack, Personal Communication, Permission granted on July 12, 2015.

These stories illustrate the Crisis/Non-Crisis continuum. This value continuum is particularly important for the coach because it is critical to planning and how planning is approached by the client. Goals, action planning, action steps, and progress reporting, as well as several other coaching issues, are impacted. The concept of Crisis and Non-Crisis values comes from Marvin Mayers Basic Values Questionnaire and is described beautifully in Sherwood Lingenfelter's book, Ministering Cross-Culturally.[81]

Brief Explanation of the Value Set

Crisis value cultures, whether they are organizational, national, or generational, will prefer planning how to deal with potential problems and crises in advance. Time and money will be spent on expert advice and research. Decisions regarding the plan will then be made clearly and quickly. Plans formulated ahead of time will be honored and dutifully carried out. This planned response will ensure quick, authoritative, efficient procedures are put in place ahead of time. The strength of this value is planning ahead, which will come naturally. Clients who have this value may seem overly pessimistic to coaches with the opposite value. The icon for Crisis is an outline, carefully prepared and researched, which can be checked off as the plan is implemented.

Non-Crisis cultures will work with a problem when it comes up rather than beforehand. Suspicious of expert advice and tolerant of some lack of clarity, Non-Crisis cultures may delay or put off decision-making until it is necessary. When the crisis or problem does occur, Non-Crisis cultures are adept at improvisation of creative solutions and immediate fixes, using whatever resources are at hand. This adaptive response opens the door for on-the-spot solutions that fit current conditions. The strength of this value is adapting naturally and easily. Non-Crisis clients may seem overly optimistic to coaches with the opposite value. The icon for this value is a question mark, which denotes openness to possibility and opportunity in the moment.

---

81   Sherwood G. Lingenfelter and Marvin K. Mayers, *Ministering Cross-Culturally: An Incarnational Model for Personal Relationships* (Grand Rapids: Baker Academic, 2007), 65-76.

The tricky thing about the Crisis/Non-Crisis continuum is that it might sound as if a country or culture high on the Risk scale would be high in Non-Crisis, or that a Crisis client would be a Long-Term thinker rather than a Short-Term one. Sometimes that is the case, and sometimes it is not. For instance, according to Hofstede, Hofstede and Minkov, China plots high on Risk and Long-Term while the U.S. plots high on Risk and Short-Term.82 China ranks strongly Non-Crisis, while the U.S. ranks strongly Crisis.

National cultures often display their Crisis or Non-Crisis orientation in how they handle natural disasters. Those who have a Crisis orientation are more likely to believe it is responsible to plan for potential problems and to make those plans based on expert advice and research. Those with a Non-Crisis orientation are more likely to believe it is better not to waste time and resources on planning for things that may not happen, but to have faith things will work out.[83]

Take a Minute

- *Based on what you just learned about Crisis and Non-Crisis cultures, what kind of retirement planning would you expect in each? What about leadership succession? Stretch yourself and really think about how a client with a Crisis/Non-Crisis orientation would look and act differently than one with Risk/Caution orientation.*
- *As you begin the section on application of this value continuum, think about a conversation you've had with someone of the opposite value than yourself. Consider as you read what you could do and say differently (CQ Action) based on what you are learning about Crisis and Non-Crisis values (CQ Knowledge)*

Applying Crisis and Non-Crisis Values to Coaching

Crisis/Non-Crisis is a continuum that will show up more quickly than some of the other value continuums and will be more easily identified in the coaching relationship, if you are tuned in to look for it. Following are ways to adapt to and leverage Crisis and Non-Crisis values in coaching conversations.

---

82   Geert Hofstede, Gert Jan Hofstede, and Michael Minkov, Cultures and Organizations: Software of the Mind, Intercultural Cooperation and its Importance for Survival. 3rd ed. (New York: McGraw Hill, 2010), 192-194 & 236.
83   Sherwood G. Lingenfelter and Marvin K. Mayers, Ministering Cross-Culturally: An Incarnational Model for Personal Relationships. 2nd ed. (Grand Rapids, MI: Baker Academic, 2007), 71.

Introducing Coaching

As with the example of Peter at the beginning of this chapter, Non-Crisis leaders may find coaching more appealing if it is presented as a way to debrief and address current issues rather than to do future planning. Probably the easiest way to lose a strongly Non-Crisis client is to try to get them to work on an abstract multi-stage growth plan at the start of the relationship. Conversely, Crisis oriented individuals, teams, and organizations will find value in hearing that coaching can help them with life planning, strategy planning and business plans.

Later in the relationship, the opposite approach can be leveraged for the benefit of both Crisis and Non-Crisis clients. Non-Crisis clients may be happy to learn that if they have longer-term goals, coaching can help provide a structure to attain them. Crisis clients may be surprised to find that taking time out from discussing their overall or long term goal to debrief a current critical issue is very helpful.

Motivation

Keisa, a CMI master coach and trainer, shared this story:

> Two female leaders had been asked to lead short term teams to Thailand in the months leading up to the tsunami in 2004. They had both set up tentative plans for their teams before arrival, but once they arrived all of that changed due to the relief and reconstruction after the tsunami. The two no longer had a contact to work with and had to come up with team ministry on their own on a daily basis.
>
> The Crisis value leader panicked and felt that the real reason they had no ministry lined up was because the local contacts had dropped the ball. She had difficulty moving forward and keeping her team motivated. The Non-Crisis leader loved the fact that they were able to create the ministry on the spot each day. This second leader was excited that all their plans were trashed, because now they did not seem relevant to what was going on in Thailand in reconstruction. She became very motivated and got her team excited about all the potential opportunities to engage and serve the community.[84]

The Crisis value leader in this account was motivated by the plan, and the Non-Crisis leader was motivated by on-the-spot conditions. It's easy to feel when

---

84   Keisa Capers, Head Coach of CMI, Personal Communication, Permission granted on June 30, 2015.

> *The Crisis value leader was motivated by the plan, and the Non-Crisis leader was motivated by on-the-spot conditions.*

you have been trained in Western coaching technique that Non-Crisis clients are not motivated. They are! They are simply motivated by different things. For instance, Non-Crisis clients will not be motivated by "what ifs". Obstacles that may or may not be thrown in their path in the future do not seem important. Why waste time and resources dealing with something that might not happen? But these same hypothetical future obstacles will seem vitally important to the Crisis client, since they could interfere in the client's well-crafted plans. It is therefore most helpful to work through obstacles with Crisis clients ahead of time and with Non-Crisis clients when they actually happen.

In terms of motivation for long-term goals, clients of both values will flag at times, but Non-Crisis clients will generally lose steam faster in favor of current issues. How does a coach help Non-Crisis clients maintain their motivation for future, multi-stage goals they have set? Several expert cross-cultural coaches have graciously shared some of the questions they use to motivate such clients:

- Dimitri: "What benefits would you see in your life if this goal is reached? What could you do to ensure it happens? How could you partner with God in seeing this accomplished?"[85]
- Heather: "What do you think would happen if you didn't prepare for that? What might go wrong if you do nothing?"[86]
- Patty: "Leverage another value—in this case Relationship/Task—with a Relationship value client. If you do not accomplish this, what kind of conflict or lack of harmony will it bring?"[87]
- Kevin[88] and Ted[89]: "What impact will reaching this goal have on you or others when this goal is a *present reality*?"

Other techniques that will increase motivation for both Crisis and Non-Crisis clients are the use of envisioning as well as fleshing out what a goal will look like when it is accomplished and integrated into the coachee's daily life. In working through current obstacles with Non-Crisis clients, encourage their creativity and

---

85 Dimitri, Personal Communication, Permission granted on January 25, 2016.
86 Heather Hicks, Personal Communication, Permission granted on October 14, 2015.
87 Patty, Personal Communication, Permission granted on July 17, 2015.
88 Kevin Sutter, Personal Communication, Permission granted on July 16, 2015.
89 Ted, Encompass World Partners, Personal Communication, Permission granted on September 28, 2016.

adaptability. This is a great place for brainstorming. When dealing with flagging motivation in Crisis clients dealing with unexpected obstacles, here are some additional questions you can ask:

- What would happen if you really believed that having your plan fall through was in *God's* plan all along? How would you respond differently?
- What is a new plan you could make given these circumstances?
- What new information, resources, and expert advice do you need to make a new plan?
- What opportunities might be hidden within these obstacles?

Options and Obstacles

Crisis clients can sometimes see all too well how potential obstacles can ruin their vision and dreams. When clients begin to dismiss every option they identify based on multiple potential obstacles, the coaching process runs aground. Linda, an Indonesian coach and coach trainer working in the U.S., observes:

> Because your Crisis value client may believe that his/her environment can be controlled, there may be over-anticipation in taking preventative measures of planning. Explore the benefits of looking at obstacles when they arise rather than pre-planning. Encourage your client to explore an optimistic outlook.[90]

For those Non-Crisis clients whose lack of planning is the result of a strong belief in fate or destiny (meaning they feel they have little control over circumstances or goal attainment) or from a cultural history of hardship, repression, or poverty, generating options can be very difficult. Your client may not recognize they *have* options. And in some cases, they may not. One way to work with this is to recognize the resilience and patience of your client in dealing with whatever is thrown at them or given them in life. How have they creatively dealt with circumstances in the past? How might that inform options now? Recognize too that for those clients who do not have much control over their lives, the options and decisions process may happen in fits and starts.

One final tip is from David Harper, a Canadian coach working in Jamaica and South Africa, who adds:

> Spend more time processing options rather than moving too quickly towards finishing off the funnel. Non-Crisis clients need to "feel the gap" in order to set goals for the future rather than just for the present.[91]

---

90   Linda, Personal Communication, Permission granted on January 28, 2016.
91   David Harper, Personal Communication, Permission granted on August 15, 2015.

For Crisis coaches working with Non-Crisis clients, the concept of "working around" obstacles (changing internal attitudes rather than external circumstances) is a very important concept to understand. This adaptable response to obstacles may also be related to Indirect, Community, and Status values. Patty offers the following story about "working around", which demonstrates the overlap of these values:

> Chinese [people] believe most problems will work themselves out if given time. There's a general feeling that we are at the mercy of fate, and decisions are best made in the midst of the situation, not beforehand. An oft-heard phrase is "mei ban fa" – meaning "it can't be helped", or nothing can be done about it. There is not a lot of urgency to fix something; it's more how to live with it. How does that play out? In a school where we were working, the Overseer opposed everything the English teachers did, which was very frustrating for our teachers. One of our leaders had a conversation with this leader's boss. He said regarding this leader that she is difficult to work with and that they too are unhappy with how she does her job, but it is her job. So, rather than putting someone else in the role, we will all make the best of it and work around it. Westerners would ask, "Couldn't you do an intervention or assign someone different to work with us?" But Chinese are extraordinarily creative at working around. As a coach, I want to believe in my Non-Crisis clients that they can find a way of moving around it, rather than having to change the situation.[92]

Westerners more typically respond to obstacles by trying to change external circumstances. Eastern clients may be more likely to first respond by changing internal attitudes. In his book, *Coaching Questions*, expert Tony Stoltzfus offers several questions that aid in the process of changing inner attitudes, which can be used with Non-Crisis clients or leveraged with Crisis clients:

- What would need to change in your attitudes or responses for you to function at your best in the midst of this, even if circumstances don't change?
- If this circumstance is beyond your control, how can you choose to experience it differently?
- What is this experience teaching you? What is the gift this pain brings?[93]

---

92   Patty, Personal Communication, Permission granted on July 17, 2015.
93   Tony Stoltzfus, *Coaching Questions: A Coach's Guide to Powerful Asking Skills* (Redding, CA: Coach22, 2008), 65.

Decision-Making

Coach Linda, who works with both Western and Eastern clients, observes, "For Crisis clients, decision-making is at its best *before* the situation happens."[94] Capitalize on the future-planning capability of your Crisis client whenever possible. Recognize and be patient with the stress they feel when plans go awry. Be ready to take time for a longer decision-making process when the current situation demands a change of plan.

Westerners typically respond to obstacles by trying to change external circumstances; Eastern clients, by changing internal attitudes.

However, if you are a Crisis coach working with Non-Crisis clients, recognize that your client will be much more comfortable with their not deciding than you will be. As Patty, who coaches in China, writes: "Embrace ambiguity!" In other words, don't force decisions.[95]

Conversely, the time may come when your Non-Crisis client does need to decide about a future goal or major life choice. Anne, a coach working in Asia, suggests: "Gently support the client through that process."[96] Many coaches report that pushing the Non-Crisis client to a decision too quickly damages the relationship. Jon Taylor, a pastor and coach who travels and coaches in many cultures, suggests asking the client how *they* will know when they'll be ready to make a decision.[97]

Dealing with Coach Discomfort

Coach discomfort on this value continuum can be high due to the tendency to attach character, degree of faith, or maturity judgments to cultural values. Crisis coaches will tend to feel that Non-Crisis clients are not being responsible enough or are not practicing good stewardship. Non-Crisis coaches may think that their Crisis clients believe they have more control than they actually do and see their efforts to avert potential problems as lack of faith and trust in God.

Many coaches share the need for accepting what we might feel uneasy or even mildly distressed about on this continuum. One such is Wendy Beery, a former missions coach who now works in Christian education: "I have to accept planning options that would not be comfortable for me if they are relevant to my

---

94   Linda, Personal Communication, Permission granted on January 28, 2016.
95   Patty, Personal Communication, Permission granted on July 17, 2015.
96   Anne, Personal Communication, Permission granted on September 17, 2015.
97   Jon Taylor, Personal Communication, Permission granted on July 2, 2015.

client."[98] Non-Crisis coaches may deal with fatigue or discouragement in the face of what they experience as undue pessimism in their Crisis clients.

For more information on Crisis and Non-Crisis values at the national level, the impact of this value continuum on progress reports and session preparation, and to listen to a coaching conversation with a Crisis client living in a Non-Crisis culture, go to www.dancingbetweencultures.com.

Take a Minute

Application:

- *Go back and review the statements you underlined in the Cultural Values Chart and where you placed yourself on the continuum of Crisis/Non-Crisis. Is there anything you need to change?*
- *What new strategies occurred to you that you could deploy to be a more effective coach or conversationalist with others who differ from you on this value?*

---

98   Wendy Beery, Personal Communication, Permission granted on June 29, 2015.

Chapter Eleven

Status and Equality Values

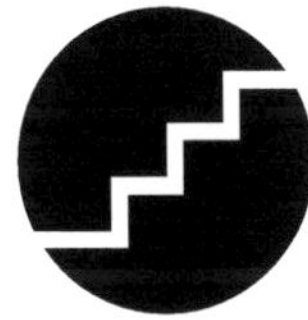 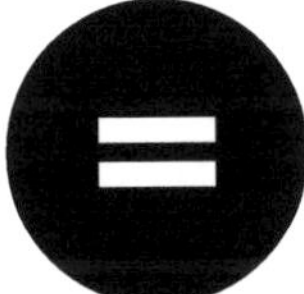

I recently spoke with three coaches who work in very different settings. James is an African who lives and works as a business coach in India. He is also the northern India regional coaching coordinator for an international sending organization, doing coach training and coaching of grassroots workers. Fiona is a coach from Ireland who works with an international missions organization in Eastern Europe. Brad is an organizational coach and VP of the Malphurs Group in the United States, but he first began coaching in South America, where he was then living and working with a missions organization. James is in his early forties, Fiona in her fifties, and Brad, in his thirties. Take note of their challenges and successes as they negotiate the Status/Equality continuum.

James shares:

> Status is a big issue here. It's all about where you belong. India is a very stratified society. People belong to a set social category. These social lines are bold and not easily dismantled or crossed. Here in my city, people want to know my family name, how much I earn, how much I pay in rent, what kind of neighborhood I live in, and what kind of school my kids go to. It is such a strong issue. I have been excluded many times. I was recently in Delhi for a training workshop and afterward sat with another leader. He said to me, "Up until I watched and observed you, I always thought there was nothing good about Africans." I deal with that a lot. It impacts other businessmen wanting to be coached by me. I have a colleague who works with me in the business, and when we go out together to local business meetings, sharing what we are offering, people clearly are not interested in what I am saying. I feel invisible. I don't exist. All the focus is on my colleague, and he has become aware of this. I am the director of the business, and my partner brings new clients to me—and then they find their way back to him! One of the issues I have dealt with in India is knowing who I am, my identity in Christ, my identity as a black African. Am I secure in that?[99]

Brad adds:

> Missions coaching in South America was much more forgiving than business coaching in the U.S. Ask a coach in a business context in the U.S. and see how much more time-centric and results-oriented it is. If you don't perform and perform quickly (and I mean, in one session: push hard, get done on time, and get results!), they will cut you from the contract. In the business world here, if I am not pressing hard, I do not have something to offer the client.[100]

---

99   James, Personal Communication, Permission granted on July 21, 2015.
100   Brad Bridges, VP of the Malphurs Group, Personal Communication, Permission granted on October 10, 2015.

Fiona offers a third perspective:

> We are trying to move away from the director title in our mission organization but it works delightfully for me. Gender issues are not a big factor in Eastern Europe (in Communist times, women worked alongside men, and that expectation of equality still exists), so if I say "I am the director" when I go to a meeting or a new setting of some kind, I get the best chair and undivided attention. It really gets a man's attention. If I have a business card that says I am the director, then I am in. Credentials are important. If I walked into a room full of men in some of the countries I travel to, they would look at the man I walked in with. But here, if I say I am the director, and I would like to coach you, that's it.[101]

Some cultures are organized by hierarchy with a value for Status and others by achievement with a value for Equality. This is the second most important continuum for the coach to understand. Some experts describe this continuum as "high power distance" and "low power distance", referring to the difference in power between leaders and subordinates in a particular culture. In high power distance (HPD) cultures, the difference between leaders and subordinates is high. In low power distance (LPD) cultures, the playing field is much flatter—i.e., there is not as much difference in power between leaders and subordinates.[102]

As in the examples shared by James, Brad, and Fiona, values in this category will significantly impact the coaching experience. This includes such aspects as gaining and keeping clients, expectations of client and coach, change/motivation, and coaching goals such as life purpose, destiny, and leadership development. Deep differences on this continuum are common in cross-cultural relationships and can lead to significant misunderstandings.

Refer to the Appendix, Cultural Values Chart, for a quick summary of this continuum or see the chart below. Icons representing this continuum are a stairway for Status, in which the top step is significantly higher than the bottom; and an equal sign, for Equality, denoting a level playing field.

We'll look at each side of this continuum and gain some CQ Knowledge to power our application of CQ Strategy and Action. As you learn more about Status and Equality values, remember the iceberg. These values are of essential importance in coaching, but are often unspoken and unconscious.

---

101   Fiona, Personal Communication, Permission granted on November 20, 2015.
102   Geert Hofstede, Gert Jan Hofstede, and Michael Minkov, *Cultures and Organizations: Software of the Mind, Intercultural Cooperation and its Importance for Survival.* 3rd ed. (New York: McGraw Hill, 2010), 61.

 **Status** (organizational arrangements) **Equality** 

I think life is a non-level playing field.	I think life is a fairly level playing field.
My identity comes from my family/birth/social status/role.	My identity comes from what I've made of my life: my achievements.
Learning is best guided by a mentor.	The best learning is self-discovery.
Don't openly challenge your leader; subordinates should follow instructions.	Leaders can, and sometimes should, be challenged; subordinates should take initiative.
It is important to give respect regardless of performance or character.	Respect is determined by accomplishments, successes, and character.
I will sacrifice for higher rank.	I will sacrifice for greater achievement.
I hold and use the authority given to me by my role to care for those that are weaker or subordinate.	I share power with those under me and expect them to take responsibility for themselves.
Men and women are treated differently.	Women and men are equal.

Take a Minute

As you read through this chapter, be intentional about trying to identify your own values and the relative strength of your preference. Take a few minutes right now and do the following quick exercises:

- *Underline or note which phrases in the Cultural Values Chart most appeal to you or match your own beliefs.*
- *Evaluate the strength of your preference for either Status or Equality. Plot a point on the line below that represents where you are on the continuum. Continue to keep this in mind as you read the chapter.*

Status   Equality

Brief Explanation of the Value Set

Confucius: The superior man does what is proper to the station in which he is; he does not desire to go beyond this. In a position of wealth and honor, he does what is proper to a position of wealth and honor. In a poor and low position, he does what is proper to a poor and low position. Situated among barbarous tribes, he does what is proper to a situation among barbarous tribes. In a position of sorrow and difficulty, he does what is proper to a position of sorrow and difficulty. The superior man can find himself in no situation in which he is not himself . . . He does not murmur against Heaven, nor grumble against men. Thus it is that the superior man is quiet and calm, waiting for the appointments of Heaven, while the mean man walks in dangerous paths, looking for lucky occurrences.[103]

U.S. Declaration of Independence: When in the course of human events, it becomes necessary for one people to dissolve the political bands which have connected them with another, and to assume among the powers of the earth, the separate and equal station to which the Laws of Nature and of Nature's God entitle them, a decent respect to the opinions of mankind requires that they should declare the causes which impel them to the separation. We hold these truths to be self-evident, that all men are created equal, that they are endowed by their Creator with certain unalienable Rights, that among these are Life, Liberty and the pursuit of Happiness. That to secure these rights, Governments are instituted among Men, deriving their just powers from the consent of the governed, That whenever any Form of Government becomes destructive of these ends, it is the Right of the People to alter or to abolish it, and to institute new Government. [104]

The values on the Status and Equality continuum can raise our hackles and our passions. It's helpful to remember that wherever we place ourselves on it, Scripture points us to the paradoxical truth that we are both equal in value before God (Galatians 3:28) and called to be content in all circumstances (I Timothy 6:6-8; Philippians 4:11-12). The rank of honor for every Christian in the kingdom of God is that of adopted child and heir. We know too that this rank does not depend on our own achievement of righteousness, but only on the righteous-

---

103   "Confucius," *Wikipedia.com*, last modified December 10, 2016. https://en.wikiquote.org/wiki/Confucius.

104   The United States Declaration of Independence, 1776.

ness of Jesus. As usual, God does a wonderful job in holding together that which we may see as poles apart. As you learn more about this continuum, keep this paradox in mind.

In Equality cultures, respect is given when performance is outstanding and respect is lost when performance is unsatisfactory. Age, experience, leadership role—none of these matter as unequivocally as performance. Brad, the coach who was reminded to deliver value or lose his coaching contract, was describing an Equality culture.

Equality culture persons are motivated towards achievement through self-determination. North Americans in particular have created a culture in which it is common to hear parents tell a child: "You can do anything if you try." While this statement is blatantly untrue, due to children having different abilities, intelligence, and personality, along with a variety of other factors, these parents may sincerely believe it. In fact, many people from Equality cultures hold this belief as almost sacrosanct.

And since status is based on achievement, there *is* significant opportunity in Equality cultures to better one's life. A child from a poor, uneducated family with the requisite intelligence and drive can indeed become a doctor, lawyer, or the president. This in turn will drastically increase their social, educational, and economic status. In consequence, there is strong motivation in Equality cultures to create one's own destiny due to a general belief that this is indeed possible. This increases incentive to achieve, but it also adds to pressures to overcome obstacles that may actually be systemic in nature.

In Equality cultures, differences in status are seen as unfair and therefore to be minimized. For instance, bosses, elderly acquaintances, and pastors are addressed by their first names in many parts of the United States. Protocol tends to be more informal. Leaders often do not want to call attention to the power and influence they have and tend to downplay it. Bosses are expected to be accessible, and leaders at any level may be openly challenged. Leaders delegate power and supervise loosely. Initiative is prized, and subordinates are expected to solve problems on their own. Junior staff may resent being "micromanaged" and may expect to be part of decision-making. An equal sign really does represent an Equality value culture.

Conversely, in Status cultures the motivation is towards harmony or contentment rather than achievement. Maturity is acceptance of your place in life. Status value persons find security in knowing their position and station and peace in not having to strive constantly to achieve. Kevin Sutter, a coach working with a branch of YWAM focused on long term work among unreached people groups, writes:

> Based upon the Karma of your previous life, you have received your current station in life—your Dharma. In order to have good Karma for the next life, you must live according to your station or caste (Dharma). Most [Hindu] people believe they are born into a certain level of status, and little needs to be or should be done to alter this through achievement. This plays out in many ways in daily life.[105]

Within a Status culture, structural and social obstacles stand in the way of dramatically changing one's station in life. Kevin goes on to describe how even in the church, high caste background members tend to rise to leadership more quickly than lower caste believers. Beliefs about fate, maturity, and serenity increase motivation for those from Status cultures to learn to be content in one's circumstances.

In Status cultures, respect is given based on role, age, rank, or birth. Giving respect is also considered a sign of good character. Those who are older are seen as wiser and more respected. Their advice and counsel is of high importance. Many coaches I know who work in Status cultures celebrate gaining gray hairs on their head because this gives them more legitimacy. Leaders are respected due to their role and the responsibility they carry, often regardless of their performance. In many Status cultures, your family's place in society matters. Neighbors and business associates of James, the African coach in India, asked questions about his family, where he lived, and where his children went to school so they could place him in the social hierarchy and know how to relate to him. Fiona was given respect simply because her business card said Director.

Those from Status cultures believe that organizations function best when a hierarchy is established and maintained. As the icon displays, there is not a level playing field: some are higher in status and power than others. Leaders are expected to make decisions from the top down and to maintain or hold onto power. They do not delegate lightly. Leaders may be expected to drive a certain kind of vehicle or live at a certain lifestyle level. Subordinates may express pride that their leader has the nicest home in the neighborhood. Protocols exist as to how to address leaders and elders. Subordinates in hierarchical cultures are expected to submit to and support the leader. They will expect to be supervised closely.

---

105   Kevin Sutter, Personal Communication, Permission granted on July 16, 2015.

Argument and open challenge of leaders is rare. In strong Status cultures, there is often little open political debate. Change is effected by changing leaders in a revolution or military takeover.[106]

 ## "That's Your Decision"

I remember swapping stories with a Status culture friend about how we made the decision to marry our future husbands. At one point in my story, I shared that I had gone home to ask my parents what they thought of Gary and whether they approved of my marrying him. My friend was astonished and upset that my parents' response was simply, "That's your decision, Tina." To her, this demonstrated a shocking absence of proper love and care from my parents. In her culture, an elder or leader has a duty of care, and dependence on their counsel is expected. For me, though I had wished for my parents' verbal approval, I deeply appreciated the confidence they were expressing in my ability to make a good decision independently.

In Status cultures, gender, race, and skin color can also limit social opportunity and power to effect change. James, our African coach, is working in India, where black skin color and African ancestry are seen as low status. Gender and racial stratification is not as accepted or limiting in Equality cultures, and opportunities for women and persons of color are greater. But there is still inequality, particularly in leadership. Because there is not as much understanding or acceptance in Equality cultures of systemic differences in power, those with less power may feel that their lack of achievement is simply due to lack of effort, motivation, or talent. Alison Ludick, a coach from South Africa, notes that those with organizational power in Equality cultures may feel that the lack of achievement by subordinates or those with less organizational clout, is also due to lack of effort, motivation or talent.[107]

One final concept that is crucial for the coach to understand is how learning and growth take place on this continuum. Equality cultures emphasize self-directed discovery, challenge, and open debate of ideas, trial and error, and self-examination. In Status cultures, wisdom is passed down the stairway to the learner through a teacher, elder, mentor, or guru. This elder or mentor is an essential part of the growth process. For Equality culture individuals, growth is a self-discovery

---

106   Geert Hofstede, Gert Jan Hofstede, and Michael Minkov, *Cultures and Organizations: Software of the Mind, Intercultural Cooperation and its Importance for Survival.* 3rd ed. (New York: McGraw Hill, 2010), 83.
107   Alison Ludick, Personal Communication. Permission granted February 20, 2017.

process in which others might play a part, but the essential action takes place with the individual.

Connections and Disconnects with Status/Equality

Cultures that have a high value for Status very often have a high value for Community, and cultures that have a high value for Autonomy, usually have a high value for Equality. You will likely have noticed some overlap between facets of these continuums and how they play out in coaching. These values tend to group together in most cases. However, this is not always true. Costa Rica, for instance, is a high Community value culture that also values Equality. France is a high Status culture that also values Autonomy.

It's important to note that there can be vast regional differences in the Status/Equality continuum. For instance, Slovakia, Russia, Romania, and Serbia are strongly Status, while Latvia, Lithuania, and Estonia rank nearly as high on Equality as the U.S. and Canada. Pakistan and Iran are near the middle of the continuum while most other Arab countries rank markedly on the Status side. France, Belgium, French-speaking Switzerland, and Portugal are on the Status side of the continuum, while German-speaking Switzerland, Denmark, and Austria are in the top five countries for Equality scores.[108]

Take a Minute

- *Based on what you just learned about Status and Equality cultures, how would each culture describe a great leader?*
- *What might you guess would be some issues within cross-cultural teams due to differences on this continuum?*
- *Think about a cross-cultural situation (preferably a coaching situation) that you are currently in where both values are operating. Jot down some factors in the situation that might be related to the values of Status and Equality. As you read through the next chapter, identify new behaviors or strategies that you could deploy to be a more effective coach in the scenario you've identified.*

---

108   Geert Hofstede, Gert Jan Hofstede, and Michael Minkov, *Cultures and Organizations: Software of the Mind, Intercultural Cooperation and its Importance for Survival.* 3rd ed. (New York: McGraw Hill, 2010), 57-59.

Chapter Twelve

Applying Status and Equality Values to Coaching

In the last chapter, we explored how Status and Equality values differ and how they are expressed in behavior, expectations, and beliefs. The Status and Equality orientation can profoundly impact the coaching relationship and conversation and is one of the top two most important continuums for the coach to be aware of. In this chapter, we'll take an in-depth look at the ways those differences shape gaining and keeping coachees, the role of the coach, setting goals, overcoming obstacles, and more.

Beginning the Relationship: How to Gain Clients

The examples at the beginning of the last chapter highlight some issues coaches will face in gaining and keeping clients in Equality and Status cultures. As noted in Fiona's example, the right credentials, title, or role in a Status society will open the door to clients. In James' case, his lack of the "right" family, ethnicity, and color impacted his ability to attract coachees. His addition of a partner who had the needed status was a strategic move.

Within a Status value organization, people who have high status are more respected. These leaders will have "cachet" and be seen as more desirable coaches. Often these are older leaders with more experience. If you are coaching in a Status value culture or organization, emphasize the credentials and professional role you do have and find a "sponsor" who is older or of higher status than you. Understanding what is important in terms of role, rank, or birth is critical as you enter a new Status culture hoping to coach others.

Recognize however, that having Status will not necessarily give you access to client's hearts. Ditmar Pauck, a German seminary director coaching in Brazil states: "You gain 'entry' from status, but you gain real access through genuine interest." He shares this story of a doctoral student approaching him for coaching based on his status in the seminary:

> He sensed someone of higher status was really interested in him. But it was by being accessible and vulnerable in sharing my personal story that trust was gained. The personal aspect of gaining trust and confidence: that's what generated potential for transformation.[109]

On the Equality end of the spectrum, the issues are a bit different. But credentials can also be helpful as a sign of achievement. Patti, an American who works in an Equality culture in Europe, writes:

> In Catalonia [Spain] they don't recognize status very much, because those with traditionally high status and roles are the ones who betrayed them historically (the king, the church, etc.). Now Catalonians have a much higher value for evidence of achievement. I have printed up my certification documents and have them on the wall and talk a lot about how much study I've done, what my training in coaching was. I will put up every certificate I get if it helps gain the client's confidence."[110]

In Equality cultures, testimonials from satisfied clients, a great presentation or website, and evidence of competency is very important. As in Brad's example, Equality value clients are looking for what coaching will help them achieve. If there is no perceived value in the relationship, the coaching will quickly be over. Coaches working with Equality value clients, particularly in the business sector, will need to connect quickly with clients, home in on what the client's priorities are, and focus on early "wins".

Dependence and Independence: The Role of the Coach

Anna, who coaches in China, writes:

> I had been coaching a woman for five sessions, and then she joined a weekend coach training event I did. In the training we talked about the difference between coaching and mentoring, and I did a demo [live demonstration] of that. Afterward, my client said, "I get it now!" For our five sessions, she was still ex-

---

109   Ditmar Pauck, Personal Communication, Permission granted on September 16, 2015.
110   Patti, Personal Communication, Permission granted on June 30, 2015.

periencing me as the teacher and herself as the student. I asked her, "How will this new knowledge change things for you the next time we coach?" The client replied, "I thought I needed to take your advice. Now I realize I can choose." I didn't even remember giving advice ever! But Chinese communication is very indirect, and Chinese are very good at reading underneath what is being said. I do not know if I can fully adjust and not send any nonverbal signals [that would lead my Chinese clients to believe that I am giving them advice]. I think that in future I want to spend the first coaching session doing some training about what the coaching relationship looks like.[111]

One coach working in Southeast Asia noted that as a coach, he was naturally given the status of a teacher and was expected by his clients to transmit knowledge to them. This expectation on his clients' part made it hard for him to implement a coaching process based on self-discovery. In many cultures, formal learning is done through memorization of facts or transmission of wisdom from a teacher or guru.

Western expectations and Equality bias have massive impact on the coaching relationship and process.

Coaching was developed in the West and has a Western value for Equality. The coaching model is based on partnership, a relationship of equals. Most professional coaches were taught in coach training to let the client lead in a process of self-discovery because the answers the client needs are within him/her. Tony Stoltzfus, director of the Leadership MetaFormation Institute, defines coaching as "helping people grow without telling them what to do."[112]

These very Western underlying expectations have massive impact on the coaching relationship and process. At best, they can create misunderstanding and disappointment when our clients do not share this value. Because coaching does have an Equality bias, we'll spend more time in this chapter discussing how to adapt coaching to Status cultures vs. to Equality cultures.

Responding to expectations to be the expert or teacher is challenging for the Equality value coach or for those who have been trained in Western coaching principles. For Asians and others from Status cultures, the perceived value in a coaching relationship is often associated with gaining wisdom and advice from

---

111   Anna, Personal Communication, Permission granted on July 17, 2015.
112   Tony Stoltzfus, "Bringing Coaching to the Church," Coach22.com, http://www.coach22. com/discover-coaching/resources/9-06BringingCoachingtotheChurch.htm

the coach. Some Asian coaches and those with much experience in Status cultures advocate strongly for adapting the coaching framework for Status clients by taking on some of the behaviors of a mentor, such as offering suggestions at times and sharing insights or experience.[113] This may be especially helpful at the beginning of the coaching relationship as the client gets adjusted to the coaching model.

Other coaches are adamant about not giving advice or suggestions. Giving advice may create the continuing expectation that the coach will act as mentor or guru, thereby leading the client to choose a particular option solely because the coach (the "expert") suggested it. Patty, who coaches in China, writes:

> Because Chinese clients will most likely view the coach as an expert with a higher status, be mindful that clients will want to please you and not let you be uncomfortable. They may give answers or choose actions they think you want. Be very cautious about making suggestions or asking leading questions. Although the client may want—and even expect—guidance and suggestions, encourage them to explore and follow their own ideas.[114]

Kevin Beery, a coach who worked in Eastern Europe, notes: "Progress may be slower when the coach is of lower status than the client."[115] When this is the case, it is important to use language, appropriate greetings and titles, and other signs of respect and honor with the client.

There are some differences and principles to keep in mind when you are working with a client from the opposite end of the continuum. Let's take a closer look at both sides of this continuum, and how each affects the coaching relationship.

Equality coaches working with Status clients: Coaches who work in Status societies must deal with clients who expect a hierarchy within the coaching relationship. If this is the case, you must decide intentionally how to respond. Here are some suggestions to facilitate the process.

First, be very clear about the coaching process and philosophy from the first session or even before. Expect that the coaching process, and particularly asking questions to which you are not expecting a pre-determined answer, may initially feel foreign to the client.

---

113   Lina Nangalia and Ajay Nangalia, "The Coach in Asian Society: Impact of Social Hierarchy on the Coaching Relationship," *International Journal of Evidence Based Coaching and Mentoring* 8, no. 1 (February 2010): 61-63.

114   Patty, Personal Communication, Permission granted on July 17, 2015.

115   Kevin Beery, Personal Communication, Permission granted on July 2, 2015.

Alternately, begin with a mentoring relationship before intentionally transitioning to a coaching relationship. This method was used successfully by a Nepali coach who first discipled, then mentored, and then coached the younger leaders he was raising up. When leaders were ready to go beyond him or begin their own ministry, he transitioned them to coaching.

When a client does ask directly for your advice, here is a great technique from Dr. Keith Webb, author and master trainer, who spent many years coaching in Asia:

> When the client asks me what I think, I reply, "I will tell you exactly what I think as soon as we discuss it together." Then I do the normal coaching process with exploring and options. When they have some ideas on the table, I reply, "The very things you mentioned were the things I think are the most important!" (Which is absolutely true—I do think that their ideas are the most important!). I do the same thing with action steps.[116]

It is important to do all you can to help the client find value in the coaching process, especially at the beginning of the relationship. To accomplish this, Dr. Keith Webb gives this suggestion as well:

> At first, [your Status value clients] may be blind to the growth process and won't recognize it. They may get great insights during a coaching session, but still not see the value because you didn't tell them what to do. Point out what they gained from the conversation and call attention to their insights. Then affirm those insights and choices and give extra acknowledgement of their efforts (for instance, saying, "That sounds like a great action step, and I believe it will really move you in the direction you want to go"). For someone who is not yet confident of the value of a non-directive coaching process, you must increase affirmation of their choices.[117]

Sharing stories of your own life experiences and how God has processed you will also be deeply appreciated. But these should always be prefaced with humility (for example, adding a qualifier such as: "This may not be the same for you or in your culture."). Never draw a conclusion or give an adage along with the story. Instead, ask the client to tell you what they see or hear in the story. You may be surprised at what they hear.

---

116   Dr. Keith Webb, Founder of Creative Results Management, Personal Communication, Permission granted on July 6, 2015.
117   Ibid.

Status coaches working with Equality clients: Status value coaches working in Equality culture societies will face challenges of their own. Here are some suggestions for dealing with an Equality client. First, recognize that you do not have the status of an expert with your client. You need to earn respect and honor by providing value to them as soon as possible. Help clients set achievable goals that result in early wins. Help your client to focus on the successes and insights they have gained through coaching. David Ausdahl II, a leadership coach, writes of coaching in Scotland:

> The progress report is a really key time. If an action step has been met, take the time to celebrate progress. It is fruitful as things progress to regularly remind the coachee of that pathway of achievement, the growing number of successes so far. Unmet action steps can easily be perceived as failure, and coaching around why it was unmet is usually very helpful for the coachee.[118]

Finally, stick to the coaching process. Giving advice will subvert the creative self-discovery of your Equality client. In one coaching demonstration done by a Status culture coach trainee with an Equality value "client", a single piece of advice from the coach shut down the client completely. After several moments of dead silence, the client observed that the coach's advice was not applicable to his situation and asked if they could return to brainstorming.

Take a Minute

Based on what you have just learned about Status/Equality, how would you expect a Status client to respond to a coach's request for feedback on the coach's performance and helpfulness? How about an Equality client?

Initiative to Set Goals and Deal with Obstacles

George Bailey, who coaches in North Africa in both business and ministry contexts, shares:

> I've been coaching a young professional from North Africa who has an advanced degree from a top French university. [He] initially appears and sounds

---

118   David Ausdahl II, Leadership Coach, Personal Communication, Permission granted on February 16, 2016.

very capable and mature, capable of making independent personal decisions in his own life for travel and faith. But as I coach him, I'm finding he is actually almost incapable of taking responsibility and initiative for problem-solving on the job and is still very submitted to his family and community in almost every way. This means that he has not been able to take delegated responsibility without his supervisor also providing him with detailed expectations, tasks, and procedures. This has been challenging as well in the coaching relationship.[119]

Taking initiative and personal responsibility is an Equality value and is also a cherished value of most Western-trained coaches. "Leaders take responsibility for their own lives." is a phrase familiar to many coaches. [120] In Equality cultures, things get done when initiative is taken and leaders or subordinates act to achieve goals and conquer obstacles. Subordinates or junior leaders will often follow the adage to "act now and apologize later", meaning that it is better to take initiative and do what you think is best, even if you must apologize to your leader and others afterwards. This may feel like very dishonoring and immature behavior to Status value coaches. However, a Status value coach needs to recognize that a client living and working in an Equality culture or organization would likely be punished or disrespected for not taking initiative.

> *Taking initiative and personal responsibility is an Equality value cherished by most Western-trained coaches.*

Coaching those in societies and organizations where initiative is punished means that extra patience and longer-term commitment will be needed in the coaching relationship. Because some Status clients will have never experienced taking significant personal responsibility to create goals and make decisions, the coaching process may produce anxiety. Trust will need to be built over a period of time. Wendy Beery, an American working in Bulgaria, writes:

> Don't fight against a person's perceived status, but ask questions that encourage clients to see themselves in ways they are comfortable with, but with a little stretching—not a big jump, but a small one.[121]

---

119   George Bailey, Personal Communication, Permission granted on June 30, 2015.
120   Tony Stoltzfus, *Leadership Coaching: The Disciplines, Skills, and Heart of a Coach* (Redding, CA: Coach22, 2005), 75.
121   Wendy Beery, Personal Communication, Permission granted on June 29, 2015.

Celebrating these small steps is key. Likewise, when working with low-status clients, coaches can ask: "What can be accomplished within your power? What are the parameters you need to work within? What within this situation is God prompting you to do or believes you can do?"

Those lower in status on their team or in their family or organization will likely not be able to set a bold goal without the input of their leader, elder, husband, or boss. This may slow down the goal setting, decision, and action step process in similar fashion to Community cultures (for additional explanation, review the section on Goals, Decision and Action Steps in the Autonomy/Community chapter).

Low status clients may also use "backdoor" methods to get things done. Subordinates can work at change in their organization or system by creating something similar to what we referenced as a "wave of influence" in our earlier discussion of Community cultures. Philippe Rosinski in *Coaching across Cultures*, pp. 123-5, calls the process "constructive politics".[122] Constructive politics is gaining the necessary resources, power, and influence through finding common cause and goals with others. Influence can come through developing allies, gaining knowledge, external networking, etc. In Status cultures, who you know in the hierarchy and how you use those connections can be powerful. Constructive politics can be a circuitous way to get things done, but can result in win-win decisions that are stronger due to their being owned by more people.

Equality coaches with low-status clients will need to tamp down their desire to encourage their client that they can "achieve the impossible dream" so that their client can live within unavoidable constraints with equanimity. Turn your achievement orientation to the character development that will occur in your client as they engage God in their circumstances.

By contrast, leaders and others of high status in Status cultures have a great deal of freedom to act and expect to have others follow them—which, by and large, they do![123] As you coach your Status value client, be aware of where they are in the hierarchy of family, tribe, and organization as you consider how to help them frame options and action steps.

Status coaches with Equality clients may need to set aside their desire to see their client become content and accepting of their circumstances to help them attain what the coach may see as unrealistic goals, but the client considers per-

---

122   Philippe Rosinski, *Coaching Across Cultures: New Tools for Leveraging National, Corporate & Professional Differences* (London: Nicholas Brealey Publishing, 2003), 48 and 62.
123   Ibid., 123-125.

fectly achievable. Build a strong relational bridge so that if the client does fail due to external circumstances, you still have relational equity to be able to help them debrief and learn afterwards. One of the strengths you will bring to your Equality client may be a natural bent towards helping them engage God in their circumstances once they are ready.

Motivation

Clients from each side of the continuum are motivated towards different kinds of outcomes and goals. Status clients will likely be more moti-vated by harmony/contentment, while Equality clients will be motivated by achievement. Once goals are established and coaching is in progress, values from the opposite side of the continuum, whether achievement or harmony, can be tapped if the client is losing motivation. For example, a coach may ask the Status client: "How will overcoming this ob-stacle help you achieve your dream?" Or conversely, ask the Equality client, "How do these action steps bring you closer to contentment and maturity?"

When conflicting priorities are in play, questions sur-rounding these deep identity-level needs for achievement and for honor or con-tentment can be deployed.

When conflicting priorities are in play, questions surrounding these deep iden-tity-level needs for achievement (in the best sense of using one's gifts well in service of God's kingdom) and for honor or contentment (again, in the best sense of developing Christ-like personal character and demonstrating respect towards others) can be deployed. For instance, you might ask a Status client: "If being respectful towards others on your team were the most important issue here, what would you do?" Or "How has God designed this circumstance to build your character?" With Equality clients, you might ask: "If the achievement of this goal were the most important priority, what would you need to do?" Of course, when clients are stuck, leveraging these values by asking the opposite value ques-tions can also be helpful.

Motivation for low-status clients may come simply from the attention and care of the coach. Chris Teague, an American who worked in urban Kazakhstan (a Status society), suggests investing time during the exploring phase to listen closely to the client. Not only will this be viewed as very honoring by lower status clients, but it can help uncover hidden desires and new perspectives that will motivate the client to move forward.[124]

---

124 Chris Teague, United World Mission, Personal Communication, Permission granted on August 13, 2015.

Obstacles and Action

"When the head is there, the knee does not wear the hat."—Cote d'Ivoire Proverb

"Just Do it!"— Nike athletic apparel ad campaign; originally targeted at North American audiences, this tag line became one of the top advertising slogans of the 20th century

Obstacles are an issue in every culture. In Equality cultures, obstacles will be dealt with directly, head-on if possible. Equality cultures will tend to believe that external obstacles can be conquered. Status cultures, Eastern cultures in particular, will be more focused on going around the obstacle or making peace with it, leading back to contentment. This is related to the concept of "working around" (see chapter on Autonomy/Community).

Dealing with Coach Discomfort

As an Equality value coach, take a moment to identify how you would feel if:

- Your low-status client with strong leadership gifts continues to be passed over for promotion. You can see and feel her leadership gifts stagnating and her motivation dimming.
- Your Status value client continues to bring up obstacle after obstacle to acting on a goal they have stated is very important to them.
- Your high-status client, living in a quite poverty-stricken nation, talks a lot about the luxury car he needs, his boat, the lovely home his wife maintains, and expects you to address him as "Mr." or "Reverend" during coaching appointments.

As a Status value coach, take a moment to identify how you would feel if:

- Your client, an intern, wants to process with you how to challenge the leader of his organization on some bookkeeping irregularities he's found.
- Your Equality value client is a senior leader twenty years older than you. He wants you to coach him on helping him design a retirement plan in the next six sessions. You realize in session one that he has no retirement savings or safety net and has some big ideas about what he wants to accomplish when retired.
- Your Equality value client, a respected leader in another organization, tells you about his plans to leave the country and close the ministry he

heads. Towards the end of the session, you realize he has made no plans for the younger leaders he has been mentoring and supporting, spiritually and financially.

As we noted when introducing the Equality/Status continuum, value for equality/equal opportunity and value for honor/respect/contentment are deeply held and can trigger intense feelings. Differing values can easily be judged as less biblical, less mature, or simply wrong. Situations our clients are in can produce in us feelings of discouragement, anger, confusion, disbelief, and frustration. When these strong feelings come up, we need to gain perspective. Supervision or peer coaching and engaging God are important mechanisms for us to have in place beforehand. Coaches would also do well to remember the strengths that are present on each side of this continuum.

For more information on evaluation and feedback in the coaching relationship, and how that relates to Status and Equality values, go to <u>www.dancingbetween-cultures.com</u>.

Take a Minute

Application:
- *Go back and review the statements you underlined in the Cultural Values Chart and where you placed yourself on the continuum of Status/Equality. Is there anything you need to change?*
- *What strengths have you discovered on each side of this continuum? What new insights and strategies have you gained that will enable you to be a better coach to your differently valued coachees?*

Chapter Thirteen

Dichotomistic and Holistic Values

Thinking patterns are deep under the surface of the iceberg. How we think about our world, how we learn, how we label our experiences, how we see connections or patterns happen are all impacted by thinking modes. Two of our continuums fall into this category of thinking modes. The first is the Dichotomistic/Holistic continuum. The second is the Conceptual/Practical continuum. Regarding Dichotomistic/Holistic values, the Holistic thinker tends to see things as whole systems while the Dichotomistic thinker sorts things into patterns and categories. On the Conceptual/Practical continuum, Conceptual thinkers begin with theory and concepts while Practical thinkers begin with experience and extrapolate concepts from there.

Each mode has a significant impact on conversational style in the coaching session and, at a deeper level, on learning. Coaches who want to help clients learn deeply and well will pay attention to these differences. For a brief description of Dichotomistic/Holistic and Conceptual/Practical values, see the Cultural Values Chart in the Appendix or the chart below.

 Dichotomistic (thinking patterns)	Holistic 
Most things are right or wrong.	There are a lot of gray areas in life.
I am a linear, logical thinker.	I am a nonlinear, holistic thinker.
I tend to organize information and experiences in my mind and sort them into patterns.	I see things as whole systems and I can talk about many disparate things at once.
I feel confident and secure when roles and categories are well defined.	I feel confident and secure when I have multiple interactions and connections to explore.

 Conceptual (thinking patterns)	Practical 
I start with theory and concept to get to practical application.	I start with experience in order to come up with theories and models.
I value logical reasoning.	I value intuition.
It's important to reason through, discuss, and understand thoroughly before acting.	I'd rather not spend too long on discussion; many things can be learned through action.
I understand facts best when they are placed within a framework of concepts.	I embrace concepts when they are substantiated by data.

The icon for Dichotomistic is a whole separated in half, with one side black and the other, white. Dichotomistic thinkers see things as either/or. The icon for Holistic is an arrow going in a circle, denoting nonlinear processing. The brain icon representing Conceptual value symbolizes beginning with theory and concept; while the Practical value icon is a hand, illustrating starting with practical, hands-on experience.

Take a Minute

Take a few minutes right now and do the following quick reflection exercises to increase self-awareness:

- *Underline or note which phrases in the Cultural Values Chart most appeal to you or match your own beliefs.*
- *Think about the relative strength of your preference for either Dichotomistic or Holistic. Plot a point on the line below that represents where you are on the continuum. Do the same for Conceptual/Practical. Continue to keep this in mind as you read the next chapters.*

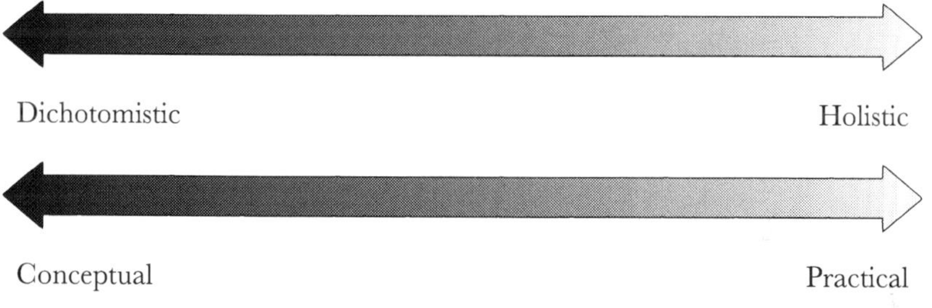

Dichotomistic and Holistic Values

Several years ago, at the end of one of CMI's onsite coach training weeks, I was observing a coaching session between two very bright trainees, both women of South Asian background. This was a full session practice, a kind of "final exam" for their coach training. I took lots of notes so I could give great feedback during debriefing. A wonderful start was made by the Indian coach Shini, who seemed to really be tracking with her "client", Moni. A broad, but workable goal was established, followed by exploration. Then Shini helped Moni develop a few options. It seemed like the session would be over quickly.

But then Shini asked an exploring question, which took the session in a new direction. It was a good question and based on something Moni had said earlier. I just wouldn't have asked it at that moment. I would have "closed the deal" and moved on to decision and action steps. I made a note to talk to Shini about this later. Shini again helped Moni explore another aspect of the complex life issue Moni wanted to be coached on. Again, they got to options, and they were good ones.

"Okay, great stuff!" I thought, "Now we'll finish up!"

But, no! Once again, Shini asked a very good question that probed a totally different area related only tangentially to what they had just discussed. My trainer notes now had a lot of circles, arrows, and exclamation points on them. The fourth time it happened, I was beginning to wonder if this trainee was going to fail the course. Moni seemed to feel well understood, and they were having a very animated and positive conversation. But Shini was clearly not getting the whole "the coach manages the conversation" thing. Plus, it didn't seem she valued getting to decision and action steps at all. What had happened to the coaching funnel, the model of managing the conversations that we had been practicing for the last several days? I started to think through how I was going to debrief this session with them and what kind of feedback I could give to Shini without crushing her spirit.

The clock kept ticking, and with ten minutes left, I witnessed Shini pull off what seemed to me to be a miraculous turn-around. She smoothly and skillfully wove together all the threads from four completely different funnels relating to the same general life challenge that Moni faced. After summarizing Moni's exploration and options from all four, she then asked Moni what she would like to do, seamlessly moving to the decision stage of the conversation. Wow! The lights came on for this trainer. I was now wondering instead how Shini had mastered such beautiful coaching technique, well suited to her coachee, with only four days of (Dichotomistic) coach training.

Our debrief was fun. I asked Moni and Shini to talk about what the coaching session was like for them. Moni's face shone. Despite the painful subject Moni had chosen to discuss that day, she had felt loved, affirmed, and understood by her coach. She had come up with action steps she felt good about in several areas.

When I conveyed how *I* had experienced most of the session, our little room exploded with laughter. Shini and Moni shared how comfortable and "right" the conversation had felt to them. Each of the four issues they discussed, while only broadly related in my mind, were intimately related in theirs. Moni shared that she would not have felt understood without being able to explore these disparate issues, and the time spent on each enhanced the outcome and the action steps she eventually chose. Shini had done a masterful job of taking a Dichotomistic system of categorizing and separating parts of the coaching conversation and adapting it to a Holistic thinking-mode client.[125]

Dichotomistic and Holistic thinkers approach problem-solving in fundamentally different ways. Dichotomistic thinkers do it by breaking things down into component parts, Holistic thinkers by making connections or intersections within the whole. Our icons illustrate this reality: Dichotomistic thinkers create categories illustrated by the black/white of the icon; while Holistic thinkers visualize the whole, symbolized by the arrow going around the entire circle. Rosinski labels this continuum Analytical/Systemic.[126] Dichotomistic thinkers think naturally in terms of categories such as right/wrong, correct/incorrect. Systemic thinkers are more likely to see shades and consider context. A Dichotomistic style can be visualized as linear, or one dimensional, Holistic as more multi-dimensional.

I was curious about how a Holistic coach working with Dichotomistic clients would experience the coaching conversation. I asked my friend Linda, who is from Indonesian and Chinese background and has lived and coached in the States for several years. With a laugh, she responded:

> Oh, it's easy! It's just looking at one thing and following it. One line instead of five. That's easier to follow. But I do feel a bit frustrated because more things will come to my mind that I want to say because I am seeing all the other arrows that can go to that one line, while this person, my client, is not seeing them at all. I will have a lot more conversation in my head than I should. I need to watch the conversation in my head more, hold back more. I could be saying, "How about this? and how about that?" But as a coach I am not supposed to give advice!"[127]

Brief Explanation of the Value Set

Dichotomistic and Holistic thinking modes have to do with how we approach problems or process issues. I'm an American, and I did my coach training in the United States. I naturally and unconsciously create categories as I learn, think,

---

125   Shini and Moni, Personal Communication, Permission granted on July 8, 2015.
126   Philippe Rosinski, *Coaching Across Cultures: New Tools for Leveraging National, Corporate & Professional Differences* (London: Nicholas Brealey Publishing, 2003), 183.
127   Linda, Personal Communication, Permission granted on January 28, 2016.

and process. Something goes here or there. It's correct or incorrect. It belongs with this, or it most definitely doesn't. Separating the coaching conversation into clearly defined categories with a right way to manage the coaching conversation (in my case, using the coaching funnel) and a wrong way, was natural to me.

Shini, Moni, and Linda think differently than I do. When processing or problem solving, they naturally consider a whole with many parts. It's not helpful to Holistic thinkers to say that this detail doesn't belong here. It's part of their whole, so it should be considered on its own merits. For Holistic clients and coaches, considering the whole is a must for great decisions and action steps.

Another way to think about this was described by my friend Linda. If you visualize a city block with houses on four sides of the block, you could just go straight to your neighbor's house on the other side of the block by cutting through the backyards. But you could also go the long way around the block to get there. Both ways will get you to your neighbor's house. Dichotomistic thinkers will naturally see a path through by breaking down the problem: they are looking straight at the neighbor's house. Holistic thinkers will naturally see a path by looking at the whole: they are seeing the block. While cutting through the backyard is efficient, Linda pointed out that if she goes around the block and sees the neighbor's house from many vantage points, she gains context and more information on the way over to visit.[128]

Holistic thinking might be best exemplified by playing chess or maybe multiplayer online role-playing games with many moving parts and scenarios to account for. Dichotomistic thinking might be compared to playing Scrabble or the online game Wordament.

Take a Minute

Application:
- *Based on what you just learned about Dichotomistic and Holistic values, how do you expect that a client would approach a colleague who has violated an ethical boundary?*
- *Applying conceptual knowledge to real life situations is helpful in adult learning. As you read through the remainder of the chapter, recall a time when you were talking or coaching with a group or individual with the opposite preference, either Holistic or Dichotomistic. As you*

---

128   Ibid.

read through the tips and strategies, think intentionally about how these would apply in your situation.

Applying Dichotomistic and Holistic Values to Coaching

Now that we've gained some basic CQ Knowledge, let's deploy our CQ Strategy by applying our new knowledge to the coaching relationship and coaching process. Among the first issues that come to mind is the structure of the coaching appointment itself. In the context of these contrasting values, how does a coach manage information?

One way to think about the difference between these two values in the structure of the coaching session is to consider the difference between an outline and a mind map.

I. Road Trip to Georgia
  A. What to take
       1. sunglasses
       2. snacks
  B. Where to go
       1. historic sites
       2. the beach
  C. What to do
       1. writing time
       2. romance

Coaching originated in the West in Dichotomistic societies. The GROW model (a conversational model that includes establishing a Goal, describing current Reality, developing Options, and determining a Way forward) and the coaching funnel are both ways to structure the coaching session that operate more as outlines. This piece goes here. That one follows. There is a linear progression from one element to another.

Mind maps, on the other hand, are formed around a central idea or goal with every issue or concept connected to the central idea. Each word or image, whether centrally or tangentially related to the central goal, is part of the picture (emphasizing connections); and each image is also separate in and of itself (emphasizing disparate elements).

How does that apply to the structure of the coaching session? Dichotomistic value clients will appreciate the orderly and linear approach that the coaching funnel or another traditional conversational model such as GROW brings. Holistic value clients, however, are much more likely to stretch the boundaries of these models and find them inhibiting. The exploring stage of the funnel will feel the most comfortable to Holistic clients since the exploring phase is traditionally designed to bring all kinds of potentially important information into the conversation. Holistic clients are likely to also want to explore different goals or action steps they could pursue, delve into the details of different options, and thoroughly consider obstacles that could arise and relationships between those obstacles.

For the Dichotomistic coach coaching a Holistic client, here are a few hints:

- Be prepared for exploring to happen at all stages of the coaching conversation. You may feel these are "bunny trails", but they are important for your client.
- Adapt to a series of mini-funnels as your client delves into all the factors they feel are important before settling on action steps.
- Holistic clients may not be ready to make a complex decision in one coaching appointment.

For the Holistic coach coaching a Dichotomistic client:

- Be prepared to explore the issue less thoroughly than you feel is needed.
- Your client will appreciate a structured, linear approach to managing the coaching conversation.
- Recognize that your Dichotomistic client may make a decision that seems simplistic to you or may make a decision that does not seem to take into consideration all the factors that you see influencing the issue.

Length of Coaching Appointment

Generally, my experience has been that Holistic clients are often not ready to decide fifty minutes into the session. One approach is to lengthen the session and continue to explore the topic and the obstacles. The other is, rather than force a decision, to help the client identify action steps that might take them closer to making the decision. For instance, the coach could ask the client: "By when do you want/need to make this decision? What do you still need to do/process before then? What actions do you need to take to get to the point of making the decision?" These action steps could include inner reflection, gaining counsel, prayer, research, or processing with significant others.

In contrast, a Dichotomistic client can generally move through the coaching funnel at a quicker pace.

Gaining and Managing Perspective

An uninvited guest is an angel sent from God—Tajik Proverb

A Holistic coach shared the following story:

> I coached a [Dichotomistic] client whose goal was to increase his coaching business, but he wanted to use Christian materials and resources. This coachee had had secular coach training. His thought was that he would have to develop this material himself. He never said, "I wonder if there is something out there already that links Christian values with coaching?" I kept thinking to myself as the coach: "What about Tony Stoltzfus' material? What about this author? Or that book?" I knew about plenty of resources on Christian coaching, but did not want to lead the conversation. I was patient. I asked: "What other resources are available? What have you done to research this?" But over and over, he kept going back to his first thought: "I am just going to develop this myself." At the end of the session, I shared some of my own experience with Christian coaching materials and how they have benefitted me and asked: "How might that be applicable to you?" He listened, but did not engage with the question or seem interested. Investigating Christian material already out there did not show up in his action steps. After a lot of encouragement to him to see beyond what he was seeing, I recognized I needed to just have patience that the client would get revelation himself.[129]

All of us have had clients like this who do not seem to want to look beyond their own nose. However, Dichotomistic or Holistic orientation can influence our clients' ability to engage with multiple factors and possibilities. Helping the client gain perspective is a coaching deliverable. One of the skills in Chapter 22 is called "Walk around the Castle". This technique is used by the coach to help the client explore different ways of looking at an issue; or, in my friend Linda's example, to help the client walk around the block instead of cutting through the back yard. But in reflecting on the Walk around the Castle process, Linda made this eye-opening statement to me:

---

129   Ibid.

> The Walk around the Castle technique [discussed in Chapter 22] is a paradigm
> shifter for the Westerner, but maybe not to the Easterner. It feels natural to me
> to look from all these vantage points![130]

Holistic coaches working with Dichotomistic clients can leverage the Holistic
end of the continuum by intentionally employing the Walk around the Castle
technique with clients who are not considering the complexity of the issue or
goal before them. Sometimes this works and sometimes not. In the story above,
the coach attempted to use a perspective question, but the client was simply not
interested in engaging.

On the other end of the continuum, for the Holistic client, who will gain perspective and view their goal/issue more naturally from multiple vantage points,
the coach's job is to assist the client in managing all the information on the table.
The coach can use paraphrase and summary to help the client review the data,
options, and consequences they've laid out, paying particular attention to the
relationships between them. While the Dichotomistic coach could get frustrated
and distracted trying to *categorize* the material the coachee is verbalizing, with a
Holistic client it will be more helpful to try to summarize the *connections* between
information shared by the coachee. Summary can help to direct the conversation
toward a decision.[131]

When the Holistic client is stuck and cannot make a decision, taking a different
approach can be helpful. Leveraging Dichotomistic thinking to help organize the
information into categories could catalyze decision-making. Linda shares that
when she herself is considering complex decisions, it can help her get "unstuck"
when her own coach groups options together and helps her to sort and classify
them.[132]

Dealing with Coach Discomfort

Holding intense coaching conversations with someone whose thinking mode
is very different from your own can be disorienting and has a high likelihood
of causing coach discomfort. One great coach I know, an American with an
influential international role in his organization who coaches leaders from many
countries and regions, says that for him coaching those with Holistic thinking is
like "entering into chaos!"[133]

---

130   Ibid.

131   Ibid.

132   Ibid.

133   Kevin Sutter, Personal Communication, Permission granted on July 16, 2015.

For the Dichotomistic coach working with a Holistic client, the cognitive leaps to different subjects, the amount of seemingly unrelated detail that must be delved into, can be very tiring, especially if the coach does not stop working overtime internally to classify, categorize, and outline what the client is saying. This will quickly lead to overload. As a Dichotomistic coach, it is important to recognize you will not understand why so many details or issues are important for your client to discuss before making a decision. As my friend and fellow coach Kevin Sutter says: "I as a coach do not need to make sense of all of it."[134] That's the client's work.

Conversely for Holistic coaches working with Dichotomistic clients, patience and self-discipline are also required. When exploring an issue, Holistic coaches will see more connections than their Dichotomistic clients do. They may chafe at the simplistic decision the client makes without noticing extenuating circumstances. Though perspective questions can help with this, the client may not always see how the Holistic coach's perspective questions are relevant, as in the earlier example of Linda's client. The coaching session may not seem as stimulating or interesting to the Holistic coach when it sticks to a straight line.

One additional note is necessary here. Because Holistic clients tend to see more "gray" and Dichotomistic more "black and white", coaches on opposite ends of this continuum may feel that their client is either "soft on sin" or "too rigid"[135] Holistic clients and coaches will see extenuating circumstances in a variety of situations which may seem much more definitively right or wrong to Dichotomistic clients and coaches.

Take a Minute

- *Reflect: how might your Holistic client be impacted by entering a Dichotomistic team? Your Dichotomistic client when entering a Holistic company?*
- *Based on what you just learned about Dichotomistic and Holistic values, how will you coach/converse differently with your opposite value coachee in the future? Is there a concrete action step you need to take?*

---

134   Ibid.
135   Sherwood G. Lingenfelter and Marvin K. Mayers, *Ministering Cross-Culturally: An Incarnational Model for Personal Relationships*. 2nd ed. (Grand Rapids, MI: Baker Academic, 2007), 64.

Chapter Fourteen

141

Conceptual and Practical Values

In our last chapter, we considered the first of the continuums that focus on thinking modes. In this chapter, we'll move to the second: Conceptual and Practical. Conceptual and Practical thinkers, also termed Deductive and Inductive thinkers, approach problem solving in very different ways. Conceptual, or deductive, thinkers begin with identifying principles and concepts that are important to them. Once a thorough discussion and agreement has been reached, they will then move into action. Deductive thinkers want to understand the question of why before how. Theory comes first, and data is understood in the context of concepts. Many European countries as well as the Arab and Latin American worlds are Conceptual value cultures.

In contrast, Practical thinkers start with experience, case study, and facts, then move from those to the generalization of a concept. Practical application comes first, then conceptual thinking. Theory alone is distrusted.

Brief Explanation of the Value Set

I once coached a wonderful European ministry leader, Stephe, who wanted to develop an action plan about the building they were using for ministry. They were currently leasing it, but hoped to buy. The building's owner would not come down in price, and with an active schedule of conferences and retreats on the calendar, Stephe needed to consider alternative options. Many factors were involved, and after discussing these, he was still unsure about how to move forward. Stephe identified feeling unsettled and vulnerable.

"What are some concrete practical steps you can take to deal with your feelings of unsettledness?" I asked him. But this did not produce any insight or commitment. Then I asked, "What might God be doing?"

This changed the course of the appointment. My client responded, "If I could see this clearly, if I could connect with God and get the meaning and understanding and hear how God is developing me through this . . . that is what I need." The client's action steps then centered on discovering that meaning through planning extended time for worship, prayer, and retreat. By the next appointment, Stephe had already moved into a new facility.[136] The icon representing Conceptual is a depiction of the brain, symbolizing starting with concept and understanding.

In contrast, here's a coaching anecdote that illustrates the opposite side of the continuum. A common goal for cross-cultural workers is self-care. I coached an American missionary, Ruth, who was a fundraising trainer/coach with YWAM,

---

136   Stephe, Personal Communication, Permission granted on July 18, 2015.

on her goal to become healthier. Ruth readily described the reality of her lack of healthy habits. She moved quickly and easily from exploring the current reality into action steps and plans, beginning with making better food choices and going to bed earlier so that her time in the morning with God was not compromised. She did not feel a need to investigate thoroughly concepts of self-care, weight loss, healthy eating, or the spiritual principles behind them as a Conceptual value client might have. As our icon illustrates, Ruth was ready to jump in and gain hands-on practical experience. She expressed high confidence and readiness for change.

The ensuing practical experience Ruth gained over the course of the next few months in what worked and did not work for her was grist for discussion when we met for coaching sessions. She came to realize, for instance, that her normal strategies for eating did not result in success while traveling, so she tried new ways to keep her commitments to healthy food on the road. As Ruth continued to work on self-care, she also realized that more dependency on God was required. She began to incorporate more Bible study, which helped her to remember that she could not be successful in making deep changes in her own strength.[137]

The starting point for decision-making is different for Conceptual vs. Practical thinkers.

The starting point for decision-making is different for Conceptual vs. Practical thinkers. Conceptual value clients start with concept, theory, belief, and meaning. Stephe needed to address the issue of what God was up to, gaining understanding of God's purposes and principles at work in his life. Until then he did not feel comfortable or confident in moving ahead. Conceptual thinkers need plenty of time to explore the big picture of theory and meaning. Once that is nailed down, practical action is a consequence. Stephe acted swiftly once he had thoroughly investigated the conceptual.

Ruth, the Practical thinker, began with action, which helped her learn. As she experienced lack of success in a particular area, the concept of dependence on God in this area became more real and meaningful to her.[138] For such thinkers, the process begins in the "real world" and moves to the conceptual.

Decision-making in cross-cultural teams can easily be impacted by this cultural continuum. American team members, for example, rarely feel the need for ex-

---

137   Ruth, Personal Communication, Permission granted on July 3, 2015.
138   Ibid.

tended discussion of the theory or values behind a decision. They are much more interested in the facts of a proposal or the statistics which explicate the problem and in spending time brainstorming and detailing a course of action. Africans and Asians are likely to have a similar process, starting with sharing stories and details that pertain to the decision at hand. European, Arab, and Latin American team members, by contrast, will want to spend most of the meeting time ensuring agreement and understanding of underlying principles and concepts before action can be discussed. Case studies, stories, or personal experience may seem irrelevant to them when the team could be discussing the theological underpinnings of the proposal, which for the Conceptual learner are much more important.

Connections and Disconnects with Conceptual/Practical

Once again, it's important not to make assumptions about clusters of cultures and values on this continuum. For instance, France is Dichotomistic and Conceptual; the U.S. is Dichotomistic and Practical. The African world tends to be Holistic and Practical, while Mediterranean countries are a mixed bag!

Take a Minute

- *Based on what you just learned about Conceptual and Practical values, how do you expect that a client would approach setting up a new ministry partnership?*
- *As you read through the rest of the chapter, keep in mind a coaching or training situation in which both Conceptual and Practical thinking modes were present and how strategies and tips from this chapter might apply in your situation.*

Applying Conceptual and Practical Values to Coaching

The Conceptual vs. Practical continuum impacts how to go about gaining clients, the length and structure of the coaching appointment, and client decision making. Although not as key a value to understand as Autonomy/Community or Status/Equality, familiarity with this continuum will help coaches and trainers adapt more successfully to the learning style of their clients. This continuum is particularly strategic in constructing successful training environments, especially those that mix thinkers from both values. Multicultural team coaching is also impacted significantly by Conceptual and Practical values.

Gaining Clients

Approaches to helping potential clients see the value of coaching will differ along this continuum. Potential clients from Practical value cultures will respond to personal stories, case studies in which coaching was successful, facts, graphs, and statistics. They may be more likely to appreciate the offer of a free session so they can experience coaching first, then decide if they are interested.

Potential clients from Conceptual (Deductive) cultures will likely be more interested in how coaching utilizes adult learning or leader development theory, as well as the ways in which coaching meshes with biblical theology (understandings of grace, unconditional love, responsibility, etc.). They will want more explanation of the theory and concepts of coaching before trying it.

These patterns will also be apparent in training contexts. Conceptual and Practical trainees will respond to different kinds of introductions to coaching, so the trainer with a mixed group of trainees would do well to utilize both approaches in introducing coaching.

Structure of the Coaching Appointment

One easily identifiable difference between Conceptual and Practical clients is the amount of time during the coaching appointment spent on action-oriented components vs. theoretical. The Conceptual client will spend much more time thoroughly explicating concepts and theory in the Exploring phase, while the Practical client will move much more quickly to action.

In a training context, Practical trainees will be comfortable moving into practice quickly. Conceptual clients will want deeper understanding first and may resist moving into practice sessions until their questions are answered. In general, for Conceptual (Deductive) value training contexts, much more discussion and question/answer time should be planned into the schedule than Practical (Inductive) value trainers may be used to.

Length of Coaching Appointment

My experience has been that Conceptual value cultures tend to expect the coaching conversation to last longer than Practical value cultures. While this is not always true (Asian and Arab cultures may expect a long coaching appointment due to Relationship value), in European nations (which vary in terms of Task/Relationship), the typical coaching conversation is 80 minutes. In the U.S., a Practical value culture, the typical session is 50 minutes.

Decision-Making

Decision-making looks different on this continuum, and that is vital for the coach to understand. For instance, a common goal in coaching is to define or redefine life purpose. There are many curriculums and life purpose materials to choose from, yet they have a common approach and feel. Life Purpose coaching materials, which were developed mostly in the United States, an Inductive/Practical value culture, encourage the coachee to draw on their own life experience as the starting point in defining the destiny, purpose, and trajectory of their future. Clients are encouraged to reflect on what they love to do, what they want more and less of, and how their current role does or doesn't fit. Often there is little theological underpinning, and valid criticism of this has been made in Christian coaching circles.[139]

For the Conceptual client to embrace a life focus process, discussion of theology and principles comes first, with discovery of values coming as a result of thinking through concepts and principles. Practical exercises are helpful much later in the process. In contrast, the Inductive client can discover their values through practical exercises. This marked difference changes the shape of the life focus coaching process.

Dealing with Coach Discomfort

Conceptual coaches may feel that their Practical clients are rushing too quickly to action, particularly in team or partnering situations where a deep level of understanding and shared values is needed for success. They may be particularly uncomfortable with intuitive leaps taken by Practical coachees that do not seem logical or with solutions that seem simplistic. Conversely, Practical coaches may feel that their Conceptual clients are wasting time or procrastinating with long sessions of theorizing without action and that their theories do not make real world, practical sense.

---

139   Tony Stoltzfus, *A Leader's Life Purpose Handbook: Calling and Destiny Discovery Tools for Christian Life Coaching* (Redding, CA: Coach22, 2009), Ch. 2.

Take a Minute

- *Conceptual and Practical thinking modes are deep under the waterline. Now that you have greater understanding of how these values operate, identify a few colleagues, coachees, or organizations you've worked with that display the opposite value from the one that describes you best.*
- *What new strategies have you discovered that you could deploy to be a more effective coach or trainer with your cross-cultural clients, whether they are individuals, teams, or organizations? What is one key insight you've gained in this chapter that will influence your CQ Action?*

Chapter Fifteen

149

Task and Relationship Values

Cultures differ in the varying degree of priority they give to relationships or to tasks. It is imperative that the coach understands this value difference, particularly in the early stages of the coaching relationship when trust and rapport are being established. This continuum may seem to have some resemblance to the Status/Equality continuum, and there are some minor similarities between the two. However, Task/Relationship is most easily confused with Autonomy/Community values, and there is a good deal of overlap between them. Perhaps the best way to understand the difference between Task/Relationship and Autonomy/Community is that the latter deals with where power for change resides and how identity is formed, whereas Task/Relationship is focused on lifestyle priorities and purpose.

For a summary of the Task/Relationship continuum, go to the Appendix, the Cultural Values Chart or see the chart below. For a visual representation of Task/Relationship, look at the icons below. Task is a checkmark: the purpose is to get the work done and checked off. In contrast, the icon for Relationship is a conversation bubble: the purpose is relating with others, talking and living life together.

✓ Task	(purpose)	Relationship 💬
I find satisfaction in attaining goals.		I find satisfaction in interaction.
Task or business first.		Relationship first.
I pursue friends with similar goals.		I pursue friends who value connection.
I will sacrifice for a project/goal.		I will sacrifice for people/interaction.
It's all about what you do or accomplish with what you are given.		It's all about who you are in relation to others.
I make connections with new people quickly but not always deeply.		I make connections with new people slowly, but I go deep.
I value external, measurable rewards.		I value inward and relational rewards.

As you review the Cultural Values Chart, you will see the commonalities with Autonomy/Community. In both continuums, one side tends to have relationships that are looser, while the other has more long-term relationships. It should be noted, however, that in Relationship cultures those relationships do not necessarily tend to be in the kinship or in-group, as do relationships in Community cultures.

Other commonalities tend to be only with Relationship and Community. Their opposites, Task and Autonomy, do not share as many characteristics. However, according to the Cultural Intelligence Center, though some countries share both a preference for Community and for Relationship (which CIC would call "Collectivism" and "Being"), not all do.[140] One clear example is Nordic Europe, which tends strongly towards both Autonomy and Relationship.

Take a Minute

- *Underline or note which phrases in the Cultural Values Chart most appeal to you or match your own beliefs.*
- *Think about the relative strength of your preference for either Task or Relationship. Plot a point on the line below that represents where you are on the Task/Relationship continuum.*

Task   Relationship

Brief Explanation of the Value Set

Wendy Beery, a coach working at a Christian college, shared this story:

> One of our Hispanic students, Claudia, came to me with a request to miss class due to her mother's health issues. Claudia shared that her mother was going to the doctor to talk about the possibility of doing a biopsy. In my mind, this didn't seem like a big issue that would warrant the daughter's presence and her missing another class, especially since this was not the first request for time off due to a health problem of a family member. The last time, her brother had fallen, and the student felt she needed to be home to help around the house. However, Claudia felt strongly that she needed to go to the doctor with her mom. To her this felt like a crisis. To me, this was not a crisis. Our organizational culture would say "Try to get the student to class!" However, I pulled back from my own biases and those of my organization to try to honor her cultural value for

---

140   Cultural Intelligence Center, CQ Report, Self-Assessment Basic Plus, Cultural Intelligence Center LLC, 2008-2013, p. 15.

family relationships. I needed to set this aside and ask myself, "What will help this student decide what will be best for her based on her values?"[141]

Wendy coached the student through the decision. The student chose to miss class and go to the doctor with her mother. Wendy approved the absence and later became an advocate for the student to the administration. As she reflected on her role in this situation, Wendy concluded:

> As our student body becomes more diverse, we'll encounter issues like this more and more. If we are forcing everyone to conform to a certain standard, we'll shut those from other cultures out. When we can be more flexible without damaging our integrity, we need to make allowances for culture.[142]

In the following anecdote, Task/Relationship values overlap with Time/Event values. You may remember Brad from an earlier chapter on Status and Equality. A missions coach formerly in South America, now consulting and coaching pastors in the U.S., Brad shares:

> I regularly have to make significant adjustments to my coaching style here in the U.S. when I switch between coaching those from my own culture and coaching leaders from Latin America. If I am coaching in a culture like Uruguay, which values relationship, I allow more than one hour for a coaching appointment. I need time to ask about their families and make a friendly connection. If I am coaching in a church context in the U.S., I had better stick with a one-hour appointment or less. Recently a client called and asked, 'Why are we meeting for an hour and fifteen minutes?' He was upset because I was using an extra fifteen minutes of his time. This kind of comment would never be made in a Latin American context; no one would ever say that to their coach! This client was going to end the coaching relationship if I wasn't ready to cut off his sessions at the one-hour mark.[143]

Brad was experiencing the impact of moving from a Relationship to a Task environment and from an Event to a Time culture. His North American client's value was for the task at hand, not on a relationship with Brad. If Brad was not helping him with his task, he was not interested in the relationship. And if Brad did not help him quickly and efficiently (value for Time), there would be no more coaching events.

---

141   Wendy Beery, Personal Communication, Permission granted on June 29, 2015.
142   Ibid.
143   Brad Bridges, VP of the Malphurs Group, Personal Communication, Permission granted on October 10, 2015.

The Task/Relationship continuum has to do with our choices about lifestyle priorities and purpose. These two coaching stories highlight some of the differences between those with Task and those with Relationship orientation. Relationship oriented cultures and individuals will tend to focus on and prioritize relationships over tasks (represented by the conversation bubble on the Relationship icon). Task oriented people and cultures will tend to focus on and prioritize duties or assignments over interactions with others (as illustrated by the checkmark on the Task icon). In our coaching stories above, Claudia was much more concerned with supporting her mother than in going to class. Fulfillment for the Relationship client is found in satisfying connections to others. For the Task client, it is found in effectively doing the work at hand.

Connections with others in Task cultures will most commonly center around common mission, calling, and assignment. In Relationship cultures, commitment and connection *lead to* shared tasks. Another difference between Relationship and Task clients is in their boundaries regarding work and friendship. Task coaches tend to have clear boundaries between work and home, colleagues and friends. The Relationship client will have loose boundaries between work and home/recreation/friendships. This creates interesting dynamics in cross-cultural teams.

What kind of visual pictures represent these two values? For Task persons, cultures, and organizations, an arrow that leads directly to accomplishment or a checkmark on a task list conveys the value. Relationships are often sought on the basis of goal attainment. All components of the coaching appointment are directed towards the goal/task to be accomplished.

For Relationship persons/cultures/organizations, a picture of a dialogue box or a set including all the necessary relationships is more on target. Within the set are the people who are important; dialoguing and interacting with them is the priority. Goals that benefit the people in the circle take precedence. Rewards are found in the circle of relationship. Components of the coaching appointment honor the value of the people in the set.

Take a Minute

- *Based on what you just learned about Task and Relationship cultures, how do you expect a client in each to form a team for a new ministry? What are the advantages of each approach?*
- *Based on what you just learned about Task and Relationship cultures, how would you coach each differently if the client was experiencing burnout?*

Applying Task and Relationship Values to Coaching

Let's look now at how Task and Relationship values impact the coaching relationship, coaching conversation, and coaching goals. As we do so, we'll be moving from CQ Knowledge to CQ Strategy and Action.

To help you make this transition and maximize your learning process, think about a specific situation in which you coached someone of the opposite value from yourself, either Task or Relationship, as you read through the chapter. Or keep in mind a current cross-cultural situation in which both values are operating—preferably a coaching situation.

As you read, engage adult learning principles and increase application and retention by beginning to "try on" the strategies in the following sections. Applying what you are learning to real situations and relationships is exercising your CQ Strategy and will be more likely to result in CQ Action.

Beginning the Coaching Relationship

Issues of Task and Relationship come into play from the very beginning of the coaching relationship. Fellow American coach Kevin Sutter, who has worked with YWAM across Asia, shares:

> One of my South Asian friends said this about the importance of relationship: "If you need a bridge strong enough for an elephant, build one strong enough for two elephants." Investing in relationships with people will mean you will eventually get the tasks done."[144]

David Ausdahl II, an American leadership coach working with Scots and Brits, writes:

---

144   Kevin Sutter, Personal Communication, Permission granted on July 16, 2015.

Some parts of Britain and Scotland have distinct conversational protocols—think of it as two or three light bounces, then right to task. You may go through the same routine each time—for example, a greeting, a comment on the weather, a joke, and then straight to business. It can be off-putting or feel shallow for highly Relational coaches but is often the most comfortable way for the coachee to enter into conversation.[145]

Rapport building during the coaching session can feel very different to a coach depending on whether their client is Relationship or Task. Task oriented clients will tend to get straight to business. They want help to accomplish their task/goal, and establishing rapport has a lot to do with whether you as coach demonstrate that you will be helpful to them in their endeavor. Keep in mind that for your Task client the coaching appointment is a straight line to their goal. This has some similarity to relationship-building with Equality clients. When establishing a connection at the beginning of a session with a Task client, you may want to center your own sharing or life storying less around your family and relationships and more about lessons you've learned in leadership or ways you've grown. Task oriented clients will be receptive to hearing about experiences that relate to their goal area.

Pace will also be quicker with Task clients. You will be "let in" more rapidly, and both your entrée into their lives and the tempo of the session will be swifter. Stories, metaphors, and anecdotes must have a point and will not be enjoyed simply for their own sake, especially at the beginning of the coaching relationship. Stick to the subject!

On the flip side, for clients at the extreme end of the Relationship value spectrum, you may need several sessions *simply to build relationship* before a goal is even discussed. In their article, "The Coach in Asian Society," published in the *International Journal of Evidence Based Coaching and Mentoring*, Ajay and Nina Nangalia write:

> While building rapport is important in coaching across the world, in Asia it is necessary to have a deeper emotional connection with the client before "real" coaching can begin. Often it takes as many as three to four meetings, and at times, even as long as three months, before trust is established.[146]

---

145   David Ausdahl II, Leadership Coach, Personal Communication, Permission granted on February 16, 2016.

146   Lina Nangalia and Ajay Nangalia, "The Coach in Asian Society: Impact of Social Hierarchy on the Coaching Relationship," *International Journal of Evidence Based Coaching and Mentoring* 8, no. 1 (February 2010): 61-63.

These authors go on to comment that relationship building *before the coaching relationship starts* can also be important in order to build trust and commitment. With Relationship clients, the pace is slower and the tone of the coaching conversation needs to be warmer and more personal. Stories are swapped, anecdotes shared. Family members and important players in the client's life are asked after. Ditmar Pauck, a seminary president and coach from Germany working in Brazil, writes:

> I try to make smooth natural transitions in the coaching sessions, maintaining a natural conversational tone, not mechanical. I spend time on relationship building and then try to make a smooth transition into the coaching funnel.[147]

Jessica Johnson, an American who coaches college students on life purpose, notes significant differences in regional expectations within the United States on this continuum. She shares:

> In the Midwest, the pace is slower than on the coasts. Students want to chitchat. They want to know who you are. They want to do the social thing first before business/work. They also want to stand and talk for a few minutes as they leave. I try to make the coaching session feel less "businessy" and more personal.[148]

When coaching is being introduced to a new client or group, Task clients and organizations will respond well to a presentation of how coaching will benefit them in goal attainment. Relationship value clients will respond more positively to an understanding of how a coach will walk alongside them, giving support and encouragement and being a trustworthy companion in their growth. Task clients are more likely to appreciate emailed contracts and written documents. Relational clients appreciate face-to-face interaction and explanations of coaching, accompanied by simple upfront documents through which a coach can personally walk the client. Especially when dealing with groups, detailed coaching—or ministry—contracts may be seen as offensive in Relationship as well as in Community cultures. Your interactions with the community, team, or group will be based on relational trust. Learning the balance of what to spell out in the contract and what to leave out takes intentionality.

A related issue is the medium through which coaching is conducted. North Americans and some northern Europeans are perfectly comfortable doing coaching over phone or Skype without video. Relational cultures tend to prefer face-to-face coaching or at minimum Skype with video. Paul Hillhouse, CMI's

---

147   Ditmar Pauck, Personal Communication, Permission granted on September 16, 2015.
148   Jessica Johnson, Personal Communication, Permission granted on July 2, 2015.

director of Professional Coach Training, recommends using video at least for the first few minutes of a long-distance coaching appointment even when the Skype connection is poor in order to establish face-to-face contact.[149]

Goals

Goals for Task culture clients will tend to be centered on "doing"—i.e., attaining a dream or completing a project. Clients are likely to start with performance coaching, then move into transformational goals as they hit internal obstacles to task completion.

Conversely, Relational clients will tend to ask for coaching for more flexible Relationship oriented goals such as team dynamics, mentoring, and relational conflict. Carl, our South African coach working in the Middle East, explains:

> In the Arab culture, they are so focused on the bigger picture regarding relationships that it is almost overwhelming to narrow in and focus on the task. The coach can help the client choose just one relational issue to work on and coach around that. That will help them see progress.[150]

As noted previously, in Relational cultures a client may not proffer their real goal until relational trust is built (similar to Concealment culture goal setting, which we will discuss later). The coach must remain patient until the real, heartfelt issues come to the surface. Relational clients will be more likely to be motivated towards transformational, internal goals once trust is established.

Motivation

A coach working in the Philippines once told me that reaching a goal without deepening the relationship made no sense to his clients. Our South African coach, Carl, also weighs in on motivations within Relational cultures:

> In my host culture, people and relationships are definitely the priority. When
> projects are taken on, they are always for the benefit of people, family especially!
> Very seldom will a person just do things for themselves. When one has a job,

---

149   Paul Hillhouse, Professional Coach Training Director at CMI, Personal Communication, Permission granted on June 29, 2015.
150   Carl, Personal Communication, Permission granted on August 2, 2015.

it will be so that the family can live a better life . . . In my host culture, the task is very important so long as it will be having direct impact on people. A task without benefiting the community or family has little value and will be viewed as selfish.[151]

Sir John Whitmore, founder of Performance Consultants International, in his best-selling title *Coaching for Performance*, states emphatically:

Real performance is going beyond what is expected. It is setting one's own highest standards, invariably standards that surpass what others demand or expect. It is, of course, an expression of one's potential. This comes closer to the second meaning of performance as defined by my dictionary: "a deed, a feat, a public exhibition of skill." By definition, the full expression of one's potential demands taking total responsibility or ownership. If it did not, it would not be one's own potential, it would be partly someone else's. [152]

In these two quotes, we again see what is a very common overlap of Task with Autonomy and Relationship with Community. As we talk about motivation within the Task/Relationship continuum, many of the principles and techniques for Autonomy/Community are applicable. However, there are some distinctives unique to Task/Relationship.

First, relating with the coach is itself often motivating for Relational clients. Ben Story, an English coach who has lived in the Pacific Islands, sums it up well:

The relationship with the coach should be seen as just that—a relationship—not as a project or merely a task to complete. Help your client create a journey with others that just happens to involve doing stuff.[153]

When a Relational client's motivation is flagging, Terry Lee, a life and leadership coach working internationally from Riverside, California, suggests asking questions that help the client weigh the impact on their family/important relationships/team members. One way to do this is by using scaling questions to help gauge motivation. For example, on a scale of 1-10, how important is this to your family/team? What will completing this goal do for you and your family/team? What will be gained or lost?[154]

---

151   Ibid.
152   Sir John Whitmore, *Coaching for Performance: Growing Human Potential and Purpose – The Principles and Practice of Coaching and Leadership*, 4th edition (Boston: Nicholas Brealey Publishing, 2009), 95.
153   Ben Story, Personal Communication, Permission granted on September 10, 2015.
154   Terry Lee, Leadership and Life Purpose Coach for CMI, Personal Communication, Permission granted on July 5, 2015.

Task value clients will generally be motivated by achieving excellent performance, completion, and accomplishment of milestones. Helping clients to envision external rewards can help with flagging motivation. For instance, Task value clients may be motivated towards a year-end bonus by envisioning the latest technology they have been hungering to purchase. Or they might regain energy for outreach by picturing growth in their congregation or ministry. Relationship value clients, in contrast, may be motivated to get the bonus by anticipating the feeling they will have in sharing the check with their elderly mother or their needy cousin. They may regain energy for outreach by envisioning enjoyable relationships with new parishioners.

When Task motivated clients feel they have received a commission from God to accomplish a particular task, they can be single-minded in pursuing it. Helping them get in touch with this by asking them what they have heard from God is simple and effective.

Action Steps and Accountability

My Task oriented client came to her first coaching appointment with her goal written down and a full list of action steps. My first internal response was to feel a bit paralyzed, asking myself, "What does she need me for?" However, as we confirmed the goal and moved into the exploring phase, it became clear where I could provide value to this client in the coaching process. Here is a bit of the exploration that followed:

"Ellen, what's the history behind this building project?"

"Well, we've tried to move forward with this project before. But we've had a lot of different views about it among the team, and it's gotten tied up many times in the past. I feel like God is saying yes right now, and I want to help the team move ahead. We have grant money in hand now, so we need to get a timeline in place and get started."

"How is the team feeling now? How invested are they?"

"Well, most of them know we have to do this. We had a great prayer time about it last week. Frankly, I get pretty frustrated by all the foot dragging that happens in our team meetings."

"What do you suspect the foot dragging is about?"

"Well, part of it was money. But since we got the grant, that can't be the issue anymore, and I still have a couple team members who are just not on board. I think one of them still isn't sure we need the building. Since he is our bookkeeper, he is going to be doing the grant reporting. I'm kind of worried about that. And Sasha, I'm not sure what her issue is."

"What impact will their foot dragging have on the project?"

For Task clients, action steps and accountability are fairly straightforward. Because the client is motivated by the task itself, developing a plan or dream into actionable steps will normally be a welcome process, and accountability for tasks will follow. However, Task clients may need help slowing down their sometimes-mad rush to action. The coach can assist them by helping them stay in the exploring and options phases of the conversation long enough to discover aspects of their dream or goal that they might otherwise miss. Open and perspective questions that help Task clients consider people consequences are also helpful. For more on this, go back and reread the Autonomy/Community chapter.

Helping Ellen slow down to consider team dynamics and their impact on successful implementation of the project resulted in a new phase for Ellen's plan: gaining team ownership. Her original action steps of contacting the architect and working on building permits and supplies were postponed in order to meet personally with Sasha and her bookkeeper to explore their concerns. Ellen needed encouragement and affirmation from her coach that she could still meet her goals.

Conversely for Relational clients, the relationship with the coach and the process of relating during the session may be pleasurable enough that the client will be satisfied even if no action steps have been identified. While this is certainly not the result we are looking for, it is a powerful dynamic. So, slow down and recognize that your Relational clients just enjoy talking to you!

Tasks may move slower in Relational cultures for a variety of reasons. This impacts how coaches help clients frame action steps and how they provide accountability for those steps. However, as Keisa Capers, CMI's head coach, writes: "Task completion is important in the culture I worked in [Ghana]; it's just that people come first!"[155]

On that same note, Lindsey, an American who worked in South America, writes: "When faced with the opportunity to spend time with friends/family or do a task, relationships take precedence. The task can always be done tomorrow or at a later time."[156]

---

155   Keisa Capers, Head Coach for CMI, Personal Communication, Permission granted on June 30, 2015.
156   Lindsey Bridges, Director of Communications at the Malphurs Group, Personal Communication, Permission granted on October 27, 2015."

In addition, clients in a Relational culture will also need to contend with the reality of the need for relational interaction to get anything done. A coach in India once said that nothing happens in that country without relationship; relational maintenance is essential in every area of life and keeps society running smoothly. Therefore, relationship building often precedes or must accompany any task related action steps.[157]

For more on this dynamic as it relates to Status cultures, see "Constructive Politics" in the Status/Equality chapter. Also, see the concept of "working around" in the discussion of Community cultures. Recognize that for your Relationship culture client, completing action steps may be a significant accomplishment.

Keep in mind too that in a Relational culture the relationship with the coach is a larger and more influential factor in the coaching dynamic. When the Relationship client is asked for a progress report on their action steps, there may be a strong desire to maintain harmony with the coach. This in turn may impact how the client reports on their steps. On the other hand, part of the motivation for doing those action steps will also come from relationship with the coach.[158] The coach must be careful to maintain the relationship with regular affirmation and understanding even when action steps are not completed.

Take a Minute

- *Based on what you have just learned about Task and Relationship clients, what expectations do you expect each will have about ending the coaching relationship?*

For more on this topic, review "Ending the Coaching Relationship" in the Autonomy/Community chapter.

Dealing with Coach Discomfort

For those acquainted with personality preferences, such as those found in the Myers Briggs Type Indicator (MBTI), the preferences for Task or Relationship may seem familiar. But when working with clients with whom the coach has significant "cultural distance" on this variable, the difference may feel extreme.

---

157   Anne, Personal Communication, Permission granted on September 17, 2015.
158   Nancy Harper, Youth with a Mission, Personal Communication, Permission granted on December 6, 2016.

Task value coaches may feel that Relationship value clients have few boundaries and lack the ability to get things done—or even to get down to coaching during the session. Relationship value coaches may feel that their Task oriented clients are cold and even selfish and do not consider the needs of others. For more on how MBTI preferences relate to Task and Relationship values, go to www.dancingbetweencultures.com.

It is tempting to judge the Task value culture or client as not being as spiritual as the Relationship value one. While it is true that Task cultures have much to learn about Jesus' value for people, it is also true that Scripture commends both doing good and relating to God and others as important. They are intrinsically connected. Because we relate to God, we are inspired to do good. To do what is right and good, we must continue relating to God, coming to him for direction and refreshment/in-filling. Both Task and Relationship values have a place in the Christian community.

Task value coaches working with Relationship clients may feel quite a bit of tension in the area of boundaries. Wendy Beery writes of coaching in a Relationship culture: "Your personal life is my business, and my business is your personal life!"[159] Keeping a clear internal image about the purpose of the coaching appointment can help. Ditmar Pauck, a German coach working in seminary education and church consulting in Brazil writes:

> For me personally, the challenge is to establish relationship and maintain the coach position without getting into friendship mode. At the beginning of coaching, I make sure I am very clear about the nature of the relationship. Before I start each session, I make an effort to clearly state the purpose of the conversation, trying to avoid for it to change into simply a friendly conversation. Following the structure of the coaching funnel really helps me. Sometimes I even verbalize this to the client, but it's usually just an internal conversation with myself.[160]

As in beginning the relationship, maintenance of the coaching connection in Relationship cultures may entail more informal contacts between or outside of sessions. I have found that in Community and Relationship cultures, clients may prefer to be called "coachees" rather than "clients" as this is more relational. Coachees will be more likely to send you a Facebook friend request and want

---

159   Wendy Beery, Personal Communication, Permission granted on June 29, 2015.
160   Ditmar Pauck, Personal Communication, Permission granted on September 16, 2015.

to know about your family and relational network. When coaching overseas in Community cultures, I always carry photos of my family. I accept friend requests from clients. Task coaches working with Relationship value clients will need to clarify for themselves where their boundaries lie. For more on boundaries, and on coaching Task and Relationship valued clients on burn-out, go to <u>www.dancingbetweencultures.com</u>.

Take a Minute

- *Go back and review the statements you underlined in the Cultural Values Chart and where you placed yourself on the continuum of Task/Relationship. Is there anything you need to change?*
- *What new strategies occurred to you that you could deploy to be a more effective coach with your cross-cultural client? What is one action step you are ready to commit to now because of identifying those new strategies?*

Chapter Sixteen

165

Direct and Indirect Values

Communication is a vital element of effective coaching. Two continuums have significant impact on communication and are therefore of particular interest to the coach. Those values are the Direct/Indirect continuum and the Concealment/Vulnerability continuum. As is often the case, there are areas of overlap with other continuums we've already discussed. For instance, Concealment and Indirect values share some characteristics with Community and Status in terms of how conflict is handled. Concealment also shares some traits with Caution. In the same way, Direct and Equality clients will tend to challenge others more openly.

To distinguish between these continuums, it is helpful to remember that Autonomy/Community values are about identity, power and responsibility; Status/Equality deal with organizational arrangements; and Direct/Indirect and Concealment/Vulnerability relate specifically to how people communicate. Go to the Appendix, the Cultural Values Chart, to see a summary of Direct/Indirect and Vulnerability/Concealment or see the charts below.

Direct (communication)	Indirect
What is said is what is important.	How the message is said is important.
I am frank and straightforward.	I am discreet and diplomatic.
I tend to confront difficult issues directly.	I tend to avoid contention and difficult issues.
I express concerns frankly.	I express concerns tactfully.
There is no need to interpret my non-verbals; I'll say what I mean.	It's important to listen with all your senses for the hidden meanings behind words.

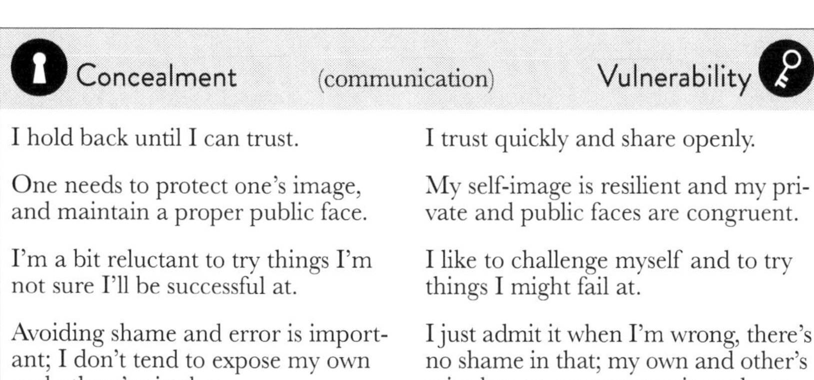

I hold back until I can trust.	I trust quickly and share openly.
One needs to protect one's image, and maintain a proper public face.	My self-image is resilient and my private and public faces are congruent.
I'm a bit reluctant to try things I'm not sure I'll be successful at.	I like to challenge myself and to try things I might fail at.
Avoiding shame and error is important; I don't tend to expose my own and others' mistakes.	I just admit it when I'm wrong, there's no shame in that; my own and other's mistakes are an opportunity to learn.
It's better not to criticize or disagree openly.	Disagreement and constructive criticism are good things for a team.

The icons representing Direct and Indirect are, for Direct, a straight line leading to the goal; and for Indirect, a line circling around the topic towards the goal. The Vulnerability icon is a key, signifying openness, and the Concealment icon is a lock, which represents protection.

We'll spend time on both these continuums so that CQ Knowledge can power our CQ Strategy and Action as we communicate with our cross-cultural coachees. These values originate at a deep "below the waterline" level, but will be more easily identifiable in clients than some of the other continuums.

Take a Minute

- *Underline or note which phrases in the Cultural Values Chart most appeal to you or match your own beliefs.*
- *Plot a point on the line below that represents where you are on the continuum. Do the same with Concealment and Vulnerability.*

Direct   Indirect

Concealment   Vulnerability

Direct and Indirect Values

My friend Onima, a skilled coach and coach trainer, shares about working with two very different coaching clients:

> I coached a Westerner, a German girl, who was always on time for her coaching, always prepared, her action steps already outlined, ready to talk about obstacles . . . I didn't have to beat around the bush. I could be direct and tell things to the face. Was it uncomfortable? Most of the time I liked it. It was easier! But sometimes I felt inside that I needed to be careful because I am Indian and this is part of my culture to be indirect. At another time, I coached a Chinese-American short-term worker. That was so different! This young man and another girl from the center seemed to be spending a lot of time together. We have a rule about this. . . so I made an announcement to everyone: "It is the rule of the center that no boys and girls are to be alone in a room. It is not appropriate for this culture." In our next coaching time, he began to talk about how he . . . had another relationship already at home, that he had made a promise to God, etc. He said this instead of just saying that there is nothing between him and this girl . . . He was even more indirect than an Indian. One day I told him: "You are not an American in the way you communicate!"[161]

Brief Explanation of the Value Set

The Direct/Indirect continuum is a fairly easy one to grasp. Those who communicate directly, as Onima's German client did, will simply say what they mean with words and will generally not flinch too much in talking openly about difficult or contentious issues. They get to the point quickly. Non-verbals are not a big part of their communication, and not much time and effort is spent trying to read nonverbal signals from others. It's a straight line to the topic at hand.

People from Indirect cultures, on the other hand, will be more tactful and diplomatic. It may take some time to "get to the point". Non-verbals such as pauses, silence, leaning backwards, eye contact or lack of eye contact, and gestures may be a crucial part of the interchange between people. What is *not* said can be as illuminating as what *is* said, as demonstrated by the Chinese-American student Onima coached. Sometimes the indirectness is more profound, and a topic may be avoided all together. Conflict and disagreement are dealt with indirectly through story, metaphor, mediators, waiting, or evasion. The visual representation of this in the icon is circling towards the topic or issue, rather than going directly there.

---

161   Onima, Personal Communication, Permission granted on July 7, 2015.

Some researchers and writers refer to this continuum as High Context (indirect communication in which non-verbals are an important part of the context of the message) and Low Context (direct communication in which non-verbals play little part in the message).[162]

Direct/Indirect: The Eyebrow Story

Michelle, a coach from a respected missions organization, shares this story from her time working with West Asians in Germany:

Many times, in our first years in the region, the younger women would say to me "Oh, you are just like a model!" I didn't know what this meant, and did not think to ask; I just took it as a compliment . . . One time, at a social gathering, the young women gathered around me and begged, "Let us 'do' your eyebrows and make you up like a bride!" . . . They took me in a room away from the men, and plucked my eyebrows as well as ALL the hair from my face . . . I was in tears, it was so painful! But all the women gathered around, oohing and ahhing at how beautiful I was. Then they got a bridal gown to dress me in. They did my makeup. I felt like a doll. With fanfare, including song and dance, I was brought out to present to my husband. I heard later, in another context, the reason why I received comments about looking like a model and the motive behind the whole bridal/eyebrow plucking experience. Evidently, in their region, women with bushy eyebrows were unmarried and available! My friends wanted me to look like a married woman . . . If they would have just told me right away to pluck my eyebrows, I would have done it myself the first month we were there![163]

Take a Minute

- *Often coaches ask for feedback from clients halfway through a coaching contract. What would feedback from a Direct client sound like? What about an Indirect client?*
- *As you read the rest of this chapter, actively engage in application by thinking about past situations or current coaching contracts in which the person you were/are relating to has the opposite value from you, either Direct or Indirect. How did that impact your relationship/coaching?*

---

162   Cultural Intelligence Center, CQ Report, Self-Assessment Basic Plus, Cultural Intelligence Center LLC, 2008-2013, 14.
163   Michelle, Personal Communication, Permission granted on March 30, 2016.

Connections and Disconnects with Direct/Indirect

The U.S., Australia, New Zealand, Canada, and the U.K, along with Germanic and Nordic Europe are Direct cultures. Arab, Asian, and African cultures are by and large Indirect. Russia, Eastern Europe, and Latin cultures tend to fall more towards the middle of this spectrum.[164] There can be, however, a good amount of variation within regions.

Generational differences within a culture for Direct/Indirect values can be significant.

An interesting cultural phenomenon is the impact that electronic devices, particularly cell phone texting, are having on the younger generation's communication preferences. Jessica Johnson, who has significant experience coaching in a university setting (with most of her students coming from the West), says of those who have grown up texting and using Facebook to communicate:

> Often, they are not comfortable sitting together in face to face conversation, especially intense conversation. They lack eye contact, and I have to watch for lots of non-verbals. They have not been taught how to have face-to-face direct conversation. This can be frustrating for me; but I remind myself, this is the reality of where they are, so I can stay patient.[165]

In other parts of the world such as South Korea, the younger generation is becoming more Direct while the older generation remains Indirect. Generational differences in these values within a culture can be significant. A very interesting phenomenon is church culture, which even in the West tends to be Indirect. Livermore notes:

> Though U.S. culture is very direct and low context, many ministry organizations are very indirect and high context. Churches in particular tend to assume a high level of understanding based on history with a church culture.[166]

---

164   Cultural Intelligence Center, CQ Report, Self-Assessment Basic Plus, Cultural Intelligence Center LLC, 2008-2013.

165   Jessica Johnson, Personal Communication, Permission granted on July 2, 2015.

166   David A. Livermore, *Cultural Intelligence: Improving your CQ to engage our Multicultural World* (Grand Rapids, MI: Baker, 2009), 136.

Applying Direct and Indirect Values to Coaching

Now that we've increased our CQ Knowledge about this continuum, let's apply what we've learned to the coaching relationship and upgrade our CQ Strategy and Action as well.

Take a Minute

Learning accelerates when application happens. Before reading further, think through the following:

- *Based on what you have just learned about Direct and Indirect values, how might each approach devotional life? Conflict with a team member?*

- *Think of a cross-cultural situation (preferably a coaching situation) you are presently in where both values are operating. Jot down some factors related to these values that might be related to this situation. As you read through the next sections, identify new behaviors or strategies you could deploy to be a more effective coach in the scenario you've identified.*

Beginning the Relationship

Wendy, a coach who has worked in Eastern Europe, says of working with Indirect clients:

> I've learned to sit back and let the relationship lead into coaching. Being uptight about accomplishing something neatly in an hour will make the Indirect client feel controlled and uncomfortable.[167]

Here is another brief anecdote I myself once heard from a trainee:

> Dutch people [well known for their bluntness] feel Americans can't be trusted because they don't say what they mean. They frame things in polite language instead of just coming out with the whole truth!

I chuckle every time I think of that anecdote about the Dutch and how they may sometimes feel about Americans. It reminds me that values occur on a continuum. In many parts of the world, Americans would be seen as unbearably blunt and lacking diplomacy. But not in the Netherlands!

---

167 Wendy Beery, Personal Communication, Permission granted on June 29, 2015.

Beginning a coaching relationship with a Direct value client is straightforward. Direct culture clients will likely let you know verbally what they are looking for in the coaching relationship and what their expectations and questions are. Beginning a coaching relationship with an Indirect client is a longer process. Time must be spent chatting to put the client at ease. The coach must get to know the Indirect client's communication patterns and personal values in order to be able to interpret their nonverbal signals. Here are some suggestions for working with Indirect clients:

- Expect a longer "getting to know you" period before working on goal setting, possibly several sessions.
- Think in terms of a longer coaching contract; instead of 6-8 sessions, think about 12 or more.
- If possible, coach or meet face to face as you begin the relationship; at minimum, use Skype with video.
- Make sure the coaching appointment starts with plenty of "room" for the Indirect client to chat about other topics at the beginning of the session.

Working with Direct Clients will in most cases call for the exact opposite. Here are some pointers to keep in mind when working with Direct Clients:

- Coaching contracts can be shorter term.
- The client will expect you to give them opportunity to say what they want early in the first session.
- You will not need face to face meetings or Skype video in order to read non-verbals.
- Don't hint about availability, scheduling, or other issues in the coaching relationship; be frank and clear.

Goal Setting and Exploring

Direct culture clients are likely to come out with their goal in the first session. Indirect culture clients are likely to circle around their real desire, especially if it is at all contentious in nature, not communicating as quickly what they really want to work on. If the client does eventually choose a challenging or painful issue to coach on, you will have been successful in building a strong relational bridge as a coach.

The exploring phase will also reflect these differences. George Bailey, coaching in North Africa in business and ministry contexts, writes:

Africans will be indirect in sharing feelings. They will be hurt by direct expression of feeling, and they will usually not come to a resolution in conflict. I find that when working with a team, it is important to listen to all the different people involved, really listen without judging. I ask them how they think the others are responding and what they think the other is trying to communicate. Helping them see that there are different ways to communicate and respond through perspective questions is helpful. Second, I leave the responsibility with them to resolve it in their context, their way. Third, I find story is very effective, like stories of team conflict, personal pain, God's redemption, and forgiveness, God giving grace to the humble.[168]

In this anecdote, George Bailey is demonstrating the use of powerful listening, perspective questions, and story or metaphor with Indirect clients in the exploring phase. It is also helpful to use third person and imagine hypothetical scenarios with the Indirect client, thus creating some distance from a challenging issue.

Direct culture clients will also respond well to perspective questions. Queries that help them see the validity of avoidance and "working around" as well as to become aware of the nonverbal high context communication of others are especially helpful. However, Direct culture clients will be much more likely to appreciate probing, challenging, and direct questions. When using story and metaphor, remember that Direct clients will not normally get "hints" and will usually want stories to end with a moral or principle (which of course you would ask for directly from the client, rather than give yourself). Indirect clients do not need to have the moral of the story nailed down.

Dealing with Coach Discomfort

A good friend and colleague of mine, Wolfgang Jani, is a Western European coach credentialed by the Swiss Coaching Association and working in Eastern Europe. He relays this story as one of his biggest failures in cross-cultural coaching:

I was coaching a leader on a major career change, and there was no significant movement forward in the twenty-five sessions over a period of three years. I

---

168   George Bailey, Personal Communication, Permission granted on June 30, 2015.

struggled with having this person pay me when he was not making significant progress from my perspective, and I did not want him to become dependent on me. I decided to summarize the themes of the last year of sessions and bring up the pattern of not making a decision. I was very direct with him in a non-confrontational and noncritical way. I said "It's really important to take steps and move forward OR make a clear decision to not do this. We are meeting but it seems we are just going around in circles, and I am not sure this is good stewardship of your resources. I would like to challenge you that we will not meet again until you have made the decision." Looking back, I wonder if he was not frank about some of the loss of community he was feeling in considering a move into a Western context, and so I underestimated this factor. I could have helped him explore if building a support network would have helped him make a good decision and then transition to a new career, since leaving the security and safety net of that Community value culture can create insecurity and anxiety. I also should have been gentler. I should have done it differently. I did not consider how my being so direct would impact him due to his culture, and so I really put it all on the line. It was a bit too much. I left it in his court on whether to continue in coaching, and he did not get in touch again. It would have been much better to set up a check-in call a few weeks later and see what had developed during that period.[169]

This story demonstrates the interplay of cultural continuums that happens in the real world for us and our clients. It also demonstrates how frustrating and at times agonizing it is for the Direct culture coach to wait for the client, to try to decipher unspoken factors, and to frame things in ways that are culturally acceptable. Coaches may struggle with ethical issues such as my friend Wolfgang did. They may be asking: "Am I serving this client well? Should they still be paying me if they are not making significant progress towards their goal? Are they becoming dependent on me?"

Direct culture coaches without cultural intelligence and cultural experience, as well as relationship with their coachee, will also have difficulty reading the language of non-verbals, which may feel very foreign to them. These coaches can easily be confused and miss key signals. This can lead to misunderstandings in the coaching relationship.

For those from Indirect cultures, it can be difficult to understand why such brashness and frankness are necessary or expedient in the Direct culture client.

---

169   Wolfgang Jani, Personal Communication, Permission granted on July 5, 2015.

Discomfort can at times be high for the Indirect leader or coach working with Direct clients, team members, or subordinates, especially when conflict issues are the topic of the coaching. Indirect culture coaches may struggle with having to put things into words that they would not want to speak aloud. They will also find it emotionally taxing to listen to frank expressions of negative feelings.

Take a Minute

- *Based on what you have learned about Direct and Indirect communication, how do you expect these two values to identify obstacles? When? How do you expect they will each respond differently?*
- *What have you learned about Direct and Indirect values that will apply in your coaching relationships? Is there an action step you need to take as a result?*

Chapter Seventeen

Concealment and Vulnerability Values

Heather Hicks, a coach working in an international relief and development organization, writes:

> There was a situation in Central America with a key leader in one of our rural offices. It was clear to both Westerners and local staff that the leader was unfair, difficult to work with, and harsh. Her behavior verged on being unethical. Over time one Westerner after another used direct communication to respectfully confront the issue with the leader, Marta. Different people also brought the issue to the attention of Marta's leader. In every situation, the weaknesses were denied or "concealed" by Marta, Marta's leader, and all the local staff that worked with Marta . . . This situation still isn't resolved today—perhaps the way we handled it was too direct and confrontational—and it became a barrier for the leaders to take action or resolve the situation. The Vulnerability value of the Western leaders gave them freedom to expose weaknesses for the purpose of dealing with an obvious problem. However, this freedom can also lead to judgmental, self-righteous, and critical attitudes towards others that elevates "us" above "them". That reaction may have felt to the local leaders to be more offensive and disrespectful than the ethical breaches and may have caused them to resist the Westerners and myself, ignoring the issues because the exposure of weakness was so direct, disrespectful and offensive from their perspective.[170]

Wolfgang Jani, a Swiss coach who worked and lived in Bulgaria for over a decade, writes:

> Due to the years of Communist rule and the fear and suspicion developed during those years, many fear to reveal something personal. They have experienced too often that others might use what they shared against them. Trusting others—leaders in particular, but colleagues as well—is difficult. Eastern and Central Europe are changing little by little in this regard. Not every client comes with that understanding or experience. I have found that it takes more time to establish trust and authenticity. As a coach, I need to reaffirm to the client from time to time that these conversations are confidential and that coaching requires openness.[171]

---

170   Heather Hicks, Personal Communication, Permission granted on October 14, 2015.
171   Wolfgang Jani, Personal Communication, Permission granted on July 5, 2015.

Brief Explanation of the Value Set

I am indebted to Sherwood Lingenfelter and Marvin Mayers as explained in their book *Ministering Cross-Culturally* for understanding of the Concealment and Vulnerability value continuum.[172] Other authors and researchers use alternate ways to understand this dynamic. For some, this dynamic is not mentioned or is subsumed under another values set. n-Culture in its *Faith & Culture* curriculum uses the cultural dimension "Expression: Conceal vs. Reveal", which relates most clearly to showing or not showing emotion.[173] Rosinski does a wonderful job of breaking down several communication-related dynamics, including Direct/Indirect, High Context/Low Context, Affective/Neutral, and Formal/Informal. He also adds a continuum related to Territories and Boundaries which he calls Protective/Sharing.[174]

I myself am drawn to the Lingenfelter and Mayers concept of Concealment and Vulnerability because I think it best illustrates this value, which has to do with communication, honor/shame, emotion, and boundaries in a way that is helpful to the coach.[175] One of the most important elements to understand about Vulnerability and Concealment is that in Vulnerability cultures, admitting mistakes and failures, sharing feelings, and putting oneself ahead of or outside of the group is perceived as strength. Trying new things that one might fail at is a sign of maturity. As in the icon of the key, Vulnerability clients "unlock" quickly to reveal emotion, weakness, and failures.

Conversely, in Concealment cultures, exposing one's own or others' vulnerabilities, being shown up by others, or admitting mistakes is seen as weak. Circumstances that are not controllable or outcomes that are unsure are avoided. When Concealment is coupled with Community culture values, Shame, which comes because of failure, can be attached not only to the individual, but to their family, team, or tribe. The natural impulse in Concealment cultures is, as in the icon, to keep things closed up and protected.

Coaching trainees often ask what the difference is between Direct/Indirect and Concealment/Vulnerability. Both have to do with communication, but Concealment/Vulnerability is powered by deep issues such as trust, protection, safety,

---

172   Sherwood G. Lingenfelter and Marvin K. Mayers, *Ministering Cross-Culturally: An Incarnational Model for Personal Relationships.* 2nd ed. (Grand Rapids, MI: Baker Academic, 2007).

173   www.n-culture.com

174   Philippe Rosinski, *Coaching Across Cultures: New Tools for Leveraging National, Corporate & Professional Differences* (London: Nicholas Brealey Publishing, 2003), 55.

175   Sherwood G. Lingenfelter and Marvin K. Mayers, *Ministering Cross-Culturally: An Incarnational Model for Personal Relationships.* 2nd ed. (Grand Rapids, MI: Baker Academic, 2007).

and resilience. As in Wolfgang's example above, Concealment value may provide real protection in cultures where personal safety is a daily issue.

Coaching has a bias toward the Vulnerability value. We want clients to find the coaching relationship a safe place to share what is really in their hearts, their deep-level hopes and dreams, and what they are struggling with. Therefore, much of our discussion in this section will center on how to work with clients from Concealment cultures. However, it is helpful to remember that there are also virtues in Concealment culture. Matthew, who has worked extensively in Asia, writes:

> In Concealment cultures, the community is protected and protects each other from unkind and unwise input from those who cannot know the whole story. There is space for mistakes to be made with less judgment. Learning can happen with less shame and loss of face. Trust can be more solidly built because we don't end up in a "too much information" environment, where others share more than we need to know about themselves—and maybe us![176]

Take a Minute

- *Based on what you have just learned about Concealment and Vulnerability values, how do you expect that a client of each value would approach a car accident or a team failure? Parenting?*
- *Keeping in mind actual situations will help you to apply CQ Knowledge and develop strategies and action that work in your context. Recall a cross-cultural relationship or coaching context in which both these values were operating as you read the rest of this chapter. Consciously apply some of the tips and strategies to that relationship or context.*

Connections and Disconnects with Vulnerability/Concealment

The Concealment value is often powered by an Honor/Shame worldview. n-Culture expresses it in this way:

> The focus of the Honor/Shame paradigm is for a person to be viewed in an honorable way, whether the perception is by society, tribe, family, or political

---

176   Matthew, Personal Communication, Permission granted on July 6, 2015.

group. Being viewed dishonorably also takes on high significance. Third-person communication and sharing information cautiously are common in these societies.[177]

Honor/Shame dynamics are related to Community values. One's dishonor/honor reflect directly on one's "we" group. Cultures in Asia and the Middle East, for instance Arab cultures, are rooted in the Honor/Shame worldview and therefore in Concealment.

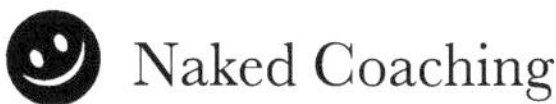 Naked Coaching

My friend Daniel shares this story:

In the Russian culture, at least with the guys I worked with, it takes a very long time to gain the trust necessary for them to be able to share deeply. I would try to model that value and share with them about areas I was involved in or struggling with, but for them it was difficult to get past that cultural block.

Finally, I figured out how I might accomplish this. The one place where these Russian men felt safe and literally "bared all" was in the sauna. You wear nothing but a loin cloth (and not always that) and generally have 2-5 people in there at once. Usually my friends would sit for twenty minutes or longer, then go take a cold shower or dive into a pool of freezing cold water. But I found that at these times, when we were all naked in a hot sauna, my friends would begin opening up. Those were great moments because we could finally talk from the heart, and I was able to coach them through some difficult times.[178]

Applying Concealment and Vulnerability Values to Coaching

Now that we've increased our CQ Knowledge about this value continuum, let's apply what we've learned to the coaching relationship and upgrade our CQ Strategy and Action. Remember, you'll learn more if you immediately apply the concepts to your own situation. As you read, keep in mind a relationship or coaching situation in which this value set is a factor.

---

177   n-Culture.com; or for more on this worldview, see Mischke, Honor and Shame in Cross Cultural Relationships: Understanding five basic cultures scales through the cultural lens of honor and shame-with application to cross-cultural relationships and partnerships, by Werner Mischke, May 2010, Copyright Mission ONE

178   Daniel, Personal Communication, Permission granted February 16, 2016.

Beginning the Relationship

Esther began the first session with her new client by sharing deeply from her own life regarding her difficult childhood, including the abuse she had suffered, how she came to Christ as an adult, and the struggles she experienced in her cross-cultural work. For Esther, these stories expressed how God formed her through adversity and personal weakness, brought glory to God, and invited understanding in this new coach/client relationship. She asked her new client, Jane, to respond with her own stories. Jane seemed withdrawn and did not share much. Jane never scheduled another session.

Coaches are often taught to build relationship with a new client by sharing stories in the first session, with the coach going first. We are encouraged to share vulnerably with our clients in order to model the level of authenticity we want to encourage in the relationship. With Vulnerability clients, it works wonderfully to dive into stories that set a high standard for authentic sharing. For instance, the coach may share how God has formed them as a leader through failure and disappointment.

For Concealment clients, this amount of vulnerability can be overwhelming—too much information! And in many Concealment cultures, sharing such highly personal information about failures and weaknesses would not only be seen as inappropriate, especially in a first meeting, but might be so discrediting in their eyes as to disqualify you as a coach.

How does one work with this dynamic successfully? Building the relationship is key. All the tips for working with Indirect clients will apply here. But here are some tips specifically for working with Concealment value clients:

Be one step ahead: When I have reason to believe my client values Concealment, I exchange a series of shorter stories during the first session. I begin with a less vulnerable story and ask the client to share one in return. Then I share another story. If the client matches my vulnerability, I continue to go a step deeper each time. If the client backs off, I do too. Many coaches who work successfully with Concealment culture clients become adept at sensing what "one step ahead" of the client in vulnerability would look like. These coaches consistently and intentionally hit that note throughout the coaching relationship, inviting their client to go deeper without overwhelming them.[179]

---

179   Celal, Personal Communication, Permission granted on July 6, 2015.

Start the relationship first: Dr. Cory Lemke, who coaches Russian speaking pastors, shares:

> Because of lack of trust, starting with a less formal relationship that allows for more natural sharing about what I would do is helpful. In other words, begin with a relationship that includes give and take so that you can share stories, ideas, and even some advice. I initially felt guilty when I did this because it went against the coaching paradigm, but I have to build trust in order for coaching to eventually work.[180]

Find shared values and experiences: Dr. Lemke goes on further to say:

> My clients hide everything and don't share until I build trust. Doing that on the ground [coaching face-to-face] is easier, but from a distance I do that by finding shared experiences and values. When I share my life story with new clients, I mold it around those. I find theological issues we agree on. I share stories about the ministry I am doing. This helps them see that I am trustworthy.[181]

Prove you care through your actions: Phil Bergey, an executive and organizational coach from the U.S. who works with a variety of clients, offers:

> Building trust may involve acts that prove your care, such as making the extra effort to meet someone thirty minutes away or committing to their cause in a concrete way. One Hispanic client asked me to become a friend of his organization and gave me an opportunity to contribute. Usually I don't do that, but in this case, I didn't think my not doing it would be understood, so I contributed.[182]

Make a case for vulnerability in a nonthreatening way: Tina Southgate, founder of Destiny Coaching Ministries, will often start her work with British groups by highlighting some of the extremes of reserve in British culture. She invites her clients to laugh at themselves, to see the downside of this cultural preference, and then to make a conscious decision to choose greater vulnerability.[183] Another way is to employ scriptural examples such as the apostle Paul, who shared freely about his weaknesses.

Beginning the coach-client relationship with a Vulnerability value client will involve a very different initial approach. Here are some tips on how to begin the relationship with Vulnerability clients:

---

180   Dr. Cory Lemke, Personal Communication, Permission granted on July 3, 2015.
181   Ibid.
182   Phil Bergey, Personal Communication, Permission granted on July 12, 2015.
183   Tina Southgate, Founder of Destiny Coaching Ministries, Personal Communication, Permission granted on February 2, 2016.

Stretch yourself to share freely from your own life: Reveal some of your vulnerabilities and weaknesses. Vulnerability clients will tend to match your level of authenticity if you share first.

Challenge is an expected deliverable: Your Vulnerability client will expect you to challenge him/her. Invite and expect Vulnerability clients to openly share weaknesses as well as goals and respond with challenge when appropriate.

Recognize that Vulnerability clients may make unexpected leaps of authenticity: Clients with this value may simply choose to go deeper and dive in with little warning. For instance, they may suddenly announce that they want to do transformational coaching rather than performance coaching. I have experienced this on many occasions with Vulnerability value clients.

Remember that you may not need to prove your trustworthiness to your Vulnerability client: They will more likely assume the relationship is safe than you might. Only an actual demonstration of a lack of trustworthiness or integrity by the coach may change their mind.

Take a Minute

- *Based on what you just learned about Concealment and Vulnerability values, how do you expect goal setting will be impacted in Concealment cultures? In Vulnerability cultures?*

Exploring and Options

Jessica Johnson, an American life coach who has coached in a university setting for about a decade, shares this story about a Concealment client who was dealing with a difficult issue in her coaching and struggling with "saving face". Jessica writes:

> I have learned to be comfortable with her silences. I let her cry when she needs to. Often, she journals during the session [this is helpful for clients who are not able to process vulnerable things out loud]. She reads through her journal later and then plans what she will share with me next time out of what she wrote. This has really been helpful to her.[184]

---

184   Jessica Johnson, Personal Communication, Permission granted on July 2, 2015.

Exploring will be impacted by the Concealment and Vulnerability continuum. Vulnerability clients will explore freely and report weaknesses easily. Brainstorming with those clients will not be difficult. However, the Concealment coach is likely to be shocked at what the Vulnerability client is willing to try without experience, resources, or backing. Perspective questions that help the Vulnerability client more accurately assess the potential consequences of failure are a gift the Concealment coach can bring to the Vulnerability client.

For Concealment clients, perspective questions can again be very effective, but for different reasons. Dreaming may be seriously curtailed due to fear. Ask questions that help the client find the security of remembering that God has a plan and is active in their circumstances. Valerie Seely, an American CRU staffer specializing in staff care for leadership development and human resources in Eastern Europe and Russia, often asks her clients perspective questions such as: "What if you believe God wants/did . . . ? What is the worst thing that could happen? How does God see you in this circumstance or difficulty?"[185]

Because the presenting issue or goal may not actually be what the client truly desires to work on, the coach needs to be open in the exploring phase to modify an existing goal as trust grows.

In some cultures, humor can be a signal that something deeper is there to explore. Leadership coach David Ausdahl II, who works in Scotland, explains:

> Jokes and banter are an important part of Scottish conversation, which includes "taking the mick" which is like teasing each other. Light doesn't mean it's not deep. What sounds like a passing joke can be an envelope that contains a really significant issue. It serves clients immensely when you bounce it back and explore it a bit.[186]

Accountability, Obstacles, and Assigning/Admitting Fault

James, an African coaching coordinator working for an international sending organization in South Asia and North India, writes:

> I am coaching a team of five, all of them South Asian [from Uttar Pradesh, India]. In the beginning, there was dragging of feet about reporting action points. They did not want to stand out, especially when they did not follow through on doing their part. With time, the workers realized it was for their own good

---

185   Valerie Seely, Personal Communication, Permission granted on July 2, 2015.
186   David Ausdahl II, Leadership Coach, Personal Communication, Permission granted on February 16, 2015.

to admit failure and then scrutinize why it wasn't done so they could unravel it together. At the end of the day, they know these issues and goals they have set are very important to them. One of the things they say is helping them—and it comes through being held accountable—is when they share their weaknesses. This creates the opportunity to untangle external or internal obstacles that keep the team from progress. They leave with greater understanding and analysis of what to do differently. From what they are telling me, they appreciate the coaching for this, for dealing with real time challenges. When they let down their guards, powerful things happen. They are seeing things unlock before them.[187]

Anna, coaching in China, shared this story:

> I talked to my son Paul [a Third Culture Kid, or TCK, who grew up in China] about this value continuum and asked what he thought. He used the example of walking in on a woman in the shower. A polite person in a Vulnerability culture would say, "Excuse me, ma'am." A person from a Concealment value culture would say, "Excuse me, sir." The "little white lie" is an attempt to lessen the exposure and embarrassment of the woman as much as possible by feigning that you didn't even notice her gender.[188]

Acknowledging failure and dealing with obstacles looks very different on this continuum. As you might expect, Vulnerability clients will tend to tackle these head on. While certainly concerned about failures, they will be much more likely to see failure as an opportunity to learn. However, Vulnerability clients are also more likely to become self-righteous when dealing with conflicts or failure in others, to focus on being right rather than loving and protecting others. This dynamic was demonstrated in Heather's example concerning the Central American leader, Marta.

Patty, who coaches in Asia, shares that a Concealment culture coach brings to the table a desire to protect others:

> A person with this value does not want to expose another person, to shame them, to embarrass, or make them feel uncomfortable. The underlying motivation is honor. I think it's a beautiful thing to be willing to overlook another's faults, giving them the benefit of the doubt that they will grow and correct anything that could bring shame to them or their community. A Concealment

---

187   James, Personal Communication, Permission granted on July 21, 2015.
188   Anna, Personal Communication, Permission granted on July 17, 2015.

culture coach will naturally reflect the coaching principle of believing the best in the person and believing God is at work in the person.[189]

This perspective can be of great value to the Vulnerability client. Another pointer for working with Vulnerability clients is using responsibility and ownership questions to help the client see the consequences of assigning fault to others. Perspective questions can also help these clients recognize that positive outcomes can result from using avoidance and accommodation strategies.

Conversely when dealing with Concealment clients, other factors come into play. One useful strategy when applicable is to use the influence inherent in the coach's own status to build buy-in as to authenticity. Dr. Cory Lemke writes:

> I'd rather sacrifice a bit about the Status value, which has biblical basis (honoring leaders and elders for instance). I may share stories that others or my clients might see as advice. I can deal with it (correcting that) later. But initially if I don't deal with the trust issue, I will never be effective in coaching, and that coaching is not just for me. It's for them and for their own ministry.[190]

In this instance, the coach uses the weight of the authority that is given to him naturally in a Status culture to share stories and advice that promote vulnerability. Dr. Lemke makes the point that without the client understanding that the coaching conversation is a trusting and safe place to be vulnerable and real, no significant progress towards change can be made. Cory would prefer to initiate a trust relationship first and later transition to a relationship that is more equal.

In the same vein, Valerie Seely reports that as an older woman she consciously shares struggles she is having in order to reiterate that "a woman much older in life and in the faith is still being and will continue to be sanctified."[191]

With Concealment clients, it is also vital to give permission for failure. George Bailey, working in North Africa, writes:

> It's important to give permission to fail, and often it's best to do this in a group setting to empower teams to overcome fear and shame. Leaders, teams, and coaches can give this permission. If the coach senses the person is afraid of failure, a personal anecdote about a failure can be a bridge. Failure is a huge thing here.[192]

---

189   Patty, Personal Communication, Permission granted on July 17, 2015.
190   Dr. Cory Lemke, Personal Communication, Permission granted on July 3, 2015.
191   Valerie Seely, Personal Communication, Permission granted on July 2, 2015.
192   George Bailey, Personal Communication, Permission granted on June 30, 2015.

A coach can convey permission for vulnerability by carefully modeling an authentic expression of ownership, and by giving strong affirmation and support when the client does acknowledge fault or weakness. Charles Buller, an American who grew up in Africa and coaches pastors in the Democratic Republic of Congo, explains:

> In a Community value society, personal vulnerability is perceived to have implications for one's standing in the community and potentially on the community itself. So sharing authentically about weakness and struggle may inadvertently bring shame or ill-report to the community to which one belongs. From this perspective, it is important to ensure that the relationship is secure and safe enough that sharing on a more vulnerable level will not result in unintended consequences. It is of essential importance to affirm Concealment clients when they admit failure and bring out personal obstacles. Thank them for trusting you. Pray with them and express care. Point them to God who loves them unconditionally.[193]

Making an Apology

When it comes to actually making an apology, Vulnerability coaches in particular should be aware that in many cultures this may include what seems to be inordinately elaborate social and linguistic mores. At times, blame deflecting and even aggressive behavior can follow confrontation. In Croatia, there are three levels of apologizing: 1) "Don't be angry." 2) "That is unfortunate." 3) "I am sorry." In China, a verbal apology can actually escalate a conflict.

Dealing with Coach Discomfort

Carl, coaching Arabs in the Middle East, shares this reflection on coaching in Concealment cultures:

> I coached a Palestinian recently and shared more intentionally with him about struggles and just really opened up my heart. He then began exposing areas where God has given him victory, but he is still unsteady, and it's not 100%. I had worked with this guy previously, but he had never before been that vulnerable. The depth and the victory that came out of it was amazing. God was really shining his light and bringing healing. It's important to share openly, and maybe it will cause/help the other to go there as well, but maybe not. Sometimes you

---

193   Charles Buller, International Staff with AIMM, Personal Communication, Permission granted on July 2, 2015.

> never get down to those levels; the other person doesn't reciprocate and you feel like an idiot! . . . I feel so honored when someone is willing to share deep things with me and they feel it's a safe place . . . When that happens, I want to say, "Thank you for feeling that I could be trusted!"[194]

Heather's story about Marta and Carl feeling like an idiot reveal some of the uncomfortable aspects of working with clients who are different from us on this continuum. Concealment coaches can be shocked at the lack of honor and protection of others from their Vulnerability clients and very uncomfortable with the pace of increasing authenticity in the relationship. Vulnerability coaches can feel hamstrung by the lack of authentic conversation and lose patience, resulting in the coach going too far too fast. Sometimes attempts at inviting vulnerability fail. Sometimes, as in Wolfgang's comments about his client's experiences under Communism, there are good reasons for concealment of disagreement. However, the results of establishing a safe coaching relationship in which the client can share their heart and experience real transformation bring eternal rewards.

Take a Minute

- *What new insights have you had about the strengths of these two values, Vulnerability and Concealment?*
- *What strategies that you have discovered in this chapter might prove fruitful in your own cross-cultural situations and coaching relationships?*

---

194   Carl, Personal Communication, Permission granted on August 2, 2015.

Chapter Eighteen

Time and Event

Ways that different cultures relate to time are of significant interest to the coach. Here too there are two continuums that deal with issues of time: Long Term/Short Term and Time/Event. Differences between Time and Event are immediately identifiable and are close to the waterline of the iceberg. Short and Long Term orientations are further below the surface, but are very helpful for the coach. Time management, a common coaching goal in the West and often a focus for business or management coaching, is highly influenced by this value continuum.

Experts have a wide variety of opinions about these time oriented continuums, how to label them, and how to differentiate between different groups and nations. Livermore puts these continuums together.[195] Rosinski also includes Monochronic and Polychronic, which have to do with single focus or multitasking.[196] The Long Term and Short Term values orientations as described originally by Hofstede are considerably more complex than reflected in this chapter.[197] I have attempted to share only what will be practical for coaching.

Turn to the Cultural Values Chart in the Appendix for a summary of the following two continuums: Long Term/Short Term and Time/Event or look at the charts, below. The icons representing Time and Event are a clock, denoting efficiency and punctuality; and a birthday cake for Event, signifying an experience with shared participation. The Long Term icon is a set of binoculars to see far away; and for Short Term, a magnifying glass to see things that are close.

🕐 Time	(time)	Event 🎂
Time is scarce and needs to be saved.	Time is plentiful and should be enjoyed and spent.	
I value efficiency.	I value participation and completion.	
Punctuality is important.	Flexibility is important.	
I feel busy most of the time.	I have a relaxed pace of life.	

---

195 David A. Livermore, *Cultural Intelligence: Improving Your CQ to Engage Our Multicultural World* (Grand Rapids, MI: Baker, 2009), 132-135.

196 Philippe Rosinski, *Coaching Across Cultures: New Tools for Leveraging National, Corporate & Professional Differences* (London: Nicholas Brealey Publishing, 2003), 92-104.

197 Geert Hofstede, Gert Jan Hofstede, and Michael Minkov, *Cultures and Organizations: Software of the Mind, Intercultural Cooperation and its Importance for Survival.* 3rd ed. (New York: McGraw Hill, 2010), 235-276.

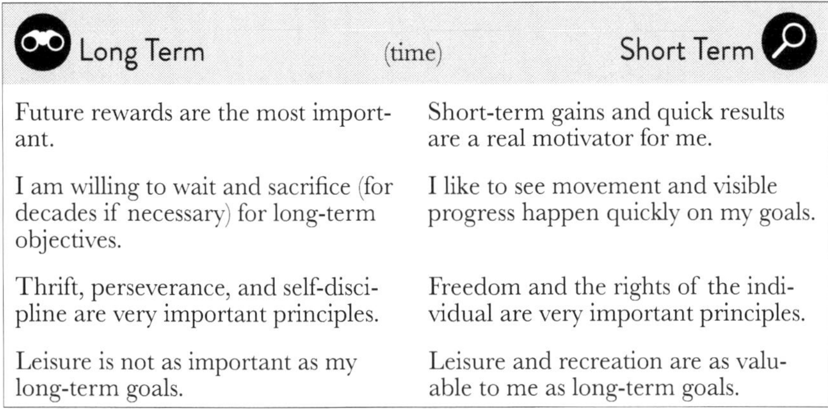

Long Term	Short Term
Future rewards are the most important.	Short-term gains and quick results are a real motivator for me.
I am willing to wait and sacrifice (for decades if necessary) for long-term objectives.	I like to see movement and visible progress happen quickly on my goals.
Thrift, perseverance, and self-discipline are very important principles.	Freedom and the rights of the individual are very important principles.
Leisure is not as important as my long-term goals.	Leisure and recreation are as valuable to me as long-term goals.

Note that groups which are Time oriented may be either Long Term or Short Term, and cultures that are Event can be either Long or Short Term oriented. For information on understanding and coaching clients with Monochronic and Polychronic values, visit www.dancingbetweencultures.com.

Take a Minute

As you read through these chapters, be intentional about trying to identify your own values and the relative strength of your preference. Take a few minutes right now and do the following quick exercises:

- *Underline or note which phrases in the Cultural Values Chart most appeal to you or match your own beliefs.*
- *Think about the relative strength of your preference for either Time or Event, Short Term or Long Term. Plot a point on the line below that represents where you are on both continuums. Continue to keep this in mind as you read the chapter.*

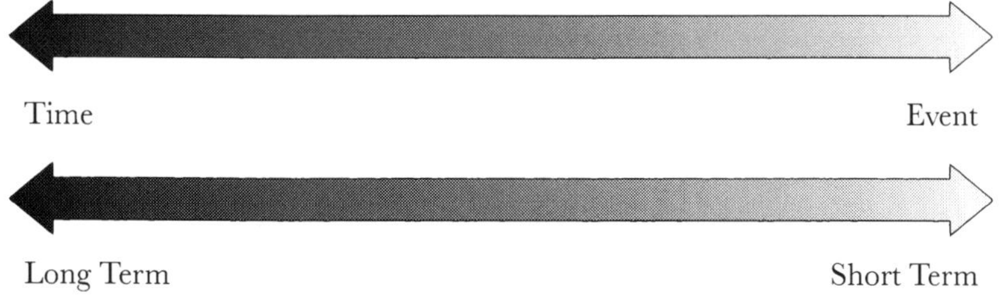

Time and Event Values

What's it like to be invited to a friend's house for dinner? Depending on whether a culture is Time or Event, this can be a very different experience. My husband Gary and I live, for example, in a Time culture. We invited our friends Pat and Kevin to join us one evening for some Thai food. Both Gary and I had to work the day before, so I went to the market over the weekend and purchased the food then.

The night before our dinner, we cooked from 6-8 p.m., since time was short and we had some other things on the agenda after 8pm. The following day, I left my home office over lunchtime to set up the table and tidy the kitchen. Gary came home early to meet with a contractor at 4:30 p.m. to deal with some drywall problems in our house. I finished up work at 5 p.m. so we'd have a half hour together to heat up the food and make a dessert for our guests. Kevin and Pat arrived right on time at 5:30 p.m. and were gone by 7:15 p.m.

Contrast that evening with a recent visit with Event culture friends who had moved to the United States from India. They encouraged Gary and I to stay for the weekend and invited another couple we both knew to join us for Sunday. We were all looking forward to a rare time together as couples. When Sunday morning came, we sat around the breakfast table with our hosts, Loren and Patricia, enjoying a leisurely breakfast with pancakes and coffee.

Though Loren was one of the pastors at the church we'd be attending that morning, neither Patricia or Loren seemed concerned about the advancing hour. Patricia called upstairs several times to wake their teenage son. The young man finally wandered downstairs, looking sleepy and rumpled. While breakfast was on, Patricia started some pots on the stove for our planned lunch of rice and curry. The other couple, Jeff and Jill, eventually arrived. We all greeted each other warmly before walking over to the church.

After the service, we returned to Patricia and Loren's home, where all of us gathered in the kitchen, since Patricia was still cooking. She had planned to make a seafood curry, but had only one bag of shrimp, so she added another curry as well to fill out the meal. While Patricia cooked, the rest of us stood around the stove, just happy to be together.

Then Loren decided it would be great to have some apple pie with our meal, so he spontaneously began cutting up apples. Jill and I helped. We set the table together. When lunch was finally ready, we all trooped into the dining room and enjoyed the curries and rice pilaf. We sat there talking for hours, finally sharing some warm apple pie, which turned out great despite Loren not consulting a recipe. Late in the afternoon, we reluctantly rose from the table and said goodbye to our friends.

Differences between Time and Event preference are some of the most obvious when interacting with those from other cultures. For those living in Time preference cultures, schedules are an integral part of life. Days are separated into hours in our Day-Timers and online calendars. Events are expected to begin on time and end on time. We believe that "time is money". We work hard to "save time". When a deadline is looming, we cut short discussion and get things moving. The icon for Time is a clock because of the focus on hours, days, and time in general. Conversely in Event cultures, the activity starts when the people arrive. The icon for Event is a birthday cake: signifying that the focus is on the event of the birthday and enjoyment of that occasion with others. Jon Taylor, an American pastor and coach who travels frequently, writes of his experience in Nepal:

> Church "starts" at 10 a.m., but people will continue to arrive until 11:30 or later. It is of no concern if church runs until 1:30 or 2 p.m. Even after the service, people will continue to socialize long after the "end" of the service time. The event is the important thing.[198]

Starting and ending times are flexible in Event cultures. Days are defined in terms of the events/activities within them, not in terms of scheduled hours. Completion of the activity with all participating is important. Flexibility is valued. Discussion of a decision or possible action will take as long as it takes. There is time for every purpose under heaven.

In an Event culture, the pace of life is often a bit slower as well. Event oriented cultures see time as something to be spent, enjoyed, and savored. There is a sense that there is plenty of time for everything and there is no need to hurry. Time with friends and family is not constrained by a tight schedule, but intended to be relished. Participation and flexibility are priorities. In contrast, in a Time value culture, people are often busy, and the pace can be frantic as people shoehorn in as many activities as possible into a short amount of time.

---

198   Jon Taylor, Personal Communication, Permission granted on July 2, 2015.

Applying Time and Event Values to Coaching

Let's look now at how Time and Event values impact the coaching relationship, coaching funnel, and coaching goals, which will in turn increase our CQ Strategy and Behavior.

Take a Minute

- *Think of a situation when you coached (or related to) someone of the opposite value than yourself, either Time or Event. Think back to the dynamics of that relationship. Is there anything you would interpret differently now based on your new CQ Knowledge? Keep this situation in mind as you read through some CQ Strategies and Action and think about how they would apply.*

Scheduling and Punctuality

Tina Southgate, a British coach and founder of Destiny Coaching Ministries, shared:

> I was coaching a guy who was a TCK [Third Culture Kid]. His home, or passport, culture was Time, but his host culture where he grew up was Event. He didn't turn up on time, didn't confirm appointments. It was very, very, frustrating. I ended up letting my client know that I couldn't continue to coach him because my schedule dictated the need for prompt confirmation of appointments and punctuality. In a sense, you could say I failed him. I got fed up with his always being late. I didn't want to adapt. He asked if he could continue with me, and I emailed him with my conditions. He didn't respond and went with a different coach.[199]

 ## Scheduling Panic

I once had a coaching client who had lived most of his childhood and adult life in India. He asked me: "Instead of scheduling a date and time for our next session, can we just meet on Skype whenever we are both on?" For him, this was

---

199 Tina Southgate, Founder of Destiny Coaching Ministries, Personal Communication, Permission granted on February 2, 2015.

the most natural way to relate that he could think of. Why couldn't we simply connect when the right moment for both of us came?

I cannot begin to describe my internal response to this request. Since I am a Time oriented person, both in terms of culture and temperament, this idea created immediately elevated levels of stress and even panic in me. With adrenaline flowing through my body, I took some deep breaths, paused, and responded that I did not believe this method of scheduling would work for me.

Punctuality is a particular sore point between coaches and clients who come from differing Time/Event cultures. Because Time value persons believe that "time is money", we become upset when others are late. We feel we dishonor others when we ourselves are late to an appointment, because this may communicate that we feel our time is more important than theirs. In Time cultures, there are often unspoken cultural norms about how late is acceptable in what situations. Generally, if you are five minutes late, it's okay. Ten minutes requires a really good excuse, while fifteen minutes is downright offensive.

In Event cultures, being late for more than fifteen minutes may hardly be considered "late" at all. In some South Pacific cultures, tension is not experienced until participants are *three hours* late.[200] On the contrary, pushing to finish something by an arbitrary time when the event, issue, or decision is not complete will be seen as quite rude.

Similarly, scheduling, confirming, or cancelling appointments will be impacted by these differences. For Time culture coaches and clients, who tend to be busy, it's efficient to plan. For Event culture coaches and clients, flexibility which honors the event is savored. The tensions that may arise in the coaching relationship over this value will appear immediately, usually in the first appointment. Time coaches who are coaching Event clients will need to make immediate adaptation in their schedules, based on what their Event culture client deems as "late". Event culture coaches will need to make it a high priority to start the coaching appointment "on time" and end it promptly.

For coaches who coach both Time and Event clients, there are further implications. Brad Bridges from the Malphurs Group shares:

Some clients say they want a 30-45-minute session. But there are others who say they want an hour, which translates in real time to 1.5 hours or longer. This is

---

200   Sherwood G. Lingenfelter and Marvin K. Mayers, *Ministering Cross-Culturally: An Incarnational Model for Personal Relationships*. 2nd ed. (Grand Rapids, MI: Baker Academic, 2007), 12.

hard! Then coaching colleagues often ask, "Why are you giving this client more time and not that one?" It's because the clients are different. Time is money to one, but time is relationship and event to another. For those clients, without the relationship there is not going to be money, especially Event-centered clients. But each hour of my time equals "x" amount of money here in the U.S.[201]

Here are a few tips for Time oriented coaches coaching Event clients. First, explain to your Event client from the outset why you need to observe discipline about starting and ending times. This can be done by leveraging another of your client's values—for instance, value for Relationship. You might say: "I have another client who really needs to meet with me today, and what works for him is to meet at 2 p.m. I value both of you and want to serve both of you well, so I have reserved ninety minutes for you, and ninety minutes for him, starting at 2 p.m."

You should also find out what is considered "late" in your client's culture. Expand your allotted time for each appointment to ninety minutes or two hours instead of one hour to adjust for "late" clients. To avoid frustration, keep work on your desk to do while you are waiting on your client.

Also, explain to Event clients why it is important to meet regularly. Tina Southgate shares:

> What I'd do differently next time [regarding her TCK client] would be to be more straightforward. I would say clearly, "The coaching you will do with me is going to change your life. It's going to be hard work! Are you ready for that? Is this right for you now? What will you need to give up or say no to in order to do coaching?"[202]

Conversely, for Event coaches with Time clients, here are some additional tips. First, it is just as important to find out what is considered "late" to your new client. Work hard at being "on time", especially for the first few appointments while relationship is built. Linda, an Indonesian coach working in the U.S., shares:

> Remember that being "on time" is a primary way to honor relationship in Time cultures. The coach's tardiness may be experienced as dishonoring and rude, even if the coach had unexpected guests or other events happen right before the client's appointment.[203]

---

201 Brad Bridges, VP of the Malphurs Group, Personal Communication, Permission granted on October 10, 2015.

202 Tina Southgate, Founder of Destiny Coaching Ministries, Personal Communication, Permission granted on February 2, 2015.

203 Linda, Personal Communication, Permission granted on January 28, 2016.

Recognize that your clients will likely perceive themselves to be very busy, so they will feel the need to schedule appointments in advance and stick to those schedules. Try not to cancel appointments with them if possible. On a positive note, Time clients will very much appreciate your flexibility in being able to flow with *their* sudden cancellations and rescheduling because they will not expect it.

Take a Minute

- *What do you expect will be the differences in pace within the coaching appointment for Time and Event clients?*

Making Decisions

Most of the impact from the Time/Event continuum will be felt in punctuality, scheduling, and pace. But there will be some impact on decision-making as well. For Event value clients, this will parallel Non-Crisis decision-making. Event clients will feel less pressure to make decisions on a time schedule or push towards a decision and will be more concerned with involving whoever needs to be involved. When coaching Event clients, recognize that the decision-making "event" might occur outside the coaching appointment or may not seem as urgent to your client as it does to you. Don't push. Your client will take as long as he or she needs to slow down and listen to themselves and to God. This is a strength. When there are inevitable time schedules to contend with, help your client to make an intentional decision about how to respond while respecting their value for completion and participation.

Time clients will feel more pressure with deadlines, so may hurry into a decision that they will need to debrief from and revise later. Allow your client to set the pace. Position yourself well so that when they are ready to debrief, you have built plenty of relational capital and can be of most use to your client.

For this continuum, using the Walk around the Castle technique as well as leveraging Time and Event values for your clients can be very helpful. For some examples, see the Walk around the Castle section in chapter 22.

Time Management and Boundaries

It is worth noting that nearly all traditional "time management" techniques originate from Time cultures. Datebooks, Day-Timers, online calendars, etc. all have a Time value bias. The underlying message is that time is scarce and must be managed. When working with Event clients, be aware that you may be able to leverage the Time value to help them when they *are* under pressure. Otherwise, traditional time management techniques will not connect with them.

Those who believe that time is scarce and must be saved or used efficiently are more likely to be drawn to the concept of having tight boundaries and being able to say "no!" Those who see time as a resource to be spent and enjoyed might be more drawn to say "yes!"

Dealing with Coach Discomfort

Most of the discomfort coaches will feel on this continuum will be near or above the waterline. In other words, fairly immediately obvious! However, it can still be highly frustrating for the coach and potentially fatal for the coach/client relationship if not identified quickly as a cultural value vs. simple rudeness or lack of caring.

Take a Minute

- *Review: What new strategies have you learned while reading this chapter that you could have deployed in your cross-cultural coaching relationship to be a more effective coach? What if any strategies do you want to commit to in the future?*

Chapter Nineteen

Long Term and Short Term Values

My brother Tony Stoltzfus is a rare Long Term value American. He has always set long-term goals, and he works towards them patiently and persistently. I remember one visit with him when he was unemployed, unpublished, and struggling with some deep hurts in work relationships. He told me that day that he felt God was directing him to set a goal of being able to generate enough income from residuals and book sales to live on his writing within five years. Because my brother is a man of faith whom I deeply respect, I settled back to watch and learn. Tony buckled down and began writing copiously and steadily. He self-published his books and watched them rise on the Amazon charts.

As to their finances, he and his wife Kathy practiced such devoted discipline that I flinched at times at their economy. They drove a vehicle for years that was given to them for free. It had no reverse gear, so they carefully parked and maneuvered it daily to get it out of their driveway. They both worked at home to save on office costs. When they began an online bookstore, they stockpiled books in their garage and hallway rather than renting a storefront or storage facility. Within five years, Tony had met his goal. Tony had his binoculars on and was taking the long view. He is a great example of a persistent, future focused, self-disciplined man with a Long Term value orientation.

Most Americans, by contrast, do not set goals further out than one year. Ned was an American entrepreneur who had a strong value for short-term gains. He and his coach worked on a series of goals that produced quick wins: a book proposal, gaining a major new business contract within a month, revamping his website, beginning a blog as a marketing tool. Each goal was completed within four to six weeks, and each brought a significant reward, usually financial. Ned did not see the need to do long-term planning for his and his family's future, and his coach's questions about retirement planning and maintenance of old contracts went unanswered. Ned was concentrating on the magnifying glass: focusing on what was in front of him.

Brief Explanation of the Value Set

Long Term value cultures, individuals, and organizations are willing to sacrifice in the present for rewards that may be decades in the future. These cultures excel at thrift and perseverance. Tony was less interested in spending resources on short-term gains such as leisure activities or current needs such as a van with a reverse gear. He was focused on the future. Often Long Term cultures, especially those typified by Confucian philosophy, will value lifelong relationships and loyalty. Long Term cultures and clients tend to value virtue which is built over time vs. knowledge or truth, which can be gained more quickly.

Short Term cultures, in comparison, will focus on quick results. Freedom, the rights of the individual, and finding truth are important values.[204] Short Term value organizations and clients find living life in the present to be just as valuable as life in the future, so they are more likely to invest in leisure and recreation or to put resources of time, energy, and money towards present desires and needs.

Connections and Disconnects with Long Term/Short Term

There are several interesting intersections of this continuum with others. Autonomy and Short Term share preference for freedom and individuality. Crisis/Non-Crisis does relate to time orientation in the sense that Crisis clients tend to plan for the future and Non-Crisis clients tend to live in the present. However, they are distinctly different value sets. Remember that Short Term/Long Term is focused on when gratification and results can/should be expected. This impacts concepts like self-discipline vs. freedom and work vs. leisure. Societies that have very high value for Long Term time orientation in the Eastern world, such as China, Japan, and Korea, also tend to have more value for Status and Community.[205]

Many African and Latin countries are strongly Short Term, while the U.S. is moderately so. East Asia and Eastern Europe are strongly Long Term, as are some European countries such as Germany, Switzerland, and Belgium. Britain, Southeast Asia, and many other countries fall towards the middle.[206]

Applying Long Term and Short Term Values to Coaching

Long Term and Short Term are usually buried further under the waterline of the cultural iceberg than are other values relating to time. Here are a few reflection questions to help you become aware of this value as you read on.

---

204   Geert Hofstede, Gert Jan Hofstede, and Michael Minkov, *Cultures and Organizations: Software of the Mind, Intercultural Cooperation and its Importance for Survival.* 3rd ed. (New York: McGraw Hill, 2010).
205   Ibid., 254.
206   Ibid., 255-258.

Take a Minute

- *Stretch yourself to identify a team, organization, or individual that you've coached or worked with who operates out of the opposite value. What stress or tension did you feel in the relationship that could have stemmed from this difference in value orientation?*
- *Be aware of the dynamics of that situation as you read through the chapter, "trying on" some of the tips or strategies to see what would have created more understanding or a better outcome.*

Introducing Coaching and Gaining Clients

Introducing coaching is often a matter of finding out what goals the client wants to work on and helping them understand how coaching can assist them. When working with Long Term vs. Short Term clients, this understanding simply needs to be tweaked and the right questions asked.

Beginning with a general question can help gain clues as to whether your potential client, team, or organization reflects Short Term or Long Term values. Listen carefully to the kind of language they use when responding to such questions as what they would like to gain from coaching or what goals they would like to accomplish.

Long Term clients will talk about accomplishments that could be decades in the future, while Short Termers want gains in the next quarter or within three months. Coaching contracts must reflect that reality. Short Term value organizations, teams, and individuals will likely not sign up when offered longer term coaching contracts, especially right away. Conversely, Long Term clients may not be interested in a coaching relationship that is framed as lasting only three months.

> *Listening carefully to the language your client uses and the time frames that seem natural to them will give clues as to their Long or Short Term value orientation.*

When you pitch your coaching services, be aware of the scope of the goals the client may want to tackle. When you suspect that your potential client may be a Long Term value person or organization, ask big questions: "What are your hopes and dreams for your children? When you retire, what do you hope to have accomplished? Where do you expect your company to be twenty-five years from now?"

These questions will successfully tap into the Long Term client's value orientation. But they may elicit yawns or blank stares from Short Term clients and organizations, who are looking for immediate gains. For the Short Term client, ask instead what they want to work on first, what would be the easiest thing to change in their life that would produce the most results, or what they'd like to accomplish in the next three months.

Motivation

Long Term oriented clients and organizations will be most motivated by lasting rewards and strategies to get them there. Expect coaching to take place over a longer period, sometimes with less frequent sessions. Use of the "ideal future" technique when clients are losing energy for goals can be a big motivator.[207] Key into your client's vocabulary and use words that would be meaningful to them, such as:

- How will the *sacrifices* you are making now pay off in a decade?
- What do you think God's perspective is about your *perseverance and staying the course* during this difficult season?
- How will your family/corporation benefit *long term* from the *thrift* you are practicing now?

Planning for quick wins when helping Short Term clients select goals and action steps is essential. Short Term clients and organizations can lose steam fast when there is no immediate progress. Help clients who need to plan longer term to build in rewards along the way to keep motivation and investment in the coaching process high. Ask questions which use their preferred vocabulary:

- How could you see *movement happen more quickly* in this area?
- What would it take to *feel free* to respond to this challenge right now?
- How are you *enjoying life in the present* during this challenge?

Dealing with Coach Discomfort

Coach discomfort on this continuum will center around where the client's vs. the coach's attention is. Coaches may feel clients are missing a big piece of life (whether it is planning for long term gratification or enjoying the present moment). Perspective questions and leveraging this value can help, but coaches will need to make peace with where the client chooses to put their effort and resources.

---

207   Tony Stoltzfus, Coaching Questions: *A Coach's Guide to Powerful Asking Skills* (Redding, CA: Coach22, 2008), 42.

Take a Minute

- *How do you suspect that Long and Short Term value clients might handle coming to the end of a coaching contract differently?*
- *What new strategies or tips that you "tried on" while reading this chapter will work for you with differently valued clients on this continuum? Is there an action step you want to take?*

Completing the Dance

Chapter Twenty

Virtues of the Culturally Intelligent Christian Coach

Becoming a great cross-cultural coach takes more than knowledge, motivation, strategy, and action. It takes character. We've talked a lot so far about adding CQ Strategy and Action/Behavior to CQ Knowledge. We've spent a good bit of time learning about cultural values and specific coaching strategies and behaviors to adapt to those values. This chapter is about another area vital to the culturally intelligent Christian coach, which is the character attributes or virtues that position you for real impact in the Kingdom.

Here's an early story from my own cross-cultural coaching journey. I was sitting at my dining room table with my Skype headset on and my laptop in front of me. It was a beautiful early morning in fall, the sun shining brightly through my east window. In contrast, it was already evening on the other side of the planet where my coaching clients live. We had only a few hours a day of overlap in which we could conveniently schedule our coaching sessions, and we had not met for two months. Their home is in a high mountain region, and their own Skype connection had proved unworkable, so after several tries, we had given up.

On this day, S and her husband J had traveled down the steep, treacherous mountain road, an eight-hour drive, into town where they had arranged a Skype connection for our appointment. Their SUV dodged pedestrians, heavily-laden trucks and carts, buses crammed with people, and the occasional group of roving monkeys, as they negotiated a zigzag of narrow, slippery switchbacks that dropped more than fifteen hundred meters in elevation. S and J would be in town for several days, so we had scheduled multiple sessions before they had to leave again for the trip home.

On this morning, the internet connection was fairly good, and we only had a few disconnects during the call. Both S and J came on the line at the beginning of the call. It was good to hear their voices crackle down the line, though I had to strain a bit to make out the words. We exchanged greetings, then spent the first half hour trading news to which email cannot do justice. The progress of their small son's new reading skills. Their concerns for parents and those to whom they minister. How much Gary and I missed our son away at college. Updates and greetings from common friends. It's important to slow down and take time for relationship. We shared. We prayed together. Then we settled into coaching, first S, then J.

Though S's English is accented and her sentence structure is sometimes more Eastern than Western, we always coach in English, our common language. S delights in every insight gained during her appointments. Her joy in life and in God comes through in every sentence. She is always right on task, punctual, and eager to glean every bit of learning she can in each minute of our time to leverage that learning to serve her neighbors, family, and friends. Her coaching times are electric with energy, creativity, and inspiration.

Coaching with J is just as energizing, but quieter. J thinks deeply and reflects on obstacles to application. He consistently takes on difficult goals. In fact, at times I must bite my tongue at what he believes is realistic. But he perseveres with determination and faith until completion. He understands duty and sacrifice and lives out the best in these values practically and faithfully. Though of high rank and status due to his birth family, he regularly takes on the task of cleaning the toilets in the community house they share with others in their organization. He feels a deep sense of responsibility for those he leads. Serious about multiplying leaders, he gives himself to mentoring. He lives out servanthood in a hands-on way that speaks volumes in the culture he is working in.

J and S met in a ministry context and come from very different cultural backgrounds. They live in a host country that is home to neither of them, and their ministry is with immigrants. They are constantly dancing between cultures—in their marriage, their families, among their colleagues, in their organization, and even with me, their American coach. Their ability to shift gears with such grace, warmth, and love (and for S, such enthusiasm!) is a bit overwhelming to me, a neophyte.

That morning I listened past the accents and the static on the Skype line with 150% of all the concentration I could muster. I struggled to hear their hearts and enter their experience of the world, their values, and their vision. I learned much while they were learning. When several hours later we finally said our last goodbyes for the day, I was physically exhausted.

Character is not an optional attribute for the coach. Great coaching is practiced by people who have paid a price for great character.

For a period of eighteen months, I coached J and S and trained them to coach others. When I finished a call with them, I would usually sit by my window and wait for tears to come. Yes, I was exhausted, but more than that, I was grateful. What a privilege to coach these leaders! How fortunate I have been to know them and to come alongside them in some small way. How grateful I feel for the opportunity to learn from and with them. Coaching them has been as much a process of growth and transformation for me as it has been for them. I am grateful for the rich blessing of having been "coach" to S and J.

Character

> Philippians 2:5-8, ***The Message:*** Think of yourselves the way Christ Jesus thought of himself. He had equal status with God but didn't think so much of himself that he had to cling to the advantages of that status no matter what. Not at all. When the time came, he set aside the privileges of deity and took on the status of a slave, became human! Having become human, he stayed human. It was an incredibly humbling process. He didn't claim special privileges. Instead, he lived a selfless, obedient life and then died a selfless obedient death.

Character is not an optional attribute for the coach. Great coaching is practiced by people who have paid a price for great character. This may seem obvious, but it is surprising how little we often focus on this absolutely essential part of our growth as coaches. Who we *are* as people is foundational to how we coach. Tony Stoltzfus, director of the Leadership Metaformation Institute, has written and spoken extensively on developing the "heart of a coach", which comes from embracing, experiencing, and then modeling God's heart towards us to our clients. Tony identifies faith, believing the best, humility, extending unconditional love and acceptance, and spiritual discipline, among others, as some of the essential virtues of the Christian coach.[208]

---

208   Tony Stoltzfus, *Leadership Coaching: The Disciplines, Skills, and Heart of a Coach* (Redding, CA: Coach22, 2005), 47-60.

I believe three character qualities in particular are essential for the coach who works cross-culturally: humility that results in a desire to learn and grow, sacrifice, and flexibility. All of these attributes are helpful in coaching, and some have been identified by other authors, but each of these has unique application in cross-cultural coaching. Dr. Cory Lemke, who coaches pastors and church planters in Ukraine, sums up these qualities as "servanthood".[209] We'll look at each of these virtues, referring to the example of coaching S and J for some specific examples.

Humility

Philippians 2:3b: In humility value others above yourselves.

Proverbs 18:15, **_The Message:_** Wise men and women are always learning, always listening for fresh insights.

When I became a coach, I needed to learn to let go of shaping the outcome for my clients. I needed to realize at a much deeper level that others had wisdom that I didn't have. That my client's solutions and ideas were much more applicable than my own. That I didn't have or need all the answers. Tony Stoltzfus identifies humility as an element of the coach's heart:

> Coaching is about having faith in the heart-changing power of the Holy Spirit.
> This discipline of faith also leads us to a place of humility: our part in changing
> people is much smaller than what we've become accustomed to thinking.[210]

Coaching itself is a humbling discipline. However, cross-cultural coaching takes humility to a whole new level. Humility is defined as modesty and respect, not behaving as though you are more important than the other. Humility in cross-cultural coaching means being willing to enter the cross-cultural relationship as a learner who must acquire the basics. Jesus modeled this for us by coming to earth as a baby, a child.[211]

We come into the coaching relationship with our cross-cultural clients with the awareness that we need to learn from them about what works in their culture, what values are important to them, what pace and elements of the coaching funnel will serve them best. We will need to learn basic things like what words

---

209   Dr. Cory Lemke, Personal Communication, Permission granted on July 3, 2015.
210   Tony Stoltzfus, *Leadership Coaching: The Disciplines, Skills, and Heart of a Coach* (Redding, CA: Coach22, 2005), 47-60.
211   Sherwood G. Lingenfelter and Marvin K. Mayers, *Ministering Cross-Culturally: An Incarnational Model for Personal Relationships.* 2nd ed. (Grand Rapids, MI: Baker Academic, 2007), 16.

are significant to them, how to greet them properly, how to enter into heartfelt communication, and how to express concern. We cannot assume, as we do when coaching someone of our own culture, that we have the basic knowledge we need to relate.

Sherwood Lingenfelter explains the concept of incarnation, of embodying Christ, as we connect with others of different cultures. He links our willingness to learn as if we were helpless infants with the practice of incarnation.[212] To truly embody Christ, we must humble ourselves and enter a new cultural environment, acknowledging the depth of our ignorance, ready to learn from our coachees.

Relating to, or entering into, a new culture is never easy. I hate losing the ability to communicate well when I leave the English-speaking world. I am a good communicator in my own language, and it is humbling to admit my terrible ineptitude for foreign language. Owning up to my inability to speak well, using broken phrases, pointing, and being constantly corrected are difficult for me. I also really like knowing the answers. Entering another culture means a lot of the answers I take for granted in my own culture don't apply. In either case, both in terms of language ability and general knowledge, I can take comfort in Jesus' example of coming as a learner.

When I began coaching S and J, I needed to learn what worked for them in the structure of a coaching session. I needed to understand why it was so difficult for them to schedule sessions, so I needed to learn about their environment and their ministry. Visiting a client's location is not always possible, but taking that trip up the mountain and down again myself to visit J and S was an eye-opening perspective shift about how hard they were trying to make their coaching work and what their commitment level was.

Because I invited them to help me understand their context, S and J took joy in teaching me. They gently led me back to friendly conversation when I jumped too quickly into the coaching appointment without giving enough time for personal sharing. I learned from J's reflections about the challenges of bringing coaching to a Status value culture and gained some needed humility through

---

212   Ibid., 23-24.

that process. As I heard how he related to his colleagues, other leaders, and those working for him, I learned better how to relate to him.

I also discovered how to greet S and J appropriately. Though to my chagrin, on a visit to their location, I forgot protocol and greeted J in front of his friends with a two-handed handshake, a huge faux pas I have regretted to this day. We may not always get the details of culture right with our clients, as I didn't in greeting J, but when our attitude is humble and we are ready to learn and try again, there is more grace for our inevitable mistakes.

Take a Minute

- *Jesus entered Jewish culture as a baby, learning the language, values and customs from his elders. Ask God what it means for you to be a humble learner in your cross-cultural coaching relationships.*
- *If you are coaching in your first language, but not your client's first language, jot down what the experience of coaching would be like for you if you were being coached in your second or third language. Then think about how you might coach/relate differently with your client because of thinking this through.*
- *Work through the following Capacity-building exercises for Humility:*
    - *Ask your cross-cultural client what mistakes you have made in greeting, language, and protocol.*
    - *Ask your client what feels foreign or uncomfortable to them about coaching. What would make it easier or more comfortable for them?*
    - *Learn to greet your client in their first language.*

Sacrifice

> Tony Stoltzfus: If you've not actively cultivated the discipline of sacrificial love in your life, you'll find it extremely difficult to coach.[213]

A willingness to sacrifice may be the most important character quality a culturally intelligent coach can have. A capacity and commitment to sacrifice for others is required. Here are some comments on this issue from cross-cultural coaches.

---

213   Tony Stoltzfus, "What Makes a Coach?" last modified 2006, http://www.coach22.com/discover-coaching/resources/what_makes_a_coach_2-07.pdf.

Toby, who coaches Hispanic ministry leaders and pastors, shares matter-of-factly with other coaches regarding his years of ministry in Mexico:

> Anything vulnerable that I share will be used against me. My advice: do it anyway.[214]

Brad, an organizational coach in the US and VP of the Malphurs Group, says:

> It's more important to be incarnational than to make more money. So I make less, and this begins to impact my ability to support my family and how many cross-cultural clients I can take. You have to have a limit to the number of cross-cultural clients or get outside funding. One way I try to deal with it is that I am not just called to make money, I am called to a greater mission. So I may not spend extra hours of my workday with that client, but I could invite them to dinner. I want to keep my integrity at work and keep integrity with the mission I feel called to. It does get dicey sometimes.[215]

Several coaches who work in the Arab world have talked about the need to build long-term relationships and invest locally before fruitful coaching can happen. One of them, Carl, explains:

> We have a lot of relational equity here because of our work in the region. Arabs respect longevity in an area more than they do newcomers. There is honor involved in being coached by someone who has been in the context a long time. Going through the same struggles, wars, and other stuff that you go through in this part of the world gives credibility. They know I can empathize with their struggles.[216]

I'm struck as I talk with successful cross-cultural coaches with how pragmatic they are about the need for routine sacrifice. This is simply a part of the work. I know in my own experience that the question of sacrifice came up early on as I started coaching cross-culturally. It felt as though God were laying down the gauntlet. Would I coach sacrificially and trust Him for the rewards?

Some of the first sacrifices required of me, as seen in the story of J and S, were sacrifices of my schedule, time, and energy. Was I willing to meet early in the morning? Schedule several long sessions with them in a period of 3-4 days? Would I accept that the energy it took to meet with them meant that I would not

---

214   Toby, Personal Communication, Permission granted on June 29, 2015.
215   Brad Bridges, VP of the Malphurs Group, Personal Communication, Permission granted on October 10, 2015.
216   Carl, Personal Communication, Permission granted on August 2, 2015.

> **Culturally intelligent coaches routinely sacrifice their physical and emotional comfort, convenience, income, time, and plans.**

be able to see as many clients or be able to accomplish as much for the rest of the day? Culturally intelligent coaches routinely sacrifice their physical and emotional comfort, convenience, income, time, and plans. Some put their reputation and, for coaches like Carl who have chosen to live cross-culturally, their personal safety and health at risk.[217]

Regardless of your situation, cross-cultural coaches of all stripes deal with the emotional, spiritual, and cognitive stretching that coaching someone from a different culture brings. This can be uncomfortable to us, and the tendency may be to go back to coaching those we know and understand. If we persist, we face the fatigue of stretching. As I began to take on more and more cross-cultural clients, I found that I was extremely tired at the end of the day. I explored this with my own coach. What was going on? Here are some of the factors I identified and where they showed up in the example of S and J:

- Communicating and listening (extremely poor Skype connections with lots of disconnections, adjusting to both J and S's accents and to S's sentence structure).
- Adjusting the pace and elements of the coaching funnel according to culture (speeding up for S, slowing down for J).
- Analyzing through the lens of culture rather than trusting my instincts for red flags (recognizing that rather than being too ambitious, J's big goals came from his Long Term value orientation; learning to interpret J's Indirect value silences correctly: recognizing when he was silently disagreeing without challenging me, when he was struggling with English, and when he was simply waiting to hear more.).
- Testing my own understandings of leadership and Scripture (rather than labeling S as not having good boundaries, understanding that leadership was exhibited differently in a Relationship rather than Task value culture).
- Switching between different cultures (with S and J, when both were on the line, switching cultures moment by moment).

Cross-cultural coaching is taxing spiritually, emotionally, mentally, and physically. We'll talk more about how to create a sustainable coaching rhythm that will

---

217   Ibid.

enable you to coach cross-culturally long-term in our final chapters on finishing well.

Coaching across cultures is an adventure that will require something of you. Jesus led the way when he came to earth to sacrifice himself as a bridge between the culture of heaven and the culture of earth. Out of love for us, he became *like* us. We have the privilege of following him when we are willing to make the smaller sacrifices necessary to bridge cultures in coaching. This is an unbelievably rewarding journey and well worth the sacrifice.

Take a Minute

- *What is your level of persistence and commitment (CQ Drive) in this area of sacrifice? How would you respond to the following situations?*
  - *The aid worker you are coaching is in Malaysia on assignment for six months, and the time difference is 13 hours. Her internet is only on during the day. Are you willing to coach her at 8 pm at night? She really wants to meet with you.*
  - *Your European business client wants 2.5-hour sessions. How do you respond?*
  - *Your North American ministry clients can pay your $200 per session; your African pastor coachees can afford $2.50. How will you allocate your time?*
  - *The Central American immigrants you coach in your church setting would prefer to walk in rather than schedule sessions ahead. How will you accommodate them?*
  - *The cross-cultural team you are coaching values face-to-face sessions. They want you to travel to their overseas location for a week of coaching and relationship building. They will pay for your ticket. You will be away from your family for a week and will not make as much as you would seeing clients at home. Will you go?*
- *Read the story of the rich young ruler in Mark 10. Jesus pinpoints the place where this young man needed to sacrifice: his money. Ask God where you need to learn to sacrifice.*
- *Complete the following Capacity-building exercises for Sacrifice:*
  - *How much of a sacrifice is your cross-cultural client making to receive coaching from you? What are you sacrificing to coach him/her/them? What is one small thing you could give up or do that would help you be a better coach to your cross-cultural client/s?*
  - *What is one thing you have not been willing to do for clients in the past that you are willing to try doing now?*

Flexibility

1 Cor. 9:19-23: Though I am free and belong to no one, I make myself a slave to everyone, to win as many as possible. To the Jews, I become like a Jew, to win the Jews. To those under the law I became like one under the law (though I myself am not under the law), so as to win those under the law. To those not having the law I became like one not having the law (though I am not free from God's law but am under Christ's law) so as to win those not having the law. To the weak I became weak, to win the weak. I have become all things to all people so that by all possible means I might save some. I do all this for the sake of the gospel that I may share in its blessings.—the apostle Paul

Without flexibility, you will go nowhere as a cross-cultural coach.

As Christian coaches, we lay down our advice, our preferences, and our ideas. As cross-cultural coaches, we lay down our cultural values and preferences. We choose to meet our coachees on their ground. That's part of what crossing cultures is about. This requires a great deal of flexibility. Without flexibility, you will go nowhere as a cross-cultural coach.

I have to say that no one who knows me well would report that flexibility is one of my natural attributes. By gifting and personality, I am someone who loves certainty and lives by her calendar. I make plans and stick to them. I am a naturally Dichotomistic thinker. There is a right way and a wrong way and an excellent way. I have had to *develop* flexibility—at times, painfully.

When I began to coach across cultures, some of my first clients were YWAMers (Youth with a Mission workers) working in Asia. YWAM is a legendarily flexible and risk-taking organization (tolerating loads of ambiguity). Asian culture is Holistic, Relationship oriented, and in the region I was working, strongly Non-Crisis. As I began to coach Asians in addition to expatriates, the cultural distance gap widened even more.

Learning to flex with my clients was hard work for me. I had to learn to become more comfortable with uncertainty and ambiguity. I had to let things go that I would normally call out. I began to build flex into my schedule. My mantra as I entered a cross-cultural coaching session or team meeting became, "My plan is to be flexible!" I began to *practice flexibility*.

In the example above of S and J, one of my first and biggest challenges was scheduling. Often, they were at the mercy of the weather, which impacted their internet. So I was also at the mercy of the weather. When they came down the mountain to meet with me, they needed several sessions in as many days, and sessions were often three hours long. So I learned to do marathon coaching. The first challenges we face in flexibility are often about these obvious things: scheduling, payment, contracts and so on.

As we gain more experience with cross-cultural coaching, the greater challenge is flexing our mental understanding of things like what makes good coaching and what makes a great leader. The term researchers use for this is "increasing category width".[218] Rather than having a narrow band of what we think is good or right, cross-cultural situations help us see the broad array of good and right possibilities. We must learn to enter the gray of uncertainty with our clients and find the way that works for them. This takes mental flexibility.

Some of you are naturally flexible and can step it up when coaching cross-culturally with only a little effort. Others of us must work harder and more diligently to develop flexibility. In either case, God is gracious to give us the experiences we need in order to fulfill our calling. If you, like me, need more flexibility to coach well cross-culturally, don't hesitate to ask God for help.

Take a Minute

- *Re-read the passage above written by Paul. Put yourself in his shoes. What would it have been like for Paul to be like a Jew, then a Gentile, then under the law, and then free of it? How about being weak, then strong? Jot down a few thoughts about what that experience would have been like. Then ask Jesus where you need to grow in flexibility. Listen and make an action step. Ask God for help as you grow in flexibility.*

- *Increase your "category width". Write down a one-paragraph description of a good leader or a good parent. After reviewing the values chapters, re-visit your description. Or compare your answer to that of a good friend from a different culture.*

- *Complete the following Capacity-building exercises for Flexibility:*
  - *Practice doing a coaching funnel in fifteen minutes, then in 1.5-2 hours, either with a client, or over coffee/tea with a friend or family member.*

---

218   David A. Livermore, Cultural Intelligence: *Improving Your CQ to Engage Our Multicultural World* (Grand Rapids, MI: Baker, 2009).

> - *Some cultures prefer to be coached in pairs or groups rather than individually. Try this by asking two clients if you can meet with them together for more synergy (a married couple could work), or coach two individuals from a team at the same time. Volunteer to provide a coaching session for a ministry team at your church. If you are accustomed to working only with pairs or teams, schedule an individual session.*
> - *Identify several areas that you think are "givens" in your coaching practice, ministry or business (perhaps it's where you meet clients, what you charge, when you work, how you do coaching agreements). List several ways you could become flexible in each of these. Make at least one of these an action step.*

Becoming the Cross-cultural Coach God Intends You to Be

Tony Stoltzfus: The primary thing you have to give to others in ministry is what Christ has done in you. Great coaching springs out of fully embracing the work of God in your own life.[219]

2 Corinthians 3:16-18, ***The Message:*** When God is personally present, a living Spirit, that old, constricting legislation is recognized as obsolete. We're free of it! All of us! Nothing between us and God, our faces shining with the brightness of his face. And so we are transfigured much like the Messiah, our lives gradually becoming brighter and more beautiful as God enters our lives and we become like him.

It should be evident by now that coaching cross-culturally will require growth, not just in skills, but in your person and character. Our goal, as Sherwood Lingenfelter says, is to become more than we are.[220] I want to become more like Jesus. Humble as a child, but strong as a King. Teachable and curious. Willing to make great personal sacrifices to serve others. Able to flexibly minister what is needed in the moment. To be that person, in order to be that kind of coach, I must be hungry for inner transformation, not simply for the attainment of a certain level of skill. I want to be a coach whose life, and therefore whose coaching ministry, is gradually becoming brighter and more beautiful as God enters in, transforming me and through me, transforming those around me.

---

219   Tony Stoltzfus, "What Makes a Coach?" last modified 2006, http://www.coach22.com/discover-coaching/resources/what_makes_a_coach_2-07.pdf.
220   Sherwood G. Lingenfelter and Marvin K. Mayers, *Ministering Cross-Culturally: An Incarnational Model for Personal Relationships.* 2nd ed. (Grand Rapids, MI: Baker Academic, 2007), 24.

Chapter Twenty-One

Skills of the Culturally Intelligent Christian Coach: Assessment

Cross-cultural coaching is a specific type of coaching, and excelling in it requires a set of particular skills. In this chapter, we'll begin to focus on the unique competencies you'll need to cultivate as you coach cross-culturally. In an earlier chapter we focused on the elements of Cultural Intelligence (Drive, Knowledge, Strategy, and Action). There are five skills especially relevant in cross-cultural coaching (Assessment, Juggling, Walk around the Castle, Plumb Line, and Intentionality). These five skills all fall into the categories of CQ Strategy and Action. We'll start with Assessment. To find out about the fifth skill, Intentionality, go to www.dancingbetweencultures.com.

Self-Assessment

Proverbs 4:7, ***The Message:*** Above all and before all, do this: Get Wisdom! Write this at the top of your list: Get Understanding!

Galatians 6:4a, ***The Message:*** Make a careful exploration of who you are and the work you've been given.

The first vital skill for a competent coach is that of Assessment. This does not simply mean learning to administer the proper tests and evaluations, nor even just assessing clients. Self-Assessment and self-awareness, i.e., a proper understanding of oneself, can be at least as vital as understanding your cross-cultural client. Wendy Beery, an American coach with missions experience who now uses her coaching skills at the University of Valley Forge, reflects:

> Coaching is so other-focused, but you can't be that until you are self-aware, just like you can't love others well unless you love yourself. How can I be at all sensitive to others' bent if I am not aware of my own?[221]

Self-awareness is a foundational skill for the cross-cultural coach, and Assessment must start with understanding our *own* cultural biases. We've touched on this extensively in the Take a Minute exercises found in each of the Values Chapters, but it is worth saying again. You cannot adapt to the cultures of others with grace and understanding unless you are aware of and own your own cultural heritage. Culture is so deeply a part of us and so often unconscious that we are usually unaware of its power. We must intentionally, relentlessly dig down under the surface and unearth what our values, our preconceptions, our beliefs, and our attitudes really are.

What happens when we aren't aware of our own values? When we are not aware of what is below our own waterline, we will unconsciously see the client through our own cultural value lens. We will be less flexible and less able to respond appropriately and effectively. We may respond emotionally when cultural value differences surface. We are more likely to judge others. We may alienate our clients with discordant responses or questions inappropriate to their situation. We will be operating out of cultural bias.

For many years, I have taught a cross-cultural coaching course, in which most trainees were career missionaries.[222] A significant percentage of these cross-culturally experienced trainees reported that one of the most helpful and illuminating exercises they did in the entire course was the initial assessment of their own cultural values. Some commented that they did not realize how much their host cultures had influenced their values. This helped them understand why it was so hard to go "home". Others realized that even after twenty or thirty years of missions work outside of their home country, they were still an American or a Brazilian (or whatever their original home country) at heart. Others owned a set of values that was more "international" or that reflected their organization more than either their home or host country. In each case, knowing and understanding their own values was foundational to their learning to coach cross-culturally.

---

221   Wendy Beery, Personal Communication, Permission granted on June 29, 2015.
222   For more information on CMI's distance learning course, Coaching with Cultural Intelligence, go to www.cmiprograms.com or www.dancingbetweencultures.com.

You've made a great start in becoming aware of your own values by reading this book and completing the exercises and reflections in each section. However, I encourage you to go deeper in developing cultural self-awareness by completing the 360 exercise found at the end of this chapter.

Client Assessment

When we begin coaching with a new client, gathering information about who they are and what is important to them is one of the first things we do. We ask for information about their family. We ask about their gifts and their experiences. Many of us inquire about their personality profiles, either using a DISC or MBTI assessment. We request that they share about their job or ministry role and history. We like to know about their educational background and learning style. Many of us start the first session with a new client by swapping stories, either telling each other a brief version of our life stories or by sharing significant events that shaped us as leaders. This information helps us as coaches to serve our clients well and to empathize with them more quickly and deeply.

However, how many of us inquire about culture values? We've learned that along with personality, cultural values and beliefs have critical influence. They may in fact determine many of our client's responses, attitudes, behaviors, and certainly their values. How can we *not* ask about this? It's scandalous that we don't!

Just as some coaches use the MBTI or DISC assessment when the client does not know their personality profile, there are assessments available to identify cultural values when, as is most often the case, the client is unaware of their own cultural values. It is quite useful and many times essential for the coach to have this information at the *start* of the coaching relationship.

Some coaches prefer formal assessments, and some prefer informal. There are a variety of formal values assessments available to you. Here are three I recommend.

The **Mayers Basic Values Questionnaire** is based on six cultural values. Unfortunately, it is not available online, but is available only in book/print form. However, it is well worth the book price. It can be found either in Sherwood Lingenfelter's *Ministering Cross-Culturally* or as a stand-alone questionnaire from Mayers and Mayers under the title "Questionnaire for Ministering Cross-culturally: A Personal Profile of Basic Values".

Philippe Rosinski's **Cultural Orientations Framework** (COF) is a very simple assessment, but will provide insight on many different value themes. It is highly accessible. It can be found online and is available free for individual participants. The COF will produce ratings in six major categories of values with seventeen subcategories. The entire assessment will generate a five-page printed report of both your values orientation and your capabilities in each values area based on your self-report.[223]

A third option is the **CQ Self-Assessment Basic Plus** from the Cultural Intelligence Center. This instrument assesses both cultural intelligence in four categories and values preferences on seven continuums. It is an excellent assessment. Unfortunately, it is also less easily available and does have a cost attached, though the Center does have faith-based context pricing.[224]

For those who prefer on-the-spot or less formal assessment of values, I recommend using an informal Values Chart assessment. The Values Chart (see the Appendix; and available online at www.dancingbetweencultures.com) can provide an informal self-assessment for your client on the value sets you've read about in this book. Simply instruct your client to read each pair of values, underline the phrases that represent their *natural preference or their choice in an environment in which they feel at home*, then mark a point on the continuum for that value pair that best represents their answers. For instance, in the example below:

Crisis (planning)	**?** **Non-Crisis**
I anticipate potential problems (tend to be pessimistic).	<u>I tend to discount potential problems (tend to be optimistic).</u>
<u>I rely on research and expert advice.</u>	I'm a bit suspicious of "experts".
I am motivated to get clarity and so, make prompt decisions.	I have a high tolerance for ambiguity, <u>so I tend to delay decisions.</u>
I stick to the plan when the crisis hits.	I improvise when a crisis hits.

---

223   You can find it at: http://www.philrosinski.com/cof/
224   Contact the Cultural Intelligence Center for more information at: http://www.culturalq.com/faith.html

The client has marked those phrases that he feels represent him. Note that he has not marked either response on one of the pairs of phrases (motivated towards clarity vs. high tolerance for ambiguity). That's OK! He's also placed his "x" towards the Non-Crisis side, which accurately reflects that most of his responses are on that end of the continuum. Remember that some clients really will fall in the middle of some of the continuums because some cultures, individuals, and organizations do not have a clear preference for one side or the other. For instance, Iran falls almost exactly in the center for two of Hofstede's continuums: Individualist/Collectivist (Autonomy/Community) and Power Distance (Status/Equality).[225]

Based on their cultural values, some clients will prefer to receive this before the session, think about it, and fill it out ahead of time. Others will prefer to do this activity within the coaching session.

Using the Values Chart with Clients

For a quick resource, here is a check list to follow in using the Cultural Values Chart (Appendix) to do a cultural assessment with your clients.

- Ask client to underline phrases that represent his/her natural preference or the choice they would make in an environment in which they feel at home.
- Ask the client to indicate the place on the continuum arrow that best represents their preference.
- Talk briefly through each continuum, using the questions below.
- Note where culture distance is the greatest between you and your client.
- If you have opportunity, ask about strong preference values.

To hear a live Values Chart assessment session, go to <u>www.dancingbetweencultures.com</u>.

Whether you do a formal or informal assessment, it's important to talk through the results together with your client in the session. At times, the client's understandings of what a value or continuum are and the meaning they attribute to the phrases will be different than your understanding, especially when you are not coaching in the client's first language. Here are some great questions to ask in discussing results with your client:

---

225   Geert Hofstede, Gert Jan Hofstede, and Michael Minkov, *Cultures and Organizations: Software of the Mind, Intercultural Cooperation and its Importance for Survival.* 3rd ed. (New York: McGraw Hill, 2010), 58 & 96.

- What do you understand about this value or continuum?
- What is your natural preference in this area?
- How do you see this value operating in yourself or in your home/host/ organizational/other culture?

It's also important to take note in the coaching session of value preferences that seem especially strong, particularly if there is a lot of cultural distance between you and your client on that value. This is not necessarily something the coach needs to discuss with the client unless the client is interested. However, if you have opportunity, ask the client about these values and the beliefs and customs they have. Take every opportunity to follow your curiosity to greater understanding of what is important to your client and why.

If you are coaching expatriates, learning about cultural value differences and CQ is crucial to their cultural adjustment. In that case, you may choose to talk about value differences more openly in the coaching appointment. Here are some great questions to ask if you have opportunity:

- What does this value look like in your daily life? Your job/ministry? Your family?
- What makes this value important to you?
- Do you operate with different values in different settings? For instance, how do expectations shift when you are in your home and host cultures?
- Do you have any competing value sets that create conflict for you? For instance, Relationship expectations from home or host culture, but Task expectations from organizational culture.

Note that the instructions ask the client to indicate their "natural preference" when doing the values chart. You are trying to get at the "under the waterline" values that your client actually owns and operates from, which could be different than those of his/her home culture. You could also ask your client to do either an informal assessment or one of the formal assessments for their work environment, their home culture, their host culture, their generation, etc., to gain a different set of information, depending on the client's coaching goal.

This informal assessment can be used for various purposes. It can be used to:

- create more understanding between you and your client.
- help the client identify their differing cultural environments in re-entry or culture shock coaching.
- help clients understand colleagues in multicultural or multi-generational teams.

- gain understanding of competing cultural values between workers and businesses or sending organizations. Remember that your client's personal cultural values may differ by varying degrees from the dominant values of their home culture.

One thing to remember about values assessment in general is that it's important to revisit the results over time. Our category width and that of our clients can widen. Exposure to new values and possibilities can shift cultural values. Be aware that both your values and your client's values may be different than when you started the coaching relationship.

A fascinating subgroup is third culture kids (TCK's): those who have grown up between cultures. My friend Jeanette Windle, author and TCK, notes that third culture kids as well as others who have lived for many years outside of their home culture can often function on both sides of the continuums. They may see gray instead of a crisp black and white, either/or option; and may find the idea of a forced choice annoying! [226] If so, the Values Chart can be used as a springboard for a discussion of what cultural values influence them most and how this impacts attainment of their coaching goals.

Take a Minute

- *Take one of the formal assessments mentioned in this chapter and reflect on your results in your journal or with your coach, peer coach, or supervisor.*
- *Do a 360-style values assessment, using the Informal Values Chart assessment process:*
  - *Using the Values Chart in the Appendix, or online, identify your own cultural values.*
  - *On a new Chart, identify the values of your home country (for instance, if you are Brazilian, think about the values of your country or fellow Brazilians; as an example, you may personally favor Task value, but most Brazilians operate out of Relationship value).*
  - *If you are an expatriate, on a new Chart, identify the values of your host country. If you are not an expat, identify the values of your church or business/organization.*
  - *Ask someone who knows you well, a spouse or close friend, to do the Informal Values Chart assessment and mark how they see you.*

---

226   Jeanette Windle, Author, Missionary, and TCK, Personal Communication, Permission granted on February 20, 2017.

- *Gather all your results. Make a continuum for each value and plot a point on the line (using a different color for each point) representing your self-assessment; your home country; your host country or church/business/organization; and your friend/spouse's assessment of you.*
- *Spend some time reflecting in your journal or with your peer coach, coach, or supervisor on what you've learned. What cultures have influenced you the most? Where have you developed your own values, or gone against your culture?*

• *Ask a friend, spouse or client if you can practice doing the assessment with them and debrief/ discuss it as you would in an actual client coaching session.*

Chapter Twenty-Two

Skills of the Culturally Intelligent Christian Coach: Utilizing Multiple Perspectives

Dual cultural perspectives are a reality when the coach and coachee come from different cultures. But often our coachees are impacted by many differing cultural values as they set goals and take action: values from home and host culture, sending organization or corporation, ministry setting, etc. Skilled cross-cultural coaches will learn to dance gracefully with this reality and to use it for the client's benefit. Skills number two and three are Juggling and Walk around the Castle.

Juggling

The first challenge is juggling the different and sometimes competing value systems we work with in every cross-cultural coaching session. Learning to keep these balls in the air while maintaining awareness of the many different layers of values present in the coaching relationship is an art that takes practice. Ability to juggle multiple value orientations will result in two specific positive outcomes:

- Helping the client identify dissonance (tension) in competing values.
- Helping the client prioritize value orientations dependent on situation.

When coachees get stuck and seem unable to identify options or overcome obstacles, inability to recognize and prioritize values may be the root of the issue.

To help our clients in this situation, we need to keep in mind both the continuums themselves and the various contexts in which the coachee is operating. Let's look closely at one example.

Woojin is a South Korean working cross-culturally with Bangladeshi immigrants in India. His missionary sending organization is YWAM. His current coaching goal is to produce a short film he believes God has asked him to complete on the challenges immigrant communities face. His own challenge is finding time and space to do this during his other responsibilities. He is having great trouble getting started.

Woojin's values come from his own culture and from YWAM. He must also honor the values of his Bangladeshi colleagues in the rural Indian region where he lives. If we were to estimate Relationship/Task value, for instance, for his different milieus, we might come up with:

- Korea: Task-high preference
- India: Relationship–moderate to high preference
- Bangladesh: Relationship-high preference
- YWAM: Relationship-moderate preference

We can immediately see that, due to his own cultural background, Woojin has a strong value to complete the task God gave him. But he is constrained by the high preference for Relationship in his milieu, represented in the value sets of his outreach focus group, community, and sending organization. Now let's take another look at Woojin's situation, but this time estimating Autonomy/Community values:

- Korea: Community-high preference
- India: Community–extremely high preference
- Bangladesh: Community–high preference
- YWAM: Autonomy-high preference

In other words, Woojin may feel some constraint about not being free to make this decision on his own in the coaching relationship. He needs to have community/personal/colleague support and processing to move ahead with prioritizing time to make this film. However, his YWAM colleagues may not see the need for this, and his leader might not expect it.

Now add in the coach's value sets:

- U.S.: Task-high preference
- U.S.: Autonomy-very high preference

Without cultural understanding, the coach's value for Task might lead to this *internal* dialogue in the coach's mind: "You need to get started on the film. God has spoken, and you know what you are to do." The coach's value for making independent decisions might result in these thoughts: "You'll have to take initiative to get this done. You need to have boundaries with others and learn to say no. Others might not always understand this, but it is necessary." These preconceptions will impact the coach's ability to help Woojin develop culturally appropriate options.

Once we are tuned in to the fact that our coachee may be juggling value sets, and we've faced our own cultural biases about the situation, how do we help the coachee? Often this will happen during either the exploring stage of the coaching funnel or in dealing with obstacles. Open questions and perspective questions are our first choice and will help the coachee move into the options phase.

> *When we realize the coachee is juggling value sets, open and perspective questions help move them into the options phase.*

Here are a few questions you might ask to help your client in choosing options: "What is important to you? What is important to others in your community? Your leadership team? Your organization? Your family? What values do you have that influence or constrain you in meeting this goal? What are the values of your organization/spouse/community, etc.? What would your leader/spouse/national colleagues advise you to pay attention to? To what purpose?"

Once these questions have been answered, use direct questions to help the coachee determine their priority: "What is your priority in this scenario? What are the most important value/values to you in this situation?"

After helping the coachee explore the underlying values and identify their priorities, the coach can again use open questions to help the coachee uncover options: "How can you honor all the values that are important to you in this situation? What is a culturally appropriate way to express this priority? What creative ways can you think of to reconcile your top two priorities? How have you seen this work in your setting in the past? What options would create a win/win scenario?"

In summary, our procedure for Juggling looks like this:
- Recognize the coachee may be dealing with competing value sets.
- Recognize our own value sets and how they might be influencing us.

- Use open and perspective questions to explore competing values.
- Use open and direct questions to uncover priorities.
- Use open questions to help the coachee generate culturally appropriate options.

Take a Minute

Practice Juggling:

- *Identify a challenge/issue that one of your cross-cultural clients is facing that might include competing cultural values. For the purposes of this exercise, it is helpful to use an expat rather than a national or local client.*
- *Identify which one or two value continuums are most impacting your client.*
    - *Value 1:*
    - *Value 2:*
- *Identify each milieu/culture that is influencing you/your client and where they are on each continuum.*
    - *Value 1:*
        - *a. home culture:*
        - *b. host culture:*
        - *c. Local community or leadership team culture:*
        - *d. Organizational culture:*
        - *e. Other _____________:*
        - *f. Coach's (your) culture:*
    - *Value 2:*
        - *a. home culture:*
        - *b. host culture:*
        - *c. Local community or leadership team culture:*
        - *d. Organizational culture:*
        - *e. Other_____________:*
        - *f. Coach's (your) culture:*
- *Identify competing values and priorities.*
- *Identify 2 open or perspective questions which could help your coachee.*

Walk Around the Castle

Proverbs 15:22: Plans fail for lack of counsel, but with many advisers they succeed.

Philippe Rosinski, ***Coaching Across Cultures:*** Culturally trained coaches aim not only to unleash human potential (this is what traditionally trained coaches already do), they also aspire to make the most of alternative worldviews.[227]

One of coaching's most significant deliverables is perspective. This means helping coachees see and understand things in new ways that bring new opportunities, new openness, and new possibilities. Learning to flex our own perspective culturally to help our coachees do the same is invaluable.

As coaches, we need to learn to match and pace with our coachees, identifying their cultural value set and adapting to it in order to serve them. However, we also need to be able to help our coachees gain perspective on the value set of their host culture and perhaps even perspective on other cultures for the purpose of widening their options, finding more effective solutions, and overcoming stubborn obstacles. In a sense, we are helping our coachees find counsel from a variety of perspectives simply by accessing cultural values. Sometimes it is enough to merely offer information on a particular continuum, which then opens the possibility that other options are available. My own daughter Rosie offers a good example of this.

Rosie was preparing to spend some months living in Belize with a distant relative whose husband, a Belizean, had a terminal illness. Just before Rosie's arrival in country, she found out that her host couple's son, daughter-in-law, and new grandchild were coming to spend time with the ill father. The family was planning many fun outings in the country they had lived in together for twenty-five years. Rosie felt uncomfortable, wondering if she should just stay at the house by herself while her hosts enjoyed family time.

I explained to my daughter the difference between Autonomy and Community cultures. Rosie immediately caught that her hosts would see her as a part of the family/web of relationships and that it might actually offend them more

---

227   Philippe Rosinski, *Coaching Across Cultures: New Tools for Leveraging National, Corporate & Professional Differences* (London: Nicholas Brealey Publishing, 2003), 19.

if she stayed at home by herself. A new option had opened up for her, and she gained a totally different perspective on the situation simply by gaining information on the two contrasting values in play. She gladly went with the rest of the family and had a fabulous week exploring Mayan ruins and enjoying the beach as these newly-appreciated distant relatives celebrated family time with her.

In this situation, note that I offered information *only.* I did not interpret the situation from my perspective or draw a conclusion. I simply shared information about the two contrasting ends of the continuum. I let Rosie do the interpreting and application for herself.

Let's take this a step further. What if more than one value orientation would be helpful to draw from? This intriguing concept invites you as a coach to move freely between cultural values orientations and to invite your coachee to move with you, in order to identify the best viewpoint or orientation to apply in each new situation. Philippe Rosinski in his excellent book *Coaching across Cultures: New Tools for Leveraging National, Corporate and Professional Differences* does a masterful job of innovating and explaining the theory of leveraging from a Conceptual value framework. I highly recommend this pioneering book. Rosinski terms this idea of moving between values as "leveraging cultural diversity".[228]

One way to understand this is to think of the coachee's situation, challenge, or goal as a castle in their mind. We want to help the coachee walk all the way around that interior castle, seeing it from every perspective and in light of every applicable continuum. Then they can choose the best possible viewpoint or cultural value to free them to move forward.

Learning to "walk around the castle" ourselves and inviting our coachees to develop this skill as well is one of the most exciting things about cross-cultural coaching. Holistic coaches will have a head start on this process (see Coach Linda's description of going the long way around the block in the Dichotomistic/Holistic chapter). But for those of us who are not naturally Holistic, how do we do it?

In the Learning to Juggle exercises, the first step in helping our coachees who are dealing with value conflicts is to identify the value orientations they have. This is also the first step in Walk around the Castle. Second, as coaches, we must know and understand the opposing value. Third, we need to be able to frame great perspective questions that highlight and draw on the difference.

One way to do this is directly. However, the situations through which we may be coaching clients are typically a bit more complex and entrenched, and a more

---

228   Ibid., 47-187.

indirect approach may be needed. Careful listening and thoughtful questions are needed to help the coachee move towards new perspectives. Let's walk through this process using as example a missionary client from North America who is dealing with too much to do.

Hank, our missionary coachee in question, works in West Africa in a village setting. He has a wife and five young children, whom they are homeschooling. The village has great physical needs. The new believers also need much discipling and teaching at this stage of their development. Hank is constantly torn by priorities. He is beginning to have conflict with his wife over lack of time spent with the children and with her. Their home life is a fishbowl with people constantly popping in with the expectation that the missionary couple will spend time sitting with them and having tea together. Our missionary coachee appears to be averaging sixteen hours per day working, is constantly frustrated by interruptions, and is very stressed. Hank and his coach have been working hard at this in sessions for two months, but are getting nowhere.

Let's consider the value orientations at work here. Hank, being North American, doubtless has a high score on Time value and is working in an Event culture. He is most likely Task value, but is living in a Relationship culture. He has a high value for Autonomy while his West African village values Community. It is also likely that the culture he is living in is Polychronic: meaning it's normal to have lots of interruptions and to do more than one thing at once (for more on Polychronic time orientation, go to www.dancingbetweencultures.com). So how could walking around the castle help Hank? In other words, how can we help Hank draw from other value perspectives to meet this challenge?

We might simply ask Hank a question that gets to the heart of the opposite value orientation. For instance, as a Time oriented coachee, he believes that time is scarce and must be managed, putting pressure on him to get things done efficiently. What if Hank could dare to believe that time is plentiful?[229] We could ask him, "Hank, if you believed that God has given you PLENTY of time every day, how would that feel? If you really believed this, how would it change your attitude? How would it change your everyday tasks and activities?"

We could also ask Hank to draw on the perspective of someone from the host culture that embodies the opposite value. In this case, let's focus on Relationship. For instance, we could ask him about the village elder or leader, who obviously has much to do and many responsibilities. How does that elder approach their

---

229   Ibid., 94-95.

tasks? How does it look and feel different than Hank's approach? If Hank visualized himself using the elder's approach, what would change?

Let's walk to another side of the castle and look at the fishbowl situation at home with visitors dropping in all the time. Let's frame a question for each value orientation that might be in play:

- Relationship/Task: If you believed that people dropping by was not an interruption, but an opportunity, how would that change how you respond? Or, what would efficient use of time look like if relationships instead of tasks were your priority?
- Autonomy/Community: What would happen if you saw visitors as part of the family?
- Polychronic/Monochronic: I've observed that some cultures are especially good at juggling many things at once and dealing with lots of interruptions. What could you learn from West African culture about how to do that well?

Walk around the Castle is a technique we can use to help clients develop new options in any situation, even ones in which no cultural clash is taking place. For instance, a German working in a U.S. corporation and facing burnout would probably have few cultural conflicts between home and host culture in the areas of Time/ Event, Autonomy/Community, and Relationship/ Task. However, it is still worth considering what value orientations might help this coachee see her situation differently so that she doesn't burn out.

The question we asked Hank in our last example could be equally helpful to this client: "What if you dared to believe that time is plentiful and that God has given you plenty of time every day?" Conversely, if you are coaching a Pacific Islander who is having trouble getting things done, it may be helpful to ask: "If you believed God had given you limited time for this initiative, how would you approach your ministry goals differently?"

It is even helpful to use the perspective from other value orientations to bear on a totally different value. For instance, you could ask a Dichotomistic client who is stuck in the launch phase of a new business venture to think Holistically: "If this was not as black and white as you are thinking, what would be some of the 'gray' options you could consider?" But what if you asked another question using a

Non-Crisis perspective? For instance: "How would you approach this differently if you believed that God would give you what you needed in the moment?" Or Crisis: "What advantages could there be in gaining some expert advice from someone who has done this before? Who could you ask?"

This is the heart of leveraging cultural differences: being able to help clients develop new options and ways of thinking about or approaching challenges by drawing on what we know about cultural values. To summarize, Walk around the Castle looks like this:

- Identify the value orientations of the coachee.
- Identify the opposing values that might be useful to the coachee.
- Frame great questions that highlight and draw on these value differences.

For more examples of perspectives questions, see Tony Stoltzfus' *Coaching Questions*.[230]

Take a Minute

Practice Walk around the Castle:

- *Identify a goal or challenge one of your cross-cultural coachees is dealing with.*
- *Underline which value in each set best represents your coachee.*

  - *Autonomy/Community*
  - *Crisis/Non-Crisis*
  - *Dichotomistic/Holistic*
  - *Task/Relationship*
  - *Concealment/Vulnerability*
  - *Long Term/Short Term*

  - *Risk/Caution*
  - *Status/Equality*
  - *Conceptual/Practical*
  - *Direct/Indirect*
  - *Time/Event*

- *With the client's goal or challenge in mind, identify one to three opposite values that might help them develop additional options or creative solutions. Circle each in the pairs above.*
- *Frame three perspective questions that might help your coachee "Walk around the Castle" and see their goal or challenge from another perspective. Use at least one question that draws on the perspective of someone in their host culture or another culture.*

---

230   Tony Stoltzfus, *Coaching Questions: A Coach's Guide to Powerful Asking Skills* (Redding, CA: Coach22, 2008), 78-79.

Chapter Twenty-Three

Skills of the Culturally Intelligent Christian Coach: Culture Transformation

Romans 8:21: The creation itself will be liberated from its bondage to decay and brought into the glorious freedom of the children of God.

1 Peter 2:16-17a, (NRSV): As servants of God, live as free people; yet do not use your freedom as a pretext for evil. Honor everyone. Love the family of believers. Fear God.

Let's finish the story we started in Chapter Six, Cultural Values, from South African coach Andrew, who was coaching a South Asian woman. Here is what he shared earlier:

I don't fully get the culture she is from. It's very different than mine, and the bulk of my clients are from another area of the world. This client has a very successful teaching ministry, but has been dealing with intimidation and fear. She went into teaching with so much trembling, even though she was teaching on faith! Whenever a negative evaluation would come in, she would lose all steam. But as we talked, I realized that she is a younger leader teaching older persons, and I came to understand that that was strange in her culture and intimidating for her."[231]

---

231   Andrew, Personal Communication, Permission granted on August 2, 2015.

And here is the rest of Andrew's story:

> I was so impacted as a coach by Tony Stoltzfus' idea of inviting Jesus into the
> coaching session. So I asked her: "What does Jesus say about your teaching?"[232]
> She replied that she hadn't asked Him. I asked if she wanted to ask Jesus about
> this. "Yes." When would she like to do this? "Now." So we did a simple prayer.
> There was silence. I thought the internet had crashed! I said her name and
> asked if she was there. She said: "Yes. I hear applause and cheering! Jesus is
> saying, 'I trust you!'"[233]

These are the moments in coaching that I hunger for. The moments when
our clients gain insight into the heart of God, and they are transformed in the
process. These moments can refresh our spirits and our client's spirits for a good
long time.

Plumb Line

There is one final skill needed by the Christian cross-cultural
coach. As Christians, we are not only interested in adapting to
and leveraging cultural diversity, but also in seeing culture transformed in and through our individual clients. At times, cultural
values will hold us and our clients back from full freedom in Jesus.
Cultural understandings might hobble us or even prevent us from
pursuing wholeheartedly the ministry God has given us, as was
the case with Andrew's client. Every culture has both strengths
where the "God-colors" (Matthew 5:14-16, *The Message*) shine
through and weaknesses where his image is dim and clouded. But
I believe that God invites *everyone* into the culture of His family.
Just as individuals are transformed by grace, so also can cultural
elements be transformed. God's heart and his character expressed
beautifully in Scripture and the person of Jesus are our ultimate
reference point, our "plumb line".

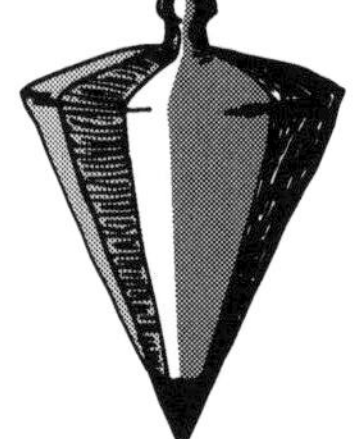

A plumb line is a cord with a weight at one end. It's a simple
carpenter's tool that will give a true straight line. In the Old Testament, Zerubbabel used this tool as he led the reconstruction
of the temple after the Israelites returned from exile in Babylon

---

232   Tony Stoltzfus, *The Invitation: Transforming the Heart Through Desire Fulfilled*
(Redding, CA: Coach22, 2015).
233   Andrew, Personal Communication, Permission granted on August 2, 2015.

(Zechariah 4:9-10). "Plumb line" is a term often used to represent the standards of God, an accurate and true measure of God's values.

Andrew helped his client to return to the plumb line of God's word. In this case, God's personal word to her. This transformed the client's understanding of what was appropriate and good in her situation and helped her go beyond cultural constraints into a new sense of freedom as she taught. Thus, this client now had a new understanding of the culture of the kingdom. Andrew didn't try to tell her that her cultural value for Status was in this case impinging on her ability to do what God wanted her to do. The client discovered this for herself.

What Are the Essential Prerequisites for Birthing Culture Transformation?

When we talk about the skill of using God's plumb line in cross-cultural coaching, I feel both excitement and a healthy dose of fear. The joy of coming into congruence with that plumb line brings freedom, and that is incredibly exciting to me. When God has freed us, as Andrew's client experienced, we are truly free. However, in no way do I want to become colonial or paternal in attitude towards my clients. I do not want to fall into the trap of patronizing them by believing that I know best how to interpret godly values for them.

> *The safeguards that guide us on this journey of culture transformation are virtues and character.*

The safeguards that guide us on this journey are virtues and character. I'll highlight two of the most important. The first is the virtue of **humility**. As coaches, we must enter humbly into dialogue about godly values with our coachee. Remember when we looked at the story of the Prodigal Son? It is easy to interpret Scripture and the model of Jesus through our own cultural lenses. Though I had read those verses countless times over forty years, I did not even see phrases in the passage that failed to match my cultural perspective. Our coachees have blind spots. So do we. Therefore, we ask respectful questions without giving advice, just as Andrew did. We challenge our coachee's perspective with humility. We believe that curiosity laced with servanthood will help our clients—and we ourselves—to find new shades of meaning in Scripture and the model of Jesus.

The second safeguard is **love**: Remember the example of Carl from the Faith and Culture chapter? Carl's love for his new people group, his deep value for the strengths he recognized in them, and his respect for Arab culture *qualified him* to look lovingly at where the culture had weaknesses.[234] That's the kind of love Jesus has for us. Love like that enables us to enter into a dialogue with our coachees. Unless you let God change your heart to love so you can see with his eyes, you'll miss the richness and strength of the other culture because it just looks different and wrong. The plumb line will get distorted. Love is like the weight at the bottom of the plumb line's string.

When Does Culture Need Transforming?

Andrew's client had "a very successful teaching ministry". Obviously, she was serving others with her gifts and very successfully. But her cultural background ingrained in her a belief common in Status cultures, i.e., that it was not proper for younger persons to teach their elders. This was creating tension and fear in her, rather than freedom and confidence.

There are more obvious examples. Perhaps you are coaching someone from a culture where there has been a history of genocide. Or perhaps, as with Haiti, there is a culture of voodoo added to the political and societal reality of a vicious secret police. In these situations, the value of Concealment is based on real fear and suspicion of others developed through generations of oppression and violence. Introducing some of the positives found within the value of Vulnerability will take time and trust-building. But just imagine what freedom a measured dose of Vulnerability could bring both to the individual you are working with and to the wider culture of that society through your client's influence.

These issues can be deep-seated and do not surface quickly. In some cases, they will prevent potential clients from choosing to be coached, as we noted in the section on Concealment/Vulnerability. At other times, readiness is not there on the client's part to deal with the transformation needed. At all times in using the Plumb Line technique, we must be attuned to what the Holy Spirit is doing. We believe that God is the one who initiates change, so we must be willing to follow God's lead.

At all times in using the Plumb Line technique, we must be attuned to what the Holy Spirit is doing. We believe that God is the one who initiates change, so we must be willing to follow God's lead.

Deploying the Plumb Line

When unhealthy or ungodly values come up in the coaching appointment, we sense

234   Ibid.

the Holy Spirit is moving, our attitude is loving and humble, and the client is ready, what steps should we then take? How can we help our clients test their values and customs against Scripture and church tradition and hear from God for themselves?

We looked earlier at the three steps involved in the Walk around the Castle technique. In the Plumb Line technique, the coach starts similarly with Step One, identifying (usually internally) the value orientation of the coachee. However, in Step Two, instead of asking the client to identify opposing values, we ask them to draw on Scripture, church history/tradition, or the example and/ or voice of Jesus to identify godly values. For Step Three, we give the coachee responsibility to define *for themselves* what best represents the freedom and transformation of Christ in their situation.

To summarize, Plumb Line looks like this:

- Identify the value orientation(s) of the coachee.
- Ask the client to draw on Scripture, church history, or the example and/ or voice of Jesus to identify godly values that could bring a different perspective.
- Allow the coachee to define what best expresses for them the freedom of Christ.

In each step, use of great coaching technique aids the process. Here's an example from Tony Stoltzfus, director of Leadership MetaFormation Institute:

I was once working with an Asian-American client who was living and working in Asia. He had a full-time job and was pastoring two churches as well. He shared with me one time in a coaching session that he felt his duty was to serve everyone who came to him for help. He said with great shame that there was one time in his life that he had not done it. There was a woman in one of his congregations who always had some kind of need and called a lot. He was in seminary at that time and had a final paper he had to get done. This woman called at 11 p.m. the night before the paper was due with another need. The client did not help her that night. He shared deep shame about his failure to do so, expressing heartfelt emotion and contrition. As a coach, I recognized the honor/shame dynamic as well as the sense of duty that leaders in Status cultures have towards those they lead [Step 1]. I asked him [Step 2], "What are some instances in the New Testament when Jesus said no when someone asked him something?" Right away, the client identified the story from Matthew 15:21-28 about the Canaanite woman who asked Jesus to heal her daughter, begging for "scraps from the master's table". The client recognized that in this story, in which Jesus initially ignored, then refused, and finally did heal the woman's daughter, that Jesus had had a choice. Jesus could say "yes" or "no". We came up with several more examples together from Scripture. This was revolutionary for the client; it changed his world. If Jesus had a choice, then he did too.[235]

In this example, Tony beautifully illustrates how simply the process works. First, identify the value orientations at work in the client's dilemma. Then ask the client to draw on (in this case) Scripture to test their own assumptions. The client immediately grasped his newfound freedom to choose, and the coaching session went on from there, to explore what that meant in his circumstances (Step 3).

The beauty of God's word and of Jesus' voice is that they often have a power of their own to change hearts. However, at times it may be helpful to add two additional steps.

One of these is sharing information about cultural value orientations/other cultural values. Helping the client see the bigger picture of culture and that there are other perspectives/ways to look at previously unquestioned ideas may help the client open the door to new viewpoints. In the Walk around the Castle section, I gave the example of how merely providing information to my daughter Rosie about differing cultural values was enough to help her see another option.

A final step here is simply to frame great questions that highlight and draw on these value differences. These will help the coachee test their values against what *they* find in Scripture, church history, etc. This technique was discussed in detail in the Walk around the Castle section (Step 3). "What if . . ." is always a useful question, or "If this (value), then what (behavior)?"

Sometimes clients are not ready to see alternatives. When that happens, we need to back off and wait. I once coached a woman in a very similar situation to Tony's client. She was overloaded and nearing burnout. After months of working on boundaries, scheduling, and reducing stress levels, she was still at an unhealthy place. It became clear over time that the underlying issue was that she felt responsible to meet the needs of a wide variety of people in her sphere who were, admittedly, very needy.

My attempts to use perspective questions failed. So, I turned to Scripture and the example of Jesus. We talked through some Scripture passages about how Jesus dealt with stress. We read about Jesus withdrawing from the crowds to pray,

---

235   Tony Stoltzfus, Director of Leadership MetaFormation Institute, Personal Communication, Permission granted on July 6, 2015.

rest, and spend time with his inner circle. We read the story of the (one) healing at the pool of Bethsaida. Though my coachee saw the passages, read them, and we talked through them, it was as if there was a huge wall between reading the words and accepting that Jesus *didn't* actually heal everyone who came to him and actually *did* withdraw from all the needs around him simply to rest and spend time with his Father in prayer. My client could not seem to apply those actions to her own situation.

At the time I was new to cross-cultural coaching. I did not have the tools to be able to see and understand the value orientation at work in this situation and be able to name it. If I had had this understanding, perhaps a more fruitful conversation might have occurred, and cultural transformation within her might have become a possibility. Perhaps even within her community as well through her leadership in business and home. However, sometimes clients are simply not ready. Conviction has not yet come. Then, our job as a coach is to wait and pray.

Going to the Heart Level

Sometimes we are not skilled enough to engage our clients in cultural value transformation. Sometimes we have the skill, but the client is not ready. But there is also a third alternative. Tony Stoltzfus shares that when a value orientation seems to be limiting or crippling a client, attempting to work at it on the cognitive level can at times only engage the client's defenses. He explains:

Helping our clients to identify the heart desire that is at work helps them to get beneath their defenses and engage God.

> Sometimes a value protects a desire. Perhaps if your client [as in the example of the Asian American pastor] stopped helping everyone, he might lose his sense of worth [as a leader in a Status culture] or meaning [for instance, in continuing to pursue Task completion]. If you sense this is the case, work with the emotional, rather than the rational brain to take the conversation to the level of heart desires. Our premise is that Jesus is the one who can fulfill our deepest heart's desires. Many times we learn to substitute things in our culture and our environment for what Jesus wants to provide to us directly. We can help our clients take those desires to Jesus, freeing them to think differently about cultural directives and norms.[236]

---

236   Ibid.

When you sense that a heart desire is hiding behind a value, you can go there directly. Ask the client what this belief or behavior does for them or gives them, what they desire, and what Jesus might say to them about that. Helping our clients to identify the heart desire that is at work helps them to get beneath their defenses and engage God. If your client finds their meaning and worth in Jesus, for instance, they will not hold on as tightly to finding it in culturally-determined norms of task completion or the status of their leadership role. Engaging clients at the level of the heart can result in deep transformation for your clients.

For more information on working at the level of heart desires, see *The Invitation: Transforming the Heart Through Desire Fulfilled*, by Tony Stoltzfus.[237]

Take a Minute

Practice Plumb Line:

- *Take ten minutes and ask God to show you where your own home culture or your own cultural values don't line up with Scripture. Think of a challenge or situation you are facing in which this value might be at play.*
- *With a peer coach, take the value and situation each of you identified in #1 above and coach each other using the Plumb Line technique. (Example: in my culture, Autonomy and Equality are highly valued, therefore I expect others to take care of their own needs. How might this impact my interaction with my staff in non-scriptural ways?)*
- *Application with Clients:*
  - *Identify a present or past coaching relationship in which your client is feeling a need for change/is stuck, and you see an ungodly value at work or a cultural value which is limiting freedom in Christ.*
  - *Identify the value orientation of the client.*
  - *Frame two questions based on Scripture or church history/tradition that might be helpful to your client.*

---

237   Tony Stoltzfus, *The Invitation: Transforming the Heart Through Desire Fulfilled* (Redding, CA: Coach22, 2015).

Chapter Twenty-Four

Challenges to Finishing Well

One day a few years into the exciting journey of coaching cross-culturally, I headed bone-tired into an appointment with my coach. I wasn't really paying attention to my tiredness until my coach asked me about it. He first asked me about my schedule and what my working hours were like. I shared with him a typical day's schedule, which at that time would have looked something like this:

- 8:30 a.m. Skype coaching session with South Asian leader of Catholic background working in lay ministry in India (1-1.5 hours).
- 10 a.m. Skype supervision coaching of Swiss coach working in Hungary (1 ¼ hour).
- 11:15 a.m. Break; returning emails and messages.
- Noon. Virtual CMI leadership team meeting over lunch, involving five leaders from three generational groups (Silent Generation, Boomer, and Gen X) and five denominations, who had served in four global regions: Africa, Asia, Central America, and the United States (2 hours).
- 2 p.m. Break.
- 3 p.m. Skype coaching with a Brit working internationally in leader development (1.5-2 hours).
- 5 p.m. Coaching face-to face with a local American businessman (1 hour).

My coach asked me what about my schedule was most tiring. Through his astute questions, I began to realize that the source of both my excitement and fatigue was the same. I was switching between cultures repeatedly each day, sometimes every hour. This was a revelation to me. I had never thought about how stressful it was to re-calibrate to different values over and over all day long. Once I realized that this was a legitimate source of fatigue, I took it into account in planning and scheduling. Moving towards wholeness meant that I became aware of what was stressful and tiring, recognized what was a legitimate and real stressor, and took steps to adjust my expectations.

To finish well as a cross-cultural coach, it's necessary to understand the particular stresses we face. So what makes cross-cultural coaching especially stressful? We began to identify some of the issues in our chapter on virtues, as we focused on sacrifice. Let's take a closer look now, starting with the obvious.

The Particular Stresses of Cross-cultural Coaching

Coaching with language challenges: It can be difficult to put important concepts and emotive meaning into a foreign language yourself or tease out what your client is trying to say in a language he/she may be less than fluent in. You may spend extra energy finding the right words or struggling with understanding your client's accent or grammar.

Coaching over phone or Skype: Not having access to all the non-verbal communication available in a face-to-face conversation, for instance, posture, foot tapping, leaning in or away, may result in misunderstandings or simply using more energy to track with your client. You may have intermittently bad phone or Skype connections, especially with international calls, which can be frustrating and stressful. A bad connection can also mean straining to hear through static and distortion.

Extreme cultural distance: The greater the cultural distance between you and your clients, especially when significant differences on multiple value continuums are present, the more challenging and stressful coaching can be.

But these "above the waterline" factors are far from the only stressors in cross-cultural coaching. Let's now take an in-depth look at some of the not so obvious "below the waterline" factors.

Letting the Client Lead: The Giant Step to Adapting to Client Values

In coaching, we learn to "go with" our clients. We let them lead the conversation and come to their own conclusions without directing them. We learn to use external techniques like open vs. closed questions that allow our clients to determine the content of the coaching session. We learn to intentionally change our internal outlook, choosing to let go of the outcome and to believe that the client can hear God for themselves.

Coaching across cultures demands significantly higher levels of flexibility and letting go. It's like letting the client lead "on steroids"! In cross-cultural coaching, we are not just letting go of the external conversation and the internal solutions we think might work for this client. We are choosing to lay aside our own cultural values that power those internal solutions.

An example here is when I was coaching by Skype with S and J, who lived on another continent and were from very different cultures from myself or even each other. I had to recognize and adapt to J's choice of big goals consistent with his Long Term value, rather than continuing to ask perspective questions to help him see how "unrealistic" his goal seemed. We take another giant step towards letting the client lead when we adapt to the values behind the client's ideas and solutions.

It takes mental energy to adjust to new values, especially if you are "switching" during the day as I was in the above sample schedule, continually adjusting with each new client to a different planning style, communication preference, thinking pattern, etc. If you are juggling multiple cultures within one coaching appointment or with one client, simply *staying aware* of the multiple value sets impacting your client related to his home country, host country, organization, team, etc., can sap energy.

Living in the Gray: Letting Cherished Assumptions Be Challenged

Kamala is a leader in a Western-based missions organization working in India. In a passing comment in a conversation with her coach, she mentioned that one of her South Asian staff had come to her and her husband to ask them to arrange a marriage for them, which was one of the tasks she was currently working on. Her Western coach was scandalized. Arranging a marriage? How could that be appropriate? But he managed to choke out an open question asking for more information. Kamala picked up her coach's tone and laughed.

"Yes, many of our Western leaders can't get their mind around that," she explained. "But our new converts have lost their whole [Hindu] family system when they became Christians, and family is how you get married in my country. We have become their new family, and as their "elders", we pray and help them find a mate. It's absolutely appropriate here."

Philipe Rosinski writes:

> Integration . . . occurs when you are able to hold different frames of reference in your mind at any time. You can look at a situation from various angles. You have acquired knowledge and mental agility, which are both very useful when working with your coachees . . . Integration is an advanced form of cultural development, and it comes with a price. Self-questioning is more difficult than living with certainties.[238]

Culturally intelligent coaches must be willing to function "in the gray". There are a good number of things that are either right or wrong in this world. But there are also a good number of things that may be wrong in one context, but aren't in another. Other things might be neither right nor wrong, but are simply "different". Those who are willing to allow more things to fall into the category of "maybe not right or wrong, but definitely different" have a much greater chance of functioning effectively cross-culturally.[239]

Culturally intelligent coaches must be willing to function in the gray; needing at times to let our cherished assumptions and expectations be challenged.

I cannot count the number of times I have held my tongue and silently processed issues that have come up in cross-cultural coaching sessions. These include corporal punishment in schools. Or the restrictions put on women leaders in Muslim countries which hamstring their effectiveness, influence, and even their travel. Or things I might consider unethical business practices. Not to mention, ideas and decisions that seem like leadership abuse of power or would definitely *be* considered abuse of power in my own cultural context. I've learned to wait, listen, and be willing to have my assumptions challenged. This stretches me, and sometimes the stretching is uncomfortable and produces negative emotions.

As cross-cultural coaches, we will need at times to let our cherished assumptions and expectations be challenged. As Rosinski noted, there is a cost to this. It is tiring and sometimes painful. It's much easier to hold onto our own culture-bound ideas of what a good leader does. It's difficult to encounter Scripture

---

238   Philippe Rosinski, *Coaching Across Cultures: New Tools for Leveraging National, Corporate & Professional Differences* (London: Nicholas Brealey Publishing, 2003), 38-39.
239   David A. Livermore, *Cultural Intelligence: Improving Your CQ to Engage Our Multicultural World* (Grand Rapids, MI: Baker, 2009), 179-180.

through another culture's eyes (the Prodigal Son story, for instance) and then face the chain of falling dominoes that is the mountain we had built from our own culture-bound assumptions about a certain Bible passage. It's hard to hear a challenge about what we hold dear in coaching when a colleague from another culture pointedly describes the biases of Western coaching theory.

Listening at Level 3: Flowing with the Spirit

Many coaches identify three levels of listening. The first level is listening to the voices in our own head. This includes noticing what thoughts and feelings we are having, being aware of distractions, and at best, being self-aware. The second level is listening to the client, i.e., being tuned fully into what the client is communicating verbally and nonverbally, being other-aware as well as self-aware. The third level involves listening to our dynamic together with God, i.e., being aware internally of what is happening between ourselves and God relationally and being tuned into the Spirit moving between us.

Level 3 listening raises the probability of truly transformational coaching conversations in which God is initiating deep change because we as coaches are dialed in to what God is doing. My friend and longtime executive coach, Phil Bergey, sums it up like this:

> "In cross-cultural coaching, you can't listen at level 1 or 2. You need to be at level 3 much of the time. This makes it more exhausting. If you don't make the effort to listen at Level 3, you can so easily be going down a trail that relates more to the coach's assumptions than to what the client means to be communicating. You need high level listening plus self-awareness, asking yourself, "Why am I feeling frustrated? What is going on between us? What is God up to?" Doing the meta-work throughout the appointment without losing the thread of the coaching conversation—this requires skill and energy, especially with accents and over Skype. But in cross-cultural coaching, I find I need to be engaged at that deeper level most of the time.[240]

Sometimes cross-cultural coaching feels like crossing the desert in bare feet with no sunglasses and half a canteen of water. To make it across, we have to be tuned in to every signpost and landmark, every nonverbal gesture or grimace, each emotion or reaction. We must depend more on the Holy Spirit. Frankly, it's hard work. But when we get across the desert successfully, that's a big "mission accomplished!"

---

240   Phil Bergey, Personal Communication, Permission granted on July 12, 2015.

Resisting the Resistance: Dealing with Spiritual Opposition

I believe that there is good and evil in the world and that we have an opponent who loves trying to thwart God's work and will. When we coach others across cultural boundaries, we are engaging in work that is reconciling and unifying in and through Christ's body, the church. Some of you have coachees who are serving cross-culturally for the express purpose of spreading God's love. Such include missionaries, cross-cultural aid workers, church planters, disaster or crisis teams, and others. As my friend and colleague Paul Hillhouse, CMI's Professional Coach Training director, reminds our trainees each year, this places you right on the front line with your coachees spiritually and relationally. Thus, spiritual opposition is real.

Such opposition can come in so many forms: discouragement, illness, technology issues, and misunderstandings, among others. I find it amazing how many times emails to and from missionaries trying to get their coaching started seem to get "lost" or never arrive. In our organization, we laugh when a new CMI coach encounters this. The percentage of times this has happened with missionaries vs. other clients, no matter where they are located or the quality of their internet, is astronomical. Thankfully, Satan is not nearly as creative as God. Often, as in the case of "lost" emails, simply naming the resistance for what it is removes its power. Other times, it is harder to identify when this is happening. At many points, focused prayer is needed. And sometimes, CQ Drive and prayerful perseverance is essential in outlasting the challenge.

I hope you are not too disheartened by this list of stressors and obstacles. If you have gotten this far in the book, you are likely up for the challenge. Philippe Rosinski, in *Coaching across Cultures*, writes:

> Coaching across cultures is a source of richness, but it does come with a price. It is much more comforting and reassuring to stay in your community and live in a "ghetto". By exploring alternative worldviews and mixing with people from different cultures, you will often feel challenged and may experience higher stress. You are venturing into new territories. Who said expanding our horizons was easy? The promise of a richer future and the excitement of learning should . . . help you accept and surmount the obstacles along the way.[241]

In our next chapter, we'll look at how to respond to the unique challenges of cross-cultural coaching.

---

241   Philippe Rosinski, *Coaching Across Cultures: New Tools for Leveraging National, Corporate & Professional Differences* (London: Nicholas Brealey Publishing, 2003), xxii.

Take a Minute

- *Which two or three of the challenges and stressors described in this chapter are most impacting you currently? Is there anything that God is highlighting in which He wants to bring change?*
- *When have you had some of your assumptions about leadership, Scripture, or ethics challenged in a cross-cultural coaching relationship? How did you respond?*
- *Think of a time in your life as a coach when you really were at a place of shalom: feeling whole, rested, motivated, and ready to coach/impact others. What did you have in place in your life at that time that brought you to that point?*

Chapter Twenty-Five

Responding to the Challenges: Discovering Shalom

Today I am struggling with how to reply to a new client, a national leader in an underground church movement. Inquiries from the police have forced him to move scheduled leadership development training to a remote location that will be safer for all involved. While he is there, no internet will be available, and my client routinely maintains a punishing schedule of travel, making appointments difficult. The only time he can meet for a mentor coaching session is either before he leaves for the leadership training event, which is during my long-awaited writing retreat, or on a Sunday three weeks from now. Otherwise, we will not be able to coach for over six weeks.

From my safe office in my safe town in a country where I can speak freely and without a speck of fear to anyone, even a stranger on the street, about my belief in Jesus, I need to respond to my client and give him my answer. What shall I say? How do I balance the demands of cross-cultural coaching ministry, of invitation to sacrifice and flexibility, with the need for retreat and rest? How do I find the rhythms of grace that can enable me to finish well while also walking alongside others in their journey to finish well, too?

This dance of trusting Jesus while sacrificing and trusting Jesus while resting and laying down the demands of ministry is what I think of as the heart of biblical "shalom". Shalom, the Hebrew word we often translate as "peace", is so much more than a simple lack of strife. Shalom as a verb is a movement towards wholeness—for ourselves, others, and the world. It's getting that tricky balance between others' needs and our own.

> *To finish well as a Christian coach, especially one doing cross-cultural work, we have to find the balance between caring deeply for our clients and caring deeply for ourselves.*

Cross-cultural coaching is such rewarding work. But it can also be demanding, challenging, and draining on so many levels. To continue to do this work takes intentional reliance on God and intentional disciplines of rest, refreshment, and self-care. To finish well as a Christian coach, especially one doing cross-cultural work, we have to find the balance between caring deeply for our clients and caring deeply for ourselves. We must discover the meaning of shalom.

Embracing the Finite and the Infinite

Ruth Haley Barton in her book *Strengthening the Soul of your Leadership* writes:

> There is finiteness to what I can do in this body. There is a finiteness to how many relationships I can engage in meaningfully at one time. There is a finiteness to time . . . There is finiteness to my energy. There comes a time when I am tired . . . These are times when I am reminded that I am human, a finite being living in the presence of an infinite God. God is the infinite one. God is the one who can be all things to all people . . . God is the one who never sleeps. I am not.[242]

Before we dive into the disciplines that will help us address the particular challenges of cross-cultural coaching so that we can finish well, we need to lay a great foundation. As coaches, we are helpers. We come alongside others to assist them in their growth. Personally, I deeply desire to help others, and I am a person who has always struggled with demanding too much of myself. That compelling desire to be helpful, which many of us as coaches share, can lead me to exhaustion, overwork, and saying yes to too many people.

I've discovered, however, a compelling reason for me to say no. Simply put, I am most definitely NOT God. I wasn't cut out to be the redeemer of the world. When I start occupying that spot, I get in the way of others being able to engage with Jesus. That's the last place in the world I want to be. Not only that, when I take the place of Jesus, I begin that downward journey into burnout that leaves me unable to be helpful to anyone. Saying yes to everyone instead of saying yes to Jesus is a recipe for disaster.

242　Ruth Haley Barton, Strengthening the Soul of Your Leadership (Downers Grove, IL: Intervarsity Press, 2008), 111.

So, what does this look like in real life? Let's go back to my underground church client who wants a new appointment. My first inclination was to set a time during my writing retreat week when I could accommodate him. After all, in five days I should be able to find a time to meet with one client. Yes, I had committed to not making any appointments during that week. Yes, I was well aware of my tendency to lose focus, getting swept away by a chain of distractions, once I lowered my guard. But after all, here was a guy who faced jail and worse every day for his faith. Couldn't I carve out ninety minutes?

Oh, the guilt! The sense of injustice that my life was so different than his! But as soon as I slowed down enough to really think, I knew what the answer had to be. I could not meet during my writing retreat. I knew what God wanted me to do that week. It was not to meet with clients. It was to focus on finishing a project that would ultimately be helpful to many people. I would trust God for His priorities for me and for my client. So, I said no.

Before we go any farther in talking about wholeness, shalom, and self-care, we must understand and embrace the reality that there are limits to our ability to flex and to sacrifice. There are limits to our energy and time. And the beauty of those limits is that they point us and those we serve to God, who has no limits. We can freely answer Jesus' call to honor the Sabbath, rest, spend time with him and with our families. We can stop and read a good book. We can turn off our phones and get a good night's sleep. We can go to the mountains and watch the sunset. We can spend time praying and journaling instead of helping and serving. We can do that when Jesus prompts us to in full confidence that he can take care of everything that he has not asked us to do!

Some of you struggle like I do. You are tempted to say yes too often. To sacrifice too much. But there is another reality. Others of you struggled back in the Virtues chapter when we discussed sacrifice. Your boundaries may instead be too rigid. You are tempted to say no too quickly.

My immediate response when my client asked to meet on Sunday was to not even consider this as an alternative. On many levels, this just felt wrong. I believe in the Sabbath, and it is an extremely rare event for me to work on a Sunday. I often advocate for Sabbath rest being included in international travel and training schedules within my own organization, CMI. I also already knew that my client struggled with rest. Should he even be entertaining the *idea* of having a mentor coaching session on a Sunday? Wouldn't I just be enabling him?

> **The underlying principle is listening for and trusting an infinite God who is wiser than we are.**

Again, stopping for a second and consulting the Holy Spirit gave a surprising response. The Sabbath is for rest. But actually, because my husband would be gone over that weekend, I had a plethora of time alone planned and plenty of time for Sabbath rest. I'd be giving up having a whole twenty-four hours devoted to rest, but I felt assured to trust God for the refreshment I needed. I was reminded that it is not my responsibility to bring conviction to my client about Sabbath. Meeting that day might open some interesting discussion with him. I can trust God to initiate change in this area with my client, and I can wait and pray for that. When the time is ripe, I will be ready to engage with him on that topic. So, my initial no turned into a thoughtful yes. I will, in this instance, meet with my client on Sunday.

In both these examples, the underlying principle is listening for and trusting an infinite God who is wiser than we are. We do this in the moment when unusual situations like my client's come up. We also do it in the bigger picture of developing long-term disciplines and strategies that fit our context and individual needs for the long haul. The foundation for doing shalom and boundaries well, both short-term and long-term, is being able to embrace our finiteness and God's infiniteness: His ability to do so much more than we can ask or imagine. We must have his perspective. God knows better than we do when we need to exercise trust in him by saying yes and when we need to exercise trust in Him by saying no.

Take a Minute

Think of the last time a cross-cultural client's request made you uncomfortable or angry, perhaps when you felt a sense of obligation or duty to respond in a certain way. Identify:

- *What is your temptation, to say no or yes too quickly?*
- *Ask Jesus how he wanted/wants you to respond in the situation you have in mind.*

We've spent a good amount of time exploring the particular stresses of cross-cultural coaching. We've gained perspective and knowledge. We've begun to explore what it means in terms of shalom to be finite helpers who serve an infinite God. Now let's turn our attention to what to do with these perspectives. What are some practical steps we can take as cross-cultural coaches to work actively towards shalom?

Spiritual Disciplines

1 Timothy 4:8: For physical training is of some value, but godliness has value for all things, holding promise for both the present life and the life to come.

Practicing spiritual disciplines is basic Christianity 101. We all know about such spiritual disciplines as fasting, worship, meditating, silence, and simplicity. We are aware of how important it is to have regular times of prayer and reading Scripture.

However, living out these disciplines is still challenging for most of those I coach and work with. It is for me as well! I am so aware that when I don't have adequate time with Jesus to bring needed perspective, reassurance, and peace, my internal well quickly runs dry. I get impatient with my clients. I am less likely to want to take the time to deal with my culturally-bound assumptions. I lose humility.

Because it is a form of spiritual reflection, journaling may be particularly helpful for the cross-cultural coach. Journaling helps us become aware of what we are thinking and feeling. To bring that to God is a form of spiritual metacognition and aids in the development of the cross-cultural coaching skill of Intentionality.[243]

This is where shalom must start: with adequate time set aside for spiritual disciplines that mature us, increase our capacity to serve, and prompt us to rub shoulders regularly with the God who created all of it.

Rhythms of Grace

Matthew 11:28-30, ***The Message:*** Come to me. Get away with me and you'll recover your life. I'll show you how to take a real rest. Walk with me and work with me—watch how I do it. Learn the unforced rhythms of grace. I won't lay anything heavy or ill-fitting on you. Keep company with me and you'll learn to live freely and lightly.

---

243   For more on the skill of Intentionality and planning in culturally intelligent coaching, go to www.dancingbetweencultures.com.

Many of us, especially those from my home country, the United States, don't know the difference between rest, refreshment, renewal, and recreation. We do recreation. We take days off and do adrenaline sports. We sit and watch TV or movies. We are entertained. But that is not rest, renewal, or refreshment.

Rest is rest. If you have gotten this far, you know that cross-cultural coaching can be really tiring on multiple levels. Rest is getting sufficient sleep so that we can do high level listening and have adequate energy to meet the challenges of cross-cultural coaching. Most new cross-cultural coaches quickly find that they can only do a couple cross-cultural coaching sessions per day without wearing out. Find the pace that works for you. In time, you'll build up the ability to do more. Rest means taking breaks when we need them. This could mean getting out of the office or maybe taking a nap. It means setting aside enough time at night (usually eight hours) for adequate sleep.

Renewal and refreshment help us stay creative, motivated, and present with our clients. I get refreshed by being out in nature. I am quickly restored by stopping to watch a sunset or smell a flower. A two-hour movie doesn't begin to touch the refreshment those simple moments in nature can bring.

Refreshment and renewal often involve creativity or activity. A quick game of basketball. An hour of photography. A group hike. Creating a painting or a beautiful piece of furniture. Whatever it may be, find out what renews/refreshes you and build it into your life without guilt. Go bird watching. Weed your garden (one of my favorites!). Make an amazing meal. Build a deck. Keep bees. This will help you bring a peaceful spirit that comes from rest, renewal, and refreshment into your coaching.

Living in Community

> Hebrews 10:24-25: And let us consider how we may spur one another on to love and good deeds. Let us not give up meeting together, as some are in the habit of doing, but let us encourage one another-and all the more as you see the Day approaching.

For most coaches I know, community is hard. Many of us work in home offices or on our own. We may live in isolated places. Perhaps we are the only coach around. But the demands of cross-cultural coaching mean we need supportive relationships more than ever. We need relationships in which we are not a helper. We need time to simply be friend or family. We need people to laugh with, be silly with. Having others to play with is fun!

We also need relationships that nourish us and help us grow. We need the outside perspective of a supervisor, mentor coach, or peer coach to help us process the assumptions that are being challenged through our cross-cultural coaching. We need continuing education. We need resourcing to better equip us. We need coaching networks and Christian coaching organizations to keep us sharp. We need as well others who pray for and with us. Spiritual opposition is real. I would not want to do cross-cultural coaching without faithful intercessors, friends, family and colleagues standing with me.

Take a Minute

- *As you think about the three areas of self-care (spiritual disciplines, rhythms of grace, and living in community), in which are you the weakest?*
- *What are two or three ways this area could be strengthened so that you will finish well?*
- *What is one action step you are willing to commit to that will help you move towards shalom?*

Summary

One of my passions—and I believe one of God's also—is to see leaders finish well. To see them complete their calling from God with joy and satisfaction. All of heaven rejoices when leaders engage God throughout life and successfully enter that convergence season when all their experiences, skills, maturity, wisdom, and character come together in a supernova of Christlikeness expressed through their unique humanness. We're not all at that convergence time of life, but my hope for you is both that you engage God along the way and that you reach convergence.

Some of us have not only been called and gifted to be coaches, but are now walking through doors God has opened for us to coach across cultures. We have an exciting and challenging calling! For us, finishing well means finding ways to make cross-cultural coaching sustainable for the long haul. It means that we need to take the challenges we encounter to God and allow him to polish and re-polish us over and over. We need to grow in character and in skill. We need others around us to support us. We need to build rhythms and patterns into our daily lives now that will enable us to flourish and to finish well for the glory of God.

An Invitation

I love to coach. Walking alongside another person, watching him or her reach for their potential in a new area, achieve a goal they have dreamed of for years, or struggle through a difficult transition and come out more virtuous, grateful, or resilient is maybe the best thing in the world. I think angels celebrate when people grow. I certainly do! We partner with God when we walk alongside others and help them develop and flourish.

Adding the dimension of culture to the already satisfying endeavor of faith-based coaching is like adding a rich dessert and gourmet coffee to a beautifully cooked meal shared with friends I hope this book has whet your appetite. As our world becomes ever more multi-cultural, we must adjust as coaches and leaders to meet the need. This is a whole new frontier in Christian coaching.

And that frontier is growing! I have not even begun to share all that has been learned in my organization, Coaching Mission International, about the unique challenges of coaching missionaries and cross-cultural workers. If you want to go deeper, CMI offers a four-month distance learning course in culturally intelligent coaching based on this book, along with full coach training programs for professional level and lay coaching (for more information, check out www.cmiprograms.org). We'd love to hear from you.

There is still much to be discovered. This book does not cover other essential topics in cross-cultural coaching such as culture stress and re-entry, coaching expats, debriefing, the challenges of coaching cross-cultural teams, or how to do coach training or mentor coaching excellently in cross-cultural settings. Learning from and sharing with each other as we tackle this new frontier in coaching is crucial. Community is not only important to self-care; it's essential to learning. If you have expertise or experience, share it! If you have new ideas and creative resources, write a post about your discoveries or comment on ours at www.dancingbetweencultures.com. Let's help each other learn and grow. Let's experience as a community of coaches and leaders the growth and transformation we long for in ourselves and in our clients, at home and around the world.

Cross Cultural Values Chart

 **Autonomy** (identity/power/responsibility) **Community** 

Autonomy	Community
My identity comes from my individual characteristics.	My identity comes from membership in a group (family, tribe, or community).
I believe that, for the most part, my choices determine my destiny.	My destiny is most often the result of my circumstances and background.
I'm responsible for my own failures.	Circumstances and destiny are often responsible for failure.
I value my independence.	I value the interdependence and dependence in my group/community/tribe.
I am responsible for my own decisions and how they impact me.	Making decisions is best done in my family/community/tribe, benefitting all.
I believe that I have distinctive and unique qualities.	Harmony and fitting in with others are most important.
My relationships evolve based on my location, job, and circumstances.	My relationships are stable; most come from family/tribe/community.

 **Risk** (change) **Caution** 

Risk	Caution
I value flexibility and adaptability.	I value rules and reliability.
I embrace change and make decisions quickly.	I prefer to have a long time to make a decision and don't change quickly.
I like to try new things and methods rather than stick to the routine.	I like to stick to what is proven and stable; I value a routine.
I value innovation: I prefer less rules and guidelines.	I value tradition: I want more rules and guidelines.
Changes and differences are interesting.	Changes and differences can make me a bit anxious.
I can handle nonlinear change.	I prefer slower, incremental change.

 **Crisis**   (planning)   **Non-Crisis** 

I anticipate potential problems (tend to be pessimistic).	I tend to discount potential problems (tend to be optimistic).
I rely on research and expert advice.	I'm a bit suspicious of "experts".
I am motivated to get clarity and so, make prompt decisions.	I have a high tolerance for ambiguity, so I tend to delay decisions.
I stick to the plan when the crisis hits.	I improvise when a crisis hits.

 **Dichotomistic**   (thinking patterns)   **Holistic** 

Most things are right or wrong.	There are a lot of gray areas in life.
I am a linear, logical thinker.	I am a nonlinear, holistic thinker.
I tend to organize information and experiences in my mind and sort them into patterns.	I see things as whole systems and I can talk about many disparate things at once.
I feel confident and secure when roles and categories are well defined.	I feel confident and secure when I have multiple interactions and connections to explore.

 **Conceptual**   (thinking patterns)   **Practical** 

I start with theory and concept to get to practical application.	I start with experience in order to come up with theories and models.
I value logical reasoning.	I value intuition.
It's important to reason through, discuss, and understand thoroughly before acting.	I'd rather not spend too long on discussion; many things can be learned through action.
I understand facts best when they are placed within a framework of concepts.	I embrace concepts when they are substantiated by data.

 **Status** (organizational arrangements) **Equality** 

I think life is a non-level playing field.	I think life is a fairly level playing field.
My identity comes from my family/birth/social status/role.	My identity comes from what I've made of my life: my achievements.
Learning is best guided by a mentor.	The best learning is self-discovery.
Don't openly challenge your leader; subordinates should follow instructions.	Leaders can, and sometimes should, be challenged; subordinates should take initiative.
It is important to give respect regardless of performance or character.	Respect is determined by accomplishments, successes, and character.
I will sacrifice for higher rank.	I will sacrifice for greater achievement.
I hold and use the authority given to me by my role to care for those that are weaker or subordinate.	I share power with those under me and expect them to take responsibility for themselves.
Men and women are treated differently.	Women and men are equal.

  **Task** (purpose) **Relationship** 

I find satisfaction in attaining goals.	I find satisfaction in interaction.
Task or business first.	Relationship first.
I pursue friends with similar goals.	I pursue friends who value connection.
I will sacrifice for a project/goal.	I will sacrifice for people/interaction.
It's all about what you do or accomplish with what you are given.	It's all about who you are in relation to others.
I make connections with new people quickly but not always deeply.	I make connections with new people slowly, but I go deep.
I value external, measurable rewards.	I value inward and relational rewards.

 **Direct**   (communication)   **Indirect** 

What is said is what is important.	How the message is said is important.
I am frank and straightforward.	I am discreet and diplomatic.
I tend to confront difficult issues directly.	I tend to avoid contention and difficult issues.
I express concerns frankly.	I express concerns tactfully.
There is no need to interpret my non-verbals; I'll say what I mean.	It's important to listen with all your senses for the hidden meanings behind words.

 **Concealment**   (communication)   **Vulnerability** 

I hold back until I can trust.	I trust quickly and share openly.
One needs to protect one's image, and maintain a proper public face.	My self-image is resilient and my private and public faces are congruent.
I'm a bit reluctant to try things I'm not sure I'll be successful at.	I like to challenge myself and to try things I might fail at.
Avoiding shame and error is important; I don't tend to expose my own and other's mistakes.	I just admit it when I'm wrong, there's no shame in that; my own and other's mistakes are an opportunity to learn.
It's better not to criticize or disagree openly.	Disagreement and constructive criticism are good things for a team.

 **Time**   (time)   **Event** 

Time is scarce and needs to be saved.	Time is plentiful and should be enjoyed and spent.
I value efficiency.	I value participation and completion.
Punctuality is important.	Flexibility is important.
I feel busy most of the time.	I have a relaxed pace of life.

 **Long Term**   (time)   **Short Term** 

Future rewards are the most important.	Short-term gains and quick results are a real motivator for me.
I am willing to wait and sacrifice (for decades if necessary) for long-term objectives.	I like to see movement and visible progress happen quickly on my goals.
Thrift, perseverance, and self-discipline are very important principles.	Freedom and the rights of the individual are very important principles.
Leisure is not as important as my long-term goals.	Leisure and recreation are as valuable to me as long-term goals.

The Cultural Values Chart draws from many sources, most notably Sherwood G. Lingenfelter and Marvin K. Mayers in *Ministering Cross-Culturally: An Incarnational Model for Personal Relationships* (Grand Rapids: Baker Academic, 2007)
CMI/CMI Programs. All rights reserved. www.cmiprograms.org.